Charismatic
Leadership

Jay A. Conger
Rabindra N. Kanungo
and Associates

Foreword by Warren Bennis

Charismatic Leadership

The Elusive Factor in Organizational Effectiveness

 Jossey-Bass Publishers

San Francisco • London • 1988

CHARISMATIC LEADERSHIP
The Elusive Factor in Organizational Effectiveness
by Jay A. Conger, Rabindra N. Kanungo, and Associates

Copyright © 1988 by: Jossey-Bass Inc., Publishers
350 Sansome Street
San Francisco, California 94104
&
Jossey-Bass Limited
28 Banner Street
London EC1Y 8QE

The lines from "Design" by Robert Frost are taken from
The Poetry of Robert Frost, edited by Edward Connery Lathem,
published by Henry Holt and Company (New York, 1979),
and are used with the kind permission of the publisher.
Permission to use this quotation in books sold throughout
the British Commonwealth and Empire, excluding Canada,
kindly granted by Jonathan Cape Ltd., publishers, London,
and the Estate of Robert Frost.

Library of Congress Cataloging-in-Publication Data

Charismatic leadership: the elusive factor in organizational
  effectiveness / [contributions by] Jay A. Conger, Rabindra N.
  Kanungo, and associates; foreword by Warren Bennis.
      p.   cm. — (The Jossey-Bass management series)
    Includes bibliographies and index.
    ISBN 1-55542-102-4 (alk. paper)
    1. Executive ability.   2. Leadership.   3. Organizational
  effectiveness.   I. Conger, Jay Alden.   II. Kanungo, Rabindra Nath.
  III. Series.
  HD38.2.C43 1988
  658.4'092—dc19   88-42784
                                                            CIP

Manufactured in the United States of America

The paper in this book meets the guidelines for
permanence and durability of the Committee on
Production Guidelines for Book Longevity of the
Council on Library Resources.

JACKET DESIGN BY WILLI BAUM

FIRST EDITION

Code 8832

The Jossey-Bass
Management Series

Consulting Editors
Organizations and Management

Warren Bennis
University of Southern California

Richard O. Mason
Southern Methodist University

Ian I. Mitroff
University of Southern California

*To Business Leaders Who Have
Enriched the Quality of Life on This Planet*

Contents

**Part One: The Nature and Dynamics
of Charismatic Leadership**

Contents

Foreword

Leaders play a significant role in our society, as in any society. They shape our morality and our ethical imperatives; they are alchemists of the mind, and they can unite the people in pursuit of the worthiest of goals. Given that, it is almost absurd to recognize that after four decades of research on leadership we still cannot claim an integrated understanding of it. Excuse the self-indulgence of self-quoting, but in 1959 I wrote: "Of all the hazy and confounding areas in social psychology, leadership theory undoubtedly contends for top nomination. And, ironically, probably more has been written and less known about leadership than about any other topic in the behavioral sciences. Always, it seems, the concept of leadership eludes us or turns up in another form to taunt us again with its slipperiness and complexity. . . . The dialectic and reversals of emphases in this area very nearly rival the tortuous twists and turns of child-rearing practices, and one can paraphrase Gertrude Stein by saying, 'a leader is a follower is a leader is a . . . ' " ("Leadership Theory and Administrative Behavior: The Problem of Authority." *Administrative Science Quarterly,* 1959, *4,* 259–260).

The beauty of this volume is that the editors, Jay A. Conger and Rabindra N. Kanungo, have mapped out the beginnings of a theory of charismatic leadership, one of the key concepts in leadership but one that has been long retired to either desuetude or idealized corruption. Yes, the editors' generalizations are in the early stage of development, and yes, there are some splendid divergences in data and in the interpretation of data. But I cannot remember a collection of chapters, on the cutting edge of such a difficult topic, that was more uniformly excellent, more fundamental in its aims and execution. For my money, no other book or collection of writings comes even close to this one in terms of advancing the state of knowledge of that venerable Weberian conundrum, charismatic leadership.

I'd be remiss in not stating that this isn't the last word, that there are many areas of healthy dissension, especially around the issue of the inner conflicts of the charismatic leader as well as the context within which charismatic leadership germinates. This is all to the good. The least and most this book offers all students and practitioners of management is that it jump-starts the mind. Can we ask more?

June 1988   Warren Bennis
                                                    Distinguished Professor
                                                        of Business Administration
                                                    University of Southern California

Preface

This volume arose out of our interest in what has been a neglected area of study in management. While the general subject of leadership has received a great deal of attention, charismatic leadership has remained a stepchild. This is ironic, since charismatic leaders are among the most profound in terms of their impact not only on nations and religions but on businesses and industries. Historically, these leaders have been the drivers of change and transformation at both societal and organizational levels. Yet they have been consistently overlooked in the world of management. In recent years, however, we have noticed the appearance of more and more stories in the popular press attributing, in part, a leader's ability to create a successful business venture or to transform a troubled organization to his or her "charisma."

Through these articles and as a result of our own observations, we became intrigued by the potential charismatic leaders seemed to hold for understanding and teaching effective leadership. We felt that unlocking the mystery behind charisma would hold important lessons for managers everywhere. Part of our interest also must be attributed to a spirit of adventure. We enjoy exploring, in being pathfinders—especially through the discovery of new frontiers in knowledge. For us, the study of charisma in business has presented the rare and wonderful opportunity to be academic entrepreneurs. With this interest, we set out to bring together the small but growing group of management theorists who have begun researching the topic. Our aim in drawing together these individuals is not only to provide a greater awareness of the phenomenon but also to explore the broad range of issues relevant to the topic. We have also sought to provide a variety of perspectives on this very rich and complex phenomenon.

In preparing this volume, we had three main objectives. The first was to bring together in one reference source the current state of knowledge on the subject. We have sought to be as comprehensive as possible. As such, the book contains contributions from scholars with different disciplinary orientations. This multidisciplinary approach offers the reader a wide spectrum of perspectives. Our second objective was to provide an initial attempt at delineating the boundaries of charismatic forms of organizational leadership as distinguished from other forms of leadership (such as participative, consideration, and task-oriented leadership) currently in vogue. This objective is partly achieved by identifying the commonalities among our contributors with respect to the questions of what the phenomenon is and what its antecedent and consequent conditions are.

Our final aim was to chart new directions for future research and management practice in the area of charismatic leadership. This can be done in two ways. First, the nature and dynamics of charismatic leadership as described in this volume require empirical verification and replication in different organizational contexts. Second, future research needs to address several areas of disagreement with the goal of bringing about a greater integration of the phenomenon. Such verification and integration of our knowledge will provide a firm footing for future management practice. It is our hope that this work will both stimulate and guide the future efforts of researchers and practitioners alike.

Given these aims, we believe this book has a broad potential audience. Academics studying and teaching leadership, organizational behavior, and other behavioral sciences should find this volume of special interest. So should their students. For this audience, the book provides, quite literally, a body of knowledge at the leading edge of this emerging field. We are unaware of any other reference book that is as comprehensive or as current.

Managers, organizational development specialists, and management training specialists should find the theoretical ideas and practical suggestions throughout this book particularly useful in terms of understanding leadership. Sections describing the characteristics, liabilities, and development of charismatic leaders will be of interest to this audience. Finally, those whose ambitions include leadership will find this book to be full of insights and possibilities. It is one of our hopes that this volume will spark greater interest in the pathways to effective leadership.

The book opens with an Introduction, which explains the rationale for studying charismatic leadership as well as the problems and prospects involved in its study. The chapters that follow are divided into four parts. Part One delves into the nature and dynamics of charismatic leadership. Examining theory and empirical research, this section's authors provide their perspectives on the qualities and forces that give rise to a charismatic leader. They offer us a wide-angle view of the phenomenon. In Part Two, the core component of charismatic leadership—strategic vision—is explored in greater depth. Part Three expands the spectrum of issues by examining the sources and limitations of charisma. For example, the role that context plays in fostering or inhibiting the expression of a leader's charisma is analyzed. In addition, the authors consider the possibility and nature of negative outcomes. Part Four explores issues of training and development of charismatic leaders, given their potentially profound impact. Possible areas for developing charismatic leaders and their unique skills are outlined. Finally, we conclude with a synthesis of the volume's contributions and reflections on the topic's future. In our editiorial efforts to bring together the contributions to this volume, the major criterion we followed was coherence—without altering the major thrust of each contribution.

We would like to offer a word of thanks to the individuals who helped make this volume possible. Our contributors are first in line for their efforts and interest in the project. In providing a review of the book, Lee Bolman played an important role. In addition, we would like to thank the Graduate Faculty and the Faculty of Management of McGill University for their generous support of this project. Finally, our special appreciation goes to three individuals: Michael Manolson, who provided the material on Lee Iacocca; Jean Hepworth, who typed several drafts with great competence and spirit; and Minati Kanungo, who showed infinite patience and understanding while the project was in progress.

Montreal, Quebec   Jay A. Conger
June 1988   Rabindra N. Kanungo

The Authors

Jay A. Conger is assistant professor of organizational behavior at the Faculty of Management, McGill University, Montreal, Quebec. He received his B.A. degree in anthropology, with honors (1974), from Dartmouth College, his M.B.A. degree (1977) from the University of Virginia, and, after a stint as an international marketing manager, his Ph.D. degree in business administration (1985) from Harvard University Graduate School of Business Administration. Conger's research centers on charisma, executive leadership, and the management of organizational change. He is particularly interested in the role that leaders play in revitalizing troubled organizations and in entrepreneurial leadership. His work on these subjects has been published in articles and book chapters, most recently in *The Handbook of Organizational Behavior* (Jay Lorsch, ed., 1987).

Rabindra N. Kanungo is professor of psychology and management at McGill University, Montreal, Quebec. He received his B.A. degree in philosophy, with honors (1953), from Utkal University, India; his M.A. degree in psychology (1955) from Patna University, India; and his Ph.D. degree in psychology (1962) from McGill University. His work experience as a university professor, researcher, and consultant spans both East (India) and West (Canada and the United States). His academic and professional honors include a Commonwealth Fellowship, a Seagram Fellowship, and a Fellowship of the Canadian Psychological Association. Kanungo has published widely in both the basic and applied areas of psychology and management. His recent books include *Management of Work and Personal Life* (Praeger, 1984),

Biculturalism and Management (Butterworths, 1980), and *Work Alienation* (Praeger, 1982).

Bruce J. Avolio is associate professor of human resource management at the School of Management, State University of New York, Binghamton. He received his B.A. degree in psychology (1975) from the State University of New York, Oneonta, and his M.A. (1978) and Ph.D. (1982) degrees in industrial and organizational psychology from the University of Akron.

Bernard M. Bass is Distinguished Professor of Management and director of the Center for Leadership Studies, State University of New York, Binghamton. He received his B.A. (1946), M.A. (1947), and Ph.D. (1949) degrees in industrial psychology from Ohio State University. He is the author of numerous books and many articles, chapters, book reviews, and monographs on organizational behavior and leadership. He is the author of *Stogdill's Handbook of Leadership* (1981) and *Leadership and Performance Beyond Expectations* (1985).

Raymond Trevor Bradley is visiting assistant professor in sociology at the University of California, Santa Cruz. He is also co-director of the Institute for Whole Social Science in Menlo Park, California. He received his B.A. (1970) and B.A. Hons. (1971) degrees in sociology and geography from Victoria University of Wellington, New Zealand, and his M.A. (1976), M.Phil. (1980), and Ph.D. (1980) degrees in sociology from Columbia University.

Eugene M. Fodor is professor of psychology at Clarkson University, Potsdam, New York. He received his B.A. degree (1960) in psychology and his Ph.D. degree (1966) in social psychology, both from Cornell University. His research interests include power and achievement motivation.

Tracy C. Gibbons is an organization development consultant at Digital Equipment Corporation in Maynard, Massachusetts, where she has been employed for the past ten years. She received her B.S. degree (1966) in community leadership and development from Springfield College, her M.S. degree (1972) in counseling psychology from George Williams College, and her Ph.D. degree (1986) in human and organizational systems from the Fielding Institute.

Robert J. House is Distinguished Professor of Organizational Behavior on the Faculty of Management at the University of Toronto. He received his B.S. (1955) and his M.B.A. (1958) degrees from the University of Detroit and his Ph.D. degree (1960) from Ohio State University, all in business administration. He has published widely on the subject of leadership and organizational behavior.

Jane M. Howell is assistant professor of business administration at the University of Western Ontario. She received her B.A. degree (1976) in psychology from the University of British Columbia, her M.A. degree (1980) in counseling psychology from the University of Western Ontario, and her Ph.D. degree (1986) in business administration from the University of British Columbia.

Manfred F. R. Kets de Vries is Raoul De Vitry D'Avancourt Professor in human resource management at the European Institute of Business Administration (INSEAD), Fontainebleau, France. He received his doctoral degree in economics (1966) at the University of Amsterdam and an M.B.A. degree (1968) and a D.B.A. degree (1970) from the Harvard Business School. He has done psychoanalytical training at the Canadian Psychoanalytic Institute and became a full-time member of the Canadian Psychoanalytic Society in 1982. He is a practicing psychoanalyst.

Henry Mintzberg is Bronfman Professor of Management at McGill University, in Montreal, where he researches and writes on management and organizations. Mintzberg received his B.S. degree (1961) in engineering from McGill University, and his M.S. (1965) and Ph.D. (1968) degrees, also in engineering, from the Massachusetts Institute of Technology. His current work involves a two-volume book on strategic formation; it is the fourth in a series under the general title *The Theory of Management Policy*. He is president-elect of the Strategic Management Society, an international association of businesspeople and academics.

Nancy C. Roberts is associate professor of organizational behavior at the Naval Postgraduate School, Monterey, California. Roberts is a co-director of the Institute for Whole Social Science at Menlo Park, California, and she is currently a visiting associate professor at the Graduate School of Business at Stanford University. She received a Diplome Annuel from the Sorbonne (1966), Paris, France, her B.A. degree (1967) in French from the University of Illinois, her M.A. degree in Latin American history and South Asian history from the University of Illinois, and her Ph.D. degree (1983) in education from Stanford University.

Marshall Sashkin is senior associate in Programs for the Improvement of Practice in the U.S. Department of Education's Office of Educational Research and Improvement, where he develops and conducts research projects on leadership in schools. He received his B.A. degree (1966) in psychology from the University of California, Los Angeles, and his Ph.D. degree (1970) in organizational psychology from the University of Michigan.

Frances R. Westley is assistant professor of policy at McGill University. She received her B.A. degree (1970) in English literature from Middlebury College, and her M.A. (1975) and Ph.D. (1978) degrees in sociology from McGill University. Her areas of investigation include strategic change, organizational culture, sociotechnical redesign, and participative management.

James Woycke is a research assistant with the Faculty of Management Studies at the University of Toronto. He received his B.A. degree (1969) from Grand Valley State College, his M.A. (1971) and M.Phil. (1973) degrees from the University of Waterloo, and his Ph.D. degree (1984) from the University of Toronto, all in history.

Charismatic Leadership

Introduction:
Problems and Prospects
in Understanding
Charismatic Leadership

Jay A. Conger
Rabindra N. Kanungo

"I am not a candidate, do not plan to become a candidate, and see no circumstances that would change my mind." These words were written by Lee Iacocca in a letter to the organizers of the Draft Lee Iacocca for President committee in July 1986. In trying to convince Iacocca to run for president of the United States, these organizers admitted that they were not acting on Iacocca's behalf but felt that they were seeking the best leadership for the country. The committee was not alone. Polls conducted and published in the summer of 1986 by the *Washington Post* and *Time* magazine pointed to Iacocca's surprisingly high level of public popularity.

Iacocca had accomplished what few, if any, North American business leaders had ever achieved: He had become a national hero. With showmanship and sharp business acumen, he had orchestrated a remarkable turnaround of the Chrysler Corporation. Impressed by his accomplishments, many Americans were hoping he would do the same for their nation.

Iacocca's success is particularly remarkable when one considers his situation. He assumed the presidency at Chrysler in

September 1979 on the day the company reported its greatest loss for any quarter in its history. Then within five months came the Iranian crisis, the energy crisis, and the most serious recession in fifty years. Chrysler continued losing money—up to $1.7 billion—and slipped dangerously close to bankruptcy at the end of 1982. But by the end of 1983, Iacocca's leadership had transformed record losses into a $925 million profit—the largest in the company's history. Through remarkable powers of persuasion, Iacocca had convinced the American people to buy his cars and the United States Congress to loan Chrysler $1.2 billion. Millions of Americans supported him, purchasing his cars and his book and even urging him to run for president.

The press attributed Iacocca's phenomenal success not only to his strong business sense but also to his "charisma." As a charismatic leader, Iacocca epitomized the power of such leaders and their profound impact on organizations and on society at large. Yet, ironically, Iacocca and charismatic business leaders like him have been largely neglected as a subject of systematic and scientific study. Although from time to time the influence of a leader's charisma has been recognized in religion and politics, even there it has retained an enigmatic association. And scholars have treated the phenomenon either as simply a manifestation of personal charm unworthy of serious attention or as an elusive event too impressionistic to be captured. The notion that charismatic leaders even exist in business organizations is a relatively new idea promoted by a handful of scholars.

Our aim is to begin to rectify this serious shortcoming by initiating an exploration of this profoundly important yet poorly understood form of leadership in management settings. Our hope is that, with this volume, social scientists and management practitioners will begin to pay serious attention to this corporate phenomenon and initiate a process of transforming what has been a mystical conception into a more scientific understanding of charisma.

Why Study Charisma?

Our opening example of Lee Iacocca and his accomplishments illustrates the potential importance of charismatic leadership for organizational effectiveness. What appears to set charismatic leaders apart is their strategic vision and their ability to motivate employees to achieve ambitious goals. They also are often associated with radical transformations of large bureaucratic organizations or the creation of successful entrepreneurial ventures. As such, the outcomes they achieve and the radical impact of their leadership on organizations and industries make them important subjects for study.

In this time of turmoil for North American industry, it is not surprising that the topic of charismatic leadership should gain popularity: Certain skills that the charismatic leader appears to possess may be essential for managing in turbulent environments. For example, one of the great dilemmas facing American corporations today is what Robert Lamb (1987) calls "tunnel vision." Many corporations are experiencing strategic failure due to a lack of vision. Part of the blame must be placed on organization leaders. As Lamb argues: "Many of the problems of U.S. companies can be traced . . . to executive constraints that foster a myopia among managers faced with a rapidly changing, competitive world. The limitations of the chief executive's training or outlook, as well as the traditions of the company or industry, can impose blinders upon the range of strategies that a particular company will consider" (p. 10). Charismatic leaders appear particularly gifted with strategic vision. They are not bound by a limited perspective or tradition. Instead, they actively seek out unforeseen opportunities in their markets and use strategies that succeed because of their unconventionality. Analyzing their talents in this area may have important implications for effective corporate strategies.

Charismatic leaders also have been associated with entrepreneurial activities. Many of the more visible entrepreneurs of the 1970s and 1980s are described as charismatic—for example, Mary Kay Ash of Mary Kay Cosmetics, Donald Burr of People's Express, Steven Jobs of Apple Computer, Ross Perot of Electronic Data Systems, and Fred Smith of Federal Express. To an extent, the entrepreneurial success of these business leaders may depend upon their charismatic qualities. The study of charismatic leadership can provide us with important clues about why certain entrepreneurs succeed or fail. And the implications for entrepreneurial success are critically important for society at large. As John Naisbitt (1982) concludes: "Recent studies have convinced government and business observers that small businesses, not big corporations, are responsible for most of the new jobs created and most of the nation's economic growth and that they are more productive and innovative as well" (p. 161).

From a motivational standpoint, there is often a profound difference in the emotional attachment and energy exhibited by followers of charismatic and noncharismatic leaders. At the annual Mary Kay sales conference in Dallas, sales representatives can be heard exclaiming, "We love Mary Kay!" or "Mary Kay has made a tremendous difference in my life." And while it is easy to dismiss such talk and adoration as the banter of restless housewives, no cynic can deny the multimillion-dollar organization Mary Kay Ash has built upon the enthusiasm and devotion of her sales force.

It would appear that charismatic leaders are unique in this ability to build emotional attachment and enthusiasm among their followers for themselves and their missions. Watching these leaders and their organizations work reminds us of a political campaign—in which workers strive tirelessly for the mission's success. If the essence of leadership is the ability to motivate subordinates, then the study of charismatic leadership can help us unravel the secrets of motivating employees and directing them toward the achievement of organizational goals.

In addition to the positive outcomes associated with charismatic leadership, there is also a dark side that needs to be understood. In recent history, charismatic religious leaders Jim Jones in Guyana (Johnson, 1979) and Bhagwan Shree Rajneesh in Oregon (Fitzgerald, 1986) fostered an extraordinary degree of psychological submission among their followers. Through their powers of persuasion and actions encouraging dependence, they developed a largely compliant followership. In the end, this dependency led to death for Jones's followers and the collapse of a multimillion-dollar communal enterprise for the followers of Rajneesh. As these examples illustrate, there is little doubt that charismatic leadership—in any setting—can foster potentially harmful levels of dependence. The study of charismatic leadership can lead us to identify conditions under which such harmful effects are manifested. Awareness of the conditions of excessive follower dependence can also help us take appropriate corrective actions.

Just as important, some charismatic leaders use their powers of persuasion in manipulative and self-seeking ways. John DeLorean's treatment of investors in his automobile venture is an example: Ultimately, investors lost $120 million in the poorly managed venture. What DeLorean did so effectively was focus investors' attention away from important investment information and onto his personal charisma: "No other entrepreneur in business history used publicity as well in amassing seed capital, and he found that investors were as unlikely to look behind his hollow hype as reporters. . . . DeLorean underwent only the most cursory check into his background before he was loaned hundreds of millions of dollars" (Levin, 1983, p. 323). These examples attest to the need to study charisma more scientifically in order to understand the negative dimensions of charismatic leadership as well as the positive.

Our day-to-day observation of charismatic and entrepreneurial leaders in business settings and their profound influence on organizations is not the only rationale for a scientific study of charisma. Certain developments within the discipline of organizational behavior also provide impetus for pushing beyond the frontiers of research on charismatic leadership.

In the management literature, the examination of leadership within organizations has been a prominent issue for almost half a century. Taking the lead from sociologists and social psychologists, different forms of leadership have been studied. For example, interest in the study of formal and informal organizations led to research focusing on formal or appointed leaders (Raven and French, 1958) and informal or emergent leaders (Bales, 1950). Interest in the nature of communication and authority between leader and subordinates led to the study of democratic versus autocratic (Lewin, Lippitt, and White, 1939) and participative versus directive styles of leadership (Vroom and Yetton, 1973). Interest in the task and social roles played by supervisors in work groups led to the famous Ohio State

University leadership studies on initiating structure versus consideration (task versus people orientations) (Halpin and Winer, 1957). Following these lines of interest, much of the current leadership research focuses on the leadership dimensions of centralizing versus decentralizing decision making and on task and people orientations of leaders (Yukl, 1981).

Recently, however, the theoretical significance and practical usefulness of this body of research have been questioned by several management theorists. Both Mintzberg (1973, 1982) and Zaleznik (1977) argue that the existing leadership research has failed to make an important distinction between leadership and managership and that most "leadership" studies, instead of dealing with true and visionary leadership roles, have dealt with only day-to-day supervisory or managerial roles. If this distinction between leaders and managers (or administrators) as advocated by these scholars is to be taken seriously, it is imperative that the focus of future leadership research change from the current preoccupation with the supervisory styles of shop floor managers or mid-level managers to the study of more profound leadership styles, such as charismatic leadership.

Charisma: A Poorly Understood Phenomenon

The distinction between charismatic and noncharismatic leaders is often detected by organization members in their day-to-day observation of business leaders. For example, it is not uncommon to hear employees casually and spontaneously describe a certain manager as a charismatic leader. Yet, as mentioned before, organizational theorists have largely ignored the existence or importance of charisma. This can be attributed in part to the fact that charismatic business leaders are not often in the limelight and thus are little known outside their organizations. Widespread unfamiliarity with business leaders and preoccupation of the media with political and religious figures may have created the popular assumption that charisma is a rare manifestation among business leaders. Such an assumption may also be responsible for the lack of interest in identifying and systematically studying charisma in business settings.

A large part of the problem can be traced to the complex and elusive nature of charisma. Historically, the term has been loosely defined and, at times, diluted. It has been attributed a mystical aura—as some special and indescribable personal quality. (For example, the media often apply the term to anything with a hint of charm or glamour.) Even among researchers, confusion surrounds the concept. Some describe it as a set of behaviors. Others consider it a cluster of traits, and still others consider it a divine gift or extraordinary ability of an unspecified nature. Multiple and vague interpretations of the phenomenon have caused problems in defining and delineating its boundaries—what it is and what it is not.

Related to the problem of defining the term *charisma* is the problem of developing a conceptual framework in which the phenomenon is related to its antecedent conditions and to its outcomes. There is a need for identifying various causal variables—personal or dispositional and environmental or contextual—that influence the development and emergence of charisma in business organizations. Likewise, there is a need for determining the effects of charisma on organizational outcomes and subordinate behavior. Ambiguities in defining charisma and the lack of a conceptual scheme have led to measurement difficulties in trying to capture the phenomenon. In addition, the phenomenon is complex and involves an interaction between important contextual factors, which adds to measurement problems. The behavioral sciences have shied away from such phenomena primarily because of problems of definition, measurement, control, and replication. As a result, existing research on the topic is limited and largely speculative.

Researchers have also encountered methodological difficulties in gaining access to charismatic leaders as objects of study. Often these individuals are time constrained and thus reluctant to be subjected to analytical probing. In lieu of direct access to leaders, researchers have had to rely on secondary sources of data, such as biographies and speeches. However, these sources have their own problems of interpretation and subjectivity: Rather than truly reflecting the intent or behavior of the leader, biographies may convey the biographer's intentions and attributions. Speeches may be the work of speech writers and thus may not present a true picture of the leader's motives that underlie the text.

The nature of charisma and methodological limitations have made the study of charismatic leadership in business difficult. However, the existence of charismatic leadership as an experiential phenomenon in organizations makes scientific investigation imperative; thus, these theoretical and methodological problems must be viewed as challenges for future research rather than as barriers. For the researcher, prospects for the future are threefold. First, it is important that theories of charismatic leadership in organizations begin to address the issues of what charisma is, how it develops, what precipitates its manifestation in organizational contexts, what its effects are, and how it relates to other leadership forms. Second, considerable research efforts must be directed toward operationalizing the concept of charisma and its causes and effects. This should encourage rigorous and systematic empirical studies of charismatic leadership within organizations. Innovative research techniques and designs must be applied in order to explicate this elusive phenomenon in comprehensible terms. Third, research should be done to develop training programs for charismatic leadership and to assess their effectiveness in achieving organizational objectives and in improving the motivational potential of organization members. The beginnings of these prospects are reflected in the various chapters in this volume.

Overview

In the Introduction, Jay A. Conger and Rabindra N. Kanungo discuss the problems and prospects of studying charismatic leadership in business organizations. Chapters in Part One treat the nature and dynamics of charismatic leadership. In Chapter One, Conger presents a literature review that provides a historical perspective, tracing conceptualizations of charismatic leadership from the pioneering work of German sociologist Max Weber to the present-day theories of organizational scholars. The chapter provides a thorough review of Weber's views on the subject, as well as a broad and integrative view of the existing literature. In Chapter Two, Bernard M. Bass provides an extensive review of conceptual and empirical work on the nature and dynamics of charisma. He examines the evolving conceptualizations of charismatic leadership, starting with Weber, and finishes with his own operationalization of the concept. His review identifies the critical leadership, followership, and contextual determinants of charismatic influence. In Chapter Three, Conger and Kanungo propose a behavioral framework for understanding the nature of charismatic leadership. They analyze different stages of the leadership process and identify within each stage a number of behavioral components that are critical for the manifestation of charisma. In Chapter Four, Robert J. House, James Woycke, and Eugene M. Fodor distinguish charismatic leaders from noncharismatic and transactional leaders in terms of a specific set of leader attributes and follower outcomes. They provide empirical evidence for their conceptualization of charismatic leadership in a study of United States presidents.

Part Two introduces the element of strategic vision, which is considered a critical component of charismatic leadership. Marshall Sashkin, in Chapter Five, analyzes the personality orientations and cognitive skills of visionary leaders. In addition, he explores through several frameworks the dimensions of strategic vision and the means for its effective communication. In Chapter Six, Frances R. Westley and Henry Mintzberg offer the reader strategic visions of two charismatic leaders in action and over time. Readers are able to witness the powerful mutual interactions between the leaders and the situations in which they find themselves. The authors conclude with configurations of strategic style characterizing the two leaders studied.

In Part Three, we shift our focus from attempting to understand the sources and character of charismatic influence to an examination of the limits of charisma. Chapters Seven (by Jane M. Howell) and Eight (by Manfred F. R. Kets de Vries) explore the potential positive power of charisma, its possible negative outcomes, and the strong dependencies that can result from this form of leadership. In Chapter Nine, Nancy C. Roberts and Raymond T. Bradley introduce the notion that forces outside of the leader may significantly influence the manifestation of charisma. They follow a charismatic leader from a situation in which she was perceived as charismatic to another in which she appeared to have lost her charismatic appeal. They offer a number of hypotheses as to why her charisma failed to transfer and suggest that context may play a critical role in the appearance of charisma.

Part Four looks at the developmental forces behind charismatic leadership and considers the possibility of training managers to be charismatic leaders. In Chapter Ten, Bruce J. Avolio and Tracy C. Gibbons examine the development of charismatic leaders from two angles: the personal development of the leader and the leader's role in developing subordinates. They remind readers of the need to examine a leader within a broad historical view of that individual's life. In Chapter Eleven, Conger and Kanungo argue that charismatic leadership may be trainable. Highlighting specific leadership skills for training, they outline a general approach to developing charismatic leaders.

Finally, in our Conclusion, we first look back over the volume to identify the areas of convergence and divergence among the contributors. We then look forward to where future research should and will be directed.

Conclusion

This book is a celebration of an emerging field. As such, it reflects the diversity of thought and perspective that characterizes a field whose identity has yet to be solidified. As the reader will discover, there are as many emerging areas of agreement as there are differences of opinion, and there are as many unanswered questions as answered. With this in mind, it is our hope that you, the reader, will join us with a spirit of inquiry that is both adventurous and open to challenge.

References

Bales, R. F. *Interaction Process Analysis*. Reading, Mass.: Addison-Wesley, 1950.

Fitzgerald, F. *Cities on a Hill*. New York: Simon & Schuster, 1986.

Halpin, A. W., and Winer, B. J. "A Factorial Study of the Leader Behavior Descriptions." In R. M. Stogdill and A. E. Coons (eds.), *Leader Behavior: Its Description and Measurement*. Columbus: Bureau of Business Research, Ohio State University, 1957.

Johnson, D. P. "Dilemmas of Charismatic Leadership: The Case of the People's Temple." *Sociological Analysis*, 1979, *40*, 315–323.

Lamb, R. B. *Running American Business*. New York: Basic Books, 1987.

Levin, H. *Grand Delusions: The Cosmic Career of John DeLorean*. New York: Viking Penguin, 1983.

Lewin, K., Lippitt, R., and White, R. K. "Patterns of Aggressive Behavior in Experimentally Created Social Climates." *Journal of Social Psychology*, 1939, *10*, 271–301.

Mintzberg, H. *The Nature of Managerial Work*. New York: Harper & Row, 1973.

Mintzberg, H. "If You're Not Serving Bill and Barbara, Then You're Not Serving Leadership." In J. G. Hunt, U. Sekaran, and C. A. Schriesheim (eds.), *Leadership: Beyond Establishment Views*. Carbondale: Southern Illinois University Press, 1982.

Naisbitt, J. *Megatrends*. New York: Warner Books, 1982.

Raven, B. H., and French, J. R. P. "Group Support, Legitimate Power, and Social Influence." *Journal of Personality*, 1958, *26*, 400–409.

Vroom, V. H., and Yetton, P. W. *Leadership and Decision Making*. Pittsburgh, Penn.: University of Pittsburgh Press, 1973.

Yukl, G. A. *Leadership in Organizations*. Englewood Cliffs, N.J.: Prentice-Hall, 1981.

Zaleznik, A. "Managers and Leaders: Are They Different?" *Harvard Business Review*, 1977, *15* (3), 67–68.

1

Theoretical Foundations of Charismatic Leadership

Jay A. Conger

As was discussed in the Introduction, our theories of charismatic leadership in management are only now beginning to take shape. To use a management metaphor, we are in the start-up phase of the venture. The topic has actually suffered from a serious lack of attention. To put its neglect in perspective, we turn to *Stogdill's Handbook of Leadership* (Bass, 1981), which is considered *the* reference book on leadership studies. Combing through the more than 5,000 studies included in the handbook, only a dozen references to charismatic leadership are to be found. This is an ironic and disheartening discovery given the profound impact of charismatic leaders. As Kanungo and I suggest in the Introduction, much of this neglect can be traced to impressions of charisma as a vague and almost mystical phenomenon. Researchers have been reluctant to face some of the methodological dilemmas associated with studying this impressionistic form of leadership.

Nonetheless, a small but growing number of individuals have begun to explore this overlooked topic. Their efforts, to date, have been largely theoretical rather than empirical—a reflection of methodological barriers—and their orientation has been principally psychological rather than sociological—a reflection of their backgrounds as ''micro'' theorists of organizational behavior. Yet, as the chapters in this book will attest, they have begun the important process of theory building and are doing so within a range of perspectives. At the same time, it would

12

appear that a critical mass of research interest has developed, and I suspect that within a few years our knowledge of charismatic leadership will be vastly deeper than and different from what it is today.

This chapter provides an overview of the development of theory up to the present. Particular attention is devoted to exploring the historical antecedents to our current theories. For while the chapters contained in this book suggest the formation of a new body of knowledge, it is important to acknowledge the profound influence of political scientists and sociologists from earlier decades. Starting with those of German sociologist Max Weber, it is possible to see how previous conceptualizations have influenced the ideas of current scholars. The chapter concludes with a review of works by organizational theorists.

Max Weber: Theory Builder

Max Weber ([1924] 1947) is the standard reference point for writers on the subject of charisma. He was the first theorist to actually use the term to describe a form of social authority. As such, his conceptualization of "charismatic authority" has had a significant influence on our notions of what a charismatic leader is and is not. It is important that we take a close look at his ideas.

Weber was particularly intrigued by the forces of authority in society. He developed a typology of three "ideal types": the charismatic, the traditional, and the rational-legal. These ideal types were not concepts in the strict sense of the word but rather theoretical systems (much like the perfectly rational model of man). In other words, the attributes the ideal types describe were meant to be taken not as defining properties but rather as propositions and heuristics (Willner, 1984).

Weber distinguished these three types of authority along several dimensions. *Charismatic authority,* he postulated, derives its legitimacy not from rules, positions, or traditions but rather from a faith in the leader's exemplary character. The holder of charisma is "set apart from ordinary men and treated as endowed with supernatural, superhuman, or at least . . . exceptional powers and qualities . . . [which] are not accessible to the ordinary person but are regarded as of divine origin or as exemplary, and on the basis of them the individual concerned is treated as a leader" (Weber, [1924] 1947, pp. 358–359). *Traditional authority,* he explains, is based on "an established belief in the sanctity of immemorial traditions," and *rational-legal authority* rests on the legality of rules—on the belief that "obedience is owed to the legally established impersonal order." Weber further distinguished between the charismatic, the traditional, and the rational-legal in four fundamental ways:

Rank Versus Personal Authority: While traditional and rational-legal forms of authority are invested in a rank or office, Weber argued that charismatic authority is found in the personal qualities of an individual leader. Unlike traditional and rational-legal leaders, who are appointed or elected under existing traditions and rules (such as a king or a president), a charismatic leader is chosen by followers out of a belief that their leader is extraordinarily gifted. The charismatic's bases of power are therefore personal, whereas traditional and rational-legal leaders derive their power from positions, expertise, rewards, coercion, rules, and traditions (Etzioni, 1961; Schein, 1980). As Weber asserted: "The charismatic hero does not deduce his authority from codes and statutes . . . , nor does he deduce his authority from traditional custom or feudal vows of faith . . . [rather, the] charismatic leader gains and maintains authority solely by proving his strength in life. If he wants to be a prophet, he must perform miracles; if he wants to be a war lord, he must perform heroic deeds" (Eisenstadt, 1968, p. 22).

The Rational Revolution Versus the Heroic Revolution. In contrast to traditional authority, both the charismatic and the rational-legal forms have their origins in revolution. According to Weber, rational-legal authority is a revolution against the tyranny of tradition. It seeks to replace the power of ancient and sacred custom with the "rationality" of man-made rules. In other words, the royal family is replaced by the elected official. Obedience is then owed to decisions determined by regulations that are devised by humans but also changeable by humans (according to constitutional procedures, and so forth). This is in contrast to traditional rule, which follows custom and tradition and usually is said to derive from some divinity.

The charismatic revolution is perceived as a radical contrast to the pretentions of rulers to a "divine right of kings" or to abstract legal statutes (Eisenstadt, 1968, pp. 23–24). It is personified in the charismatic leader: "Charismatic domination means a rejection of all ties to any external order in favor of the exclusive glorification . . . of the prophet and hero. Hence, its attitude is revolutionary and transvalues everything; it makes a sovereign break with all traditional and rational norms: 'It is written, but I say unto you'" (Eisenstadt, 1968, p. 24).

Thus, the charismatic revolution depends on beliefs in heroism and revelation. Through its emotional appeal, charismatic authority seeks to overturn an existing social order that is stagnant or in crisis. Its goals are to reorient the world to a more ideal and transcendent order. Its tools of revolution are the human mind and emotions. Such revolutions, Weber hypothesized, cannot arise from within existing institutional arrangements but rather must come from the "margins of society," since they represent such a strong break with existing traditions or rational orders. And unlike the rational-legal revolution, which is a gradual process of disenchantment with the world, the charismatic revolution appears instantaneously.

Stable Versus Transitory. Weber reasoned that charismatic authority is essentially unstable and transitory, unlike the traditional and rational-legal forms. At best, the lifetime of charismatic authority coincides with the lifetime of the charismatic leader, while the other forms of authority may persist far longer than their founders—literally for centuries. As a revolutionary force, the purpose of charismatic authority is to bridge the transition from one existing order to the next. Its role is to create and institutionalize new orders. After accomplishing this goal, charisma fades or is routinized. Rules, traditions, and institutions grow up to stabilize and guide the new social arrangements and to replace the charismatic leader who either has departed through death or other circumstances or has given in to rule by tradition or bureaucracy.

Weber also argued that success and failure contribute to this transitory nature of charismatic authority. For example, in the process of establishing a new order, the charismatic's mission may meet with failure. Failure is a serious challenge to the charismatic's authority, since it reveals a less than superhuman character on the leader's part: "Above all . . . his divine mission must 'prove' itself in that those who faithfully surrender to him must fare well. If they do not fare well, he is obviously not the master sent by the gods. . . . It is then that his mission is extinguished. . . . The charismatic holder is deserted by his following, however, [only] because pure charisma does not know any 'legitimacy' other than that flowing from personal strength, that is, one which is constantly being proved" (Eisenstadt, 1968, p. 23).

Conversely, success confirms the powers of the leader and is therefore critical to sustaining charismatic authority. Long-term success, however, creates its own problems. For in achieving the mission's goals, there is often a desire to institutionalize the new order: "Usually the wish of the master himself and always that of his disciples . . . [is] to change charisma . . . from a once-and-for-all extremely transitory free gift of grace . . . into a permanent everyday possession" (Weber, [1924] 1947, p. 236). The turning point comes as followers begin to attain positions of authority and material advantage and as the wish to institutionalize these benefits grows. With institutionalization (or routinization), authority by charisma is replaced by rules and traditions, and the charismatic life cycle ends.

Charismatic authority, then, poses a fundamental paradox: The very forms of bureaucracy and tradition that it rises up against ultimately consume it. Its essential role is to spark revolution and, in turn, the creation of a new social order; as the new order shifts through stages of stability, order, and progress, it assumes the form of a traditional or rational-legal system.

Formal Versus Informal Organization. Weber stated that while both traditional and rational-legal authority are organized around permanent and formal structures, charismatic authority operates informally through human relationships. Since it embodies a formative and revolutionary structure, charismatic authority is unencumbered by the formalities and organizational arrangements of the previous order and even rebels against such forms: "In contrast to any kind of bureaucratic organization of offices, the charismatic structure knows nothing of a form or of an ordered procedure of appointment or dismissal. It knows no regulated 'career,' 'advancement,' 'salary,' or regulated and expert training of the holder of charisma and his aides. It knows no agency of control or appeal, or local bailiwicks or exclusive functional jurisdictions; nor does it embrace permanent institutions like our bureaucratic 'departments' which are independent of persons and purely personal charisma. . . . In this respect, it is sharply opposed both to rational, and particularly bureaucratic, authority and to traditional authority" (Eisenstadt, 1968, pp. 20, 51-52). Commitment, then, is to a powerful bond to the leader rather than to a set of rules or hierarchical bodies of authority that represent the status quo.

Using these distinguishing dimensions, Weber sought to capture and explain the forces of individual creativity and responsibility through the construct of charismatic authority. By emphasizing the extraordinary and mystical, he developed a concept of authority and social organization that was in direct contradiction to the logic of rational-legal and traditional systems. At the same time, Weber was concerned with understanding the creation, maintenance, and transformation of institutional arrangements. Intrigued by the forces that stabilized and ordered society and those that brought change and disorder, he sought to categorize the two into "traditional/rational-legal" on the one hand and "charismatic" on the other. He was careful, however, to ensure that the term be considered *value free*. As political scientist Thomas Dow, Jr. (1969, p. 316), notes: "Charismatic leaders may—at the least—involve their followers in a cruel hoax, or, as in Hitler's case, an epic tragedy . . . it is a moot point whether this new order will represent an ethical improvement over the ancient regime, the outcome of such episodes being as unpredictable as their occurrence."

Implications of Weber's Theory

As political scientist Ann Ruth Willner (1984) points out, although Weber's major focus was on the transformation of charisma into other forms of authority, he did provide us with elements of its typical course: a condition under which it emerges (distress), a requirement for its maintenance (success), a probable outcome (institutionalization), and some of the means by which charismatic leaders exercise their authority (magical abilities, revelations of heroism, powers of mind and speech). Equally important, he created a category of leadership and authority that has been widely accepted as having significant validity as a heuristic.

From a managerial perspective, however, three assumptions made by Weber are at odds with organizational contexts. The first is that the charismatic leader is elected rather than imposed, the latter being the general case in most businesses. The second is his proposition that charismatic leaders arise from the margins of society, whereas business leaders generally emerge from within existing rational-legal institutions. Third, Weber stressed the anti-economic character of charismatic rule: "It [charisma] is immediately threatened in its innermost being when the economic interests of everyday life prevail" (Runciman, 1978, p. 235). Weber argued that charisma held contempt for all methodical forms of activity—especially economic activity, which was "the specific home of the patriarchal structure of domination and of the bureaucratic structure" (Runciman, 1978, p. 233). For Weber then, "charismatic business leaders" might appear to be a contradiction in terms. Yet he admitted the possibility of their existence, citing Henry Villard of Northern Pacific Railroad as a possible example: "Nevertheless, even here [the economy] there may be room for charisma" (Runciman, 1978, p. 233).

Thus, the implications of these assumptions for charismatic leaders in business have more to do with differences in the leaders' relationships with followers (on whom the leaders are more often imposed) and with their institutions (coming from within economic institutions) than with the types of relationships described by Weber. In the case of business leaders, it is presumed that the levels of devotion from their followers may be less extreme and the qualities of revolution, instability, and informality may not be of as great a magnitude or as powerful as Weber described.

In addition, Weber's hypotheses raise more research questions than they answer. Foremost is the issue of the locus of charismatic leadership. Because of Weber's sociological perspective and the resulting emphasis on social context and interaction, the issues of personal attributes and relational dynamics between leader and followers were largely overlooked. Questions surrounding the relationship of these different elements—the social context, the leader, and the followers—remained to be explored more scientifically.

Beyond Weber:
Contributions from Political Science and Sociology

In the late 1940s, translations of Weber's original work on charismatic authority appeared in the United States. An entire decade passed, however, before American sociologists and political scientists began to explore his ideas on charismatic authority seriously. From these explorations, a principle area of debate arose around the question: Where is the locus of charisma—in leaders' extraordinary qualities, in the larger social context, or in the relationship with followers?

While popular interpretations of charisma link it directly to the leader's personality, political scientists Dow (1969) and Willner (1984) demonstrated that the search for a set of universal qualities common to charismatic political and religious leaders did not yield decisive results. Instead, variations in individual personalities were so great (compare Gandhi and Hitler, for example) that a single charismatic personality type seemed highly improbable (Willner, 1984, p. 14).

Some (Blau, 1963; Chinoy, 1961; Friedland, 1964; Wolpe, 1968) believed instead that the social and historical context is the critical determinant in the emergence of charismatic leadership. Chinoy (1961, p. 247), for example, argued: "No prophet

(charismatic leader) can succeed unless the conditions are pro-
pitious. He succeeds when a political following exists because
of the problems some people face. This importance of both the
leader and the context . . . are suggested in the . . . Reforma-
tion, [when] Martin Luther found public opinion supersaturated
with revolution; all that was needed to precipitate it was a pebble
thrown in." Others (Dow, 1969; Marcus, 1961; Willner, 1984)
challenged these assertions, arguing instead that charisma resides
within the personal attributes of the charismatic leader and in
the relationship between the leader and his or her followers:
"In short, we do not believe there is any usual or necessary context within which charisma naturally develops. The situation . . .
may be relatively ordered, or it may involve . . . disorder. In
either case, . . . such situations have not uniformly produced
a revolutionary departure . . . and have as often resulted in
noncharismatic as in charismatic solutions. Thus, any analysis
which concentrates exclusively on the social context . . . risks
misunderstanding the fundamental nature of the charismatic
movement, [that is,] the relative independence of both the exceptional individual and his ideas" (Dow, 1969, p. 309).

   Much of the debate was resolved by the work of Willner
(1984), who, using in-depth case studies, demonstrated that charismatic leadership is not the product of a turbulent environment.
Willner concluded (1984, p. 46) from a review of six case studies
of charismatic political leaders that "only two, Hitler and Roosevelt, seem to conform sufficiently closely to the preconditions
of crisis and psychic distress specified in the conventional formula." In the other cases, little or no relationship existed between contexts of turmoil and charismatic leadership. Willner
argued instead that charisma is a relational and perceptual phenomenon and that the concept is most effectively defined in terms
of an individual's perceptions of and responses to a leader:
"It [is] not what the leader is but what people see the leader
as that counts in generating the charismatic relationship" (1984,
pp. 14–15). And because societies and groups differ in their
dominant definitions of extraordinary qualities, the content of
leadership images, projected and perceived, differs from group
to group. It was therefore impossible, Willner contended, to construct a universal "charismatic personality."

While a universal personality could not explain the phenomenon, Willner argued that individual personalities nonetheless play an important role, "for aspects of a leader's personality may partly determine his ability to project those images of himself that give rise to charismatic perceptions" (1984, p. 15). From her research, Willner identified four factors that, aided by individual personality, appear to be catalytic in the attribution of charisma to a leader: invocation of important cultural myths by the leader, performance of what are perceived as heroic or extraordinary feats, projection of attributes "with an uncanny or a powerful aura," and outstanding rhetorical skills (1984, p. 61). Willner's research was pivotal in understanding charismatic leadership, for it narrowed the focus to the leader and to the relational/perceptual dynamics with followers. And while context retained the potential to influence these dynamics significantly, it was not the overriding causal factor or the necessary catalyst.

Beyond the issue of charisma's locus, debate also focused on Weber's assertion that charismatic authority could arise only from outside existing institutional arrangements. Among political scientists and sociologists, there was a general belief that charismatic authority could also emerge from within existing institutions. This assumption was confirmed by Peter L. Berger (1963), who drew upon historical evidence to demonstrate that certain charismatic leaders had appeared as revolutionary forces within existing institutions. The charismatic revolution was no longer assumed to come only from the fringes of society; it also could come from within existing institutions. Political scientists and sociologists then broadened the application of charisma to leaders who were already office holders in bureaucratic organizations.

As well, there was some debate as to whether charisma belonged to the secular as well as the spiritual. Originally a Greek word meaning "gift," *charisma* was used by the early Christian church to describe gifts from God that enabled the receiver to perform extraordinary feats, such as prophecy and healing. Before Weber, the term was principally associated with such contexts.

Two political scientists, Karl Loewenstein (1966) and C. J. Friedrich (1961), argued against extending the concept beyond its religious antecedents. Loewenstein felt that the true forms of charismatic authority were not found in a modern world of technology and mass democracy but rather in the "pre-Cartesian" world—in cultures with a "magico-religious" or primitive ambiance. Only in societies "free of bureaucracy" and operating "on the level of myth" could charisma be found. To Loewenstein, Weber's true charismatic leader had been replaced by pseudocharismatics, who were master manipulators of modern mass communication (Willner, 1984, p. 12).

Friedrich (1961), however, traced his arguments back to Rudolph Sohm, a theologian who described the ecclesiastical organization of the Christian Church as based upon the distribution of God's gifts, or "charismata." Friedrich stressed that Sohm's interpretation of charisma centered on a *transcendental call by a divine being*. Charismatic authority, Friedrich insisted, had to remain linked to this original meaning. Weber misused the term in that secular leaders rarely possessed or sought a foundation in the divine.

Loewenstein undermined his own argument by acknowledging the charisma of Napoleon, a post-Cartesian leader (Willner, 1984, p. 13). Further, his contention that myth and ritual belong exclusively to the world of religion was challenged. For while religion and politics have been historically tightly intertwined, the separation of politics from religion in modern times has not ensured its divorce from myth and ritual. Rather, as Willner points out, the decline of religious influence in the modern secular world may have augmented the impact of political myth and ritual (Willner, 1984, p. 13).

In addition, the argument that mass communication and technology can create a counterfeit charisma was also challenged. Citing Richard Nixon as an example, Willner (1984) demonstrated that even the media expertise and financial resources available to a political leader could not necessarily create an image of personal charisma. And if they had, would it make any difference? The effect would be the same; only the means to achieve that effect would be different (Willner, 1984, pp. 13–14).

In Friedrich's case, again, the division between secular and religious leadership is not as clear as he would have us believe. For example, rulers in the ancient past embodied both the sacred and the secular. The pharaohs of Egypt combined these roles as a manifestation of the divine and as administrators of the state. Only in recent times have church and state separated, and only in the United States is that separation a strict matter of law. To confine charisma to the sacred would appear unrealistic, since two of the phenomenon's essential qualities of an extraordinary bond between leader and followers and a revolutionary and transcendental mission are present in both secular and religious settings. Ultimately, however, the issue of whether *charisma* belonged to the secular or to the sacred never gained momentum and was resolved by the widespread acceptance by both sociologists and political scientists that the term could include secular as well as religious leaders.

Contributions from Organizational Behavior

Organizational theorists directed considerable attention to the study of leadership (Bass, 1981) yet showed surprisingly little interest in charismatic forms. Nor did they attempt to link existing theoretical paradigms (for example, task versus social orientations) to charismatic leaders. Stock taking of the organizational behavior literature reveals only seven conceptual schemes proposed specifically for organizational settings (Bass, 1985; Berlew, 1974; Conger and Kanungo, 1987; House, 1977; Katz and Kahn, 1978; Trice and Beyer, 1986; Zaleznik and Kets de Vries, 1975). In addition, empirical studies of charismatic (and/or transformational) leadership have been reported by Avolio and Bass (1985); Bass (1985); Bass, Waldman, Avolio, and Bebb (1987); Conger (1985); Hater and Bass (1986); House (1985); Howell (1985); Pereira (1987); Roberts (1984); Smith (1982); Trice and Beyer (1986); Waldman, Bass, and Einstein (1985); and Yukl and Van Fleet (1982). Some of these will be described in greater detail by Bass in Chapter Two and House, Woycke, and Fodor in Chapter Four.

Unlike the earlier political science and sociological literature, there is little disagreement in the literature over the locus of charismatic leadership: A relational basis is widely accepted.

Charisma is believed not to reside solely in the leader and his or her personal attributes but rather in the interplay between the leader's attributes and the needs, beliefs, values, and perceptions of followers. Both Katz and Kahn (1978) and House and Baetz (1979) further postulate that the leader and followers must share basic beliefs and values in order to validate the leader's charisma.

As House, Woycke, and Fodor describe in Chapter Four, the charismatic (and/or transformational leadership) theories can be distinguished from more traditional theories of leadership along two important dimensions. First, whereas traditional theories take performance, satisfaction, and cognitions of subordinates as their dependent variables, charismatic theories generally take follower self-esteem, follower trust and confidence in the leader, follower motivation to perform beyond the call of duty, and follower emotional responses to work as their dependent variables. Second, while traditional leadership theories describe leaders in terms of social or task-oriented behavior, charismatic theories describe leaders in terms of articulating a vision and a mission, empowering followers, setting challenging expectations for followers, and creating positive and inspirational images in the minds of followers.

Unfortunately, systematic attempts at developing theories of charismatic leadership in organizations are rare. Many of the existing theories offer overlapping sets of attributes that provide pieces of the puzzle but lack comprehensive models to explain important underlying processes. Thus, there is considerable variation in the phenomenon's conceptualization. Equally important, there is limited empirical and comparative evidence to support conclusions, and explanations are based largely on theoretical speculation. As a result, the subject remains a largely unexplored topic in terms of organizational theory. Nonetheless, in order to understand the theoretical perspectives behind each of the chapters in this book, it is important that we examine the contributions of the principal organizational theorists up to this point. We can divide their work into three schools: the behavioral scientists, the institutionalists, and the psychoanalysts.

Behavioral Perspectives

The majority of charismatic leadership theorists fall into this category. As such, they have defined much of the research focus of the field. These theorists have been primarily concerned with identifying both a set of behaviors that distinguish charismatic leaders from noncharismatic leaders and a set of behavioral effects that distinguish followers of one form from the other. To a large extent, they have been influenced by the work of political scientist James MacGregor Burns (1978) and his concept of transformational leadership, as well as by psychologist David McClelland (1975) and his conception of leadership as an empowering process. There is some consensus among these theorists as to specific behaviors associated with charismatic leaders. These include vision or appealing ideological goals (see Bass, 1985; Berlew, 1974; Conger, 1985; Katz and Kahn, 1978; House, 1977; Zaleznik and Kets de Vries, 1975), behavior that instills confidence and empowers (see Bass, 1985; Berlew, 1974; House, 1977), and an ability to inspire or create inspirational activities (see Bass, 1985; Berlew, 1974; Conger, 1985; Zaleznik and Kets de Vries, 1975). In addition, there is also partial consensus on certain outcomes of charismatic leadership: heightened motivation of subordinates (Bass, 1985; Berlew, 1974; House, 1977), heightened performance of subordinates (Bass, 1985; Berlew, 1974; House, 1977), and increased confidence in the leader (Bass, 1985; Berlew, 1974; House, 1977).

Bass: Transformational Leadership. James MacGregor Burns, in his Pulitzer Prize–winning book, *Leadership* (1978), contrasted what he perceived to be the two essential forms of leadership: transactional (or exchange) and transformational (or charismatic). Under transactional leadership, followers behave in ways desired by their leaders in exchange for goods. The goods are usually specific, tangible, and calculable. The relationship lasts only as long as the needs of both leader and follower are satisfied by the continuing exchange. Thus, this is not a relationship that "binds leader and follower together in mutual and continuing pursuit of a higher purpose" (Burns, 1978, p. 20).

In contrast, transformational leadership takes place "when one or more persons engage with others in such a way that leaders and followers raise one another to higher levels of motivation and morality" (Burns, 1978, p. 20). It is a relationship built upon the deeper needs and emotional desires of followers, as well as those of their leader.

Bernard M. Bass and his associate Bruce J. Avolio conducted several studies to see if Burns's concept of transformational leadership could be applied to complex organizations. In this research, Bass (1985) discovered that managers described by subordinates as transformational leaders can be distinguished along three behavioral dimensions. The first is charismatic leadership, which, after factor analyses, accounted for 66 percent of the response variance. This dimension describes subordinate faith in the leader, inspiration and encouragement experienced by subordinates, and the respect accorded to the leader. (In Chapter Two, Bass further expands the distinguishing characteristics of charismatic leaders.) The other two behavioral dimensions of transformational leaders are intellectual stimulation (6.3 percent of response variance) and individualized consideration (6.0 percent of response variance).

In another study, Avolio and Bass (1985) found that high-potential managers rated significantly higher on the three transformational leadership dimensions than did managers rated as having less potential. In addition, Avolio, Waldman, Einstein, and Bass (1985) tested the association between team performance in a management simulation game and post-game ratings of leaders. The higher-performance, higher-satisfaction teams were those that had leaders with higher transformational leadership ratings. As Avolio and Bass (1985) pointed out, however, the teams' successful performance may have led team members to erroneously attribute transformational qualities to their leaders.

Bass and Avolio essentially operationalized Burns's concept of transformational leadership for organizational settings. Their findings demonstrated some support for a normative model of leadership. That is, in Bass and Avolio's studies, leadership effectiveness was equated with the ability to arouse followers emotionally and to inspire them to greater effort and accomplishment.

While Bass and Avolio agreed that the most significant component of transformational leadership is charisma, they nonetheless believed that it cannot stand alone in terms of organizational effectiveness. They argued that "purely" charismatic leaders could fail to be transforming: "The purely charismatic may want followers to adopt the charismatic's world view and go no further; the transformational leader will attempt to instill in followers the ability to question not only established views but eventually those established by the leader" (Avolio and Bass, 1985, p. 14). This point of view is more fully explored by Bass in Chapter Two.

Berlew: A Contingency Theory of Needs and Charismatic Leadership. The first management theorist to discuss charismatic leadership in some detail was David E. Berlew (1974). He proposed a model of three stages of organizational leadership: custodial, managerial, and charismatic. The first two stages derive from task- versus people-oriented theories of leadership (Blake and Mouton, 1964; Hersey and Blanchard, 1977); custodial leaders are task oriented, as opposed to managerial leaders, who are people oriented. Charismatic leaders are an extension of the "people" orientation, with a pronounced emphasis on their ability to provide meaning and esteem for subordinates. Four specific activities or behaviors distinguish these leaders from custodial and managerial leaders: the development of a vision shared by organizational members, the creation of activities that have value or meaning for both organizational members and the organization, the development of a sense of personal confidence and control among organizational members, and behavior that empowers subordinates (for example, setting high expectations, rewarding rather than punishing, encouraging collaboration, helping only when asked, and creating success experiences).

In essence, Berlew's three stages describe a contingency model of leadership tied to differing levels of needs. Angry or resentful workers (stage 1), Berlew felt, are concerned with meeting basic needs for food, shelter, safety, security, and respect. A custodial form of leadership can satisfy these needs by improving working conditions, compensation, and fringe benefits. As conditions improve, however, workers increasingly become concerned with a sense of belonging and a desire to do satisfying work (stage 2). To resolve these needs, managers can provide work that is less routine and more challenging, build cohesive work teams, and allow employees greater say in decisions that directly affect them. Finally, after workers' needs for membership, achievement, and recognition have been met, they desire involvement in a more personally meaningful mission (stage 3)—"the feelings of potency that accompany 'shaping' rather than being shaped." Only charismatic leaders, Berlew argued, with their sense of vision and empowering behavior, can address this set of needs (Berlew, 1974, p. 23).

While Berlew did not support his hypotheses with empirical evidence or, for that matter, describe them in substantive detail, he drew a link between charismatic leadership and human needs. He assumed that the influence process involves meeting the higher-order needs of followers. Through an interplay of these needs and the need-fulfilling actions of the leader, the relationship becomes the arena in which charismatic leadership takes place. As with Bass and Avolio, Berlew used dependent variables of follower motivation and confidence; in general, however, his theory of charismatic leadership is incomplete.

Conger and Kanungo: Behavioral Dimensions of Charismatic Leadership. In 1985, Jay A. Conger conducted a comparative field study of senior executives who were described as either charismatic and effective or noncharismatic and effective leaders. He discovered that the charismatic leaders could be differentiated from the noncharismatic according to a set of specific attributes. These include strategic vision, unconventional or countercultural management practices and tactics involving personal risk, articulation and impression management skills, and inspirational management practices. He postulated that these attributes are interrelated and as such form a constellation. Conger further theorized that the likelihood of attributing charisma to a leader increases (1) as the number of these components increases and (2) as the level of intensity or strength of individual components increases.

Building on Conger's research, Conger and Rabindra N. Kanungo (1987) presented a behavioral model that addressed the influence process involved in charismatic leadership. They argued that charismatic leadership should be viewed as another leadership dimension in addition to task, social, and participative dimensions. According to their model, the attribution of charisma to a leader depends specifically on four variables: a strategic vision shared by followers that is highly discrepant from the status quo yet within a latitude of acceptance; the leader's deployment of innovative, risky, and unconventional means to achieve the desired vision; a realistic assessment by the leader of environmental resources and constraints for bringing about the vision; and the use of articulation and impression management practices to inspire followers in pursuit of the vision. They also hypothesized that charismatic leaders influence their followers through their personal idiosyncratic power rather than through position power. And unlike consensual or directive leaders, who might also rely on personal power, charismatic leaders draw upon their idealized vision, their entrepreneurial advocacy for change, and their exemplary and unconventional expertise as the sources of their personal power. In Chapter Three, Conger and Kanungo further refine and elaborate on their model.

Katz and Kahn: Distance, Fit, and Vision. Though Daniel Katz and Robert L. Kahn (1978) proposed only a very general theory of charismatic leadership, their most intriguing insights centered on their concepts of "distance" and "membership fit." They believed that social distance is an important variable for charismatic leadership in business settings (p. 546): "Immediate supervisors exist in the workaday world. . . . They are very human and very fallible, and immediate subordinates cannot build an aura of magic about them. Day-to-day intimacy destroys illusion. But the leader in the top echelons . . . is sufficiently distant from membership to make a simplified and magical image possible." They also acknowledged the leader's need to "fit" his or her followers in certain readily perceptible dimensions to ensure bonding. He or she must share in the basic values and traits of his or her subordinates. Unfortunately, Katz and Kahn did not elaborate on this interesting insight or provide substantive examples.

Katz and Kahn did attempt to answer the larger question of how charismatic leaders are able to influence others. Rather simply, they argued that the ability to articulate or construct an emotionally meaningful vision or mission is the critical element of a leader's charisma. For Katz and Kahn, then, influence is largely dependent on the leader's appealing vision, while a relational fit along certain basic values and behavioral dimensions ensures acceptance by followers. Social distance intensifies the leader's image as a superhuman individual. Beyond these general conclusions, Katz and Kahn offered no significant details.

House: Charismatics Versus Noncharismatics. Drawing on the literature in psychology and political science, Robert J. House (1977) proposed a model of charismatic leadership that distinguishes between the behavioral and personality characteristics of charismatic leaders and those of noncharismatics. Charismatics, he argued, typically can be differentiated by their qualities of dominance, self-confidence, a need to influence, and a strong conviction in the moral righteousness of their beliefs. He also maintained that they are more likely to espouse appealing ideological goals and to engage in behaviors that create the impression of success and competence in followers and that arouse motives relevant to their mission's accomplishment.

In addition, his theory addressed the influence of charismatic leaders on subordinates' motivation. Unlike exchange theories of leadership (Evans, 1970; House, 1971; House and Mitchell, 1974), in which the effects of leaders on followers' expectancies and cognition are emphasized, House stressed that charismatic leaders have their greatest effect on the emotions and valences of followers (House, 1987, p. 14). Through emotionally appealing goals and behaviors that arouse followers' needs for achievement, affiliation, or power, charismatic leaders are able to motivate task accomplishment. In addition, House hypothesized that such leaders simultaneously communicate high performance expectations and confidence in their followers' ability to meet such expectations. These actions, in turn, enhance follower expectations that their efforts will lead to performance accomplishments (House, 1987, p. 15). House and his colleagues more fully discuss his position on charismatic leadership in Chapter Four.

Two studies—by Bryan Smith and Jane M. Howell—supported several of House's propositions. Using House's theory, Smith (1982) developed a set of eighteen constructs and thirty-eight individual scales to measure subordinate reactions to charismatic and noncharismatic leaders. Smith found that the followers of reputed effective and charismatic leaders are more self-assured, report more support from their leaders, see their leaders as more dynamic, experience their work as more meaningful, have higher performance ratings, and work longer hours than do followers of noncharismatic but effective leaders. However, as Trice and Beyer (1986) pointed out, certain of the effects—self-assurance of subordinates, back-up support, higher performance, and longer work weeks—could be relevant to any study of leadership and ultimately may not be discriminatory.

In a laboratory study that compared the effects of charismatic leader behavior on followers with those of task- or social-oriented leader behavior, Howell (1985) found that charismatic leader behavior has a more positive and stronger influence on the satisfaction, performance, and adjustment of subjects. Equally important, her study provided strong empirical support for the notion that charismatic leadership is a function of followers' perceptions and that it is possible to teach selected individuals behaviors characteristic of charismatic leaders (House, 1987, pp. 16–21). Howell's study is described in greater detail in Chapter Two.

Institutionalization Perspectives

The institutionalists were primarily concerned with the processes by which social changes introduced by a charismatic leader were formalized into more permanent institutional arrangements. For Weber ([1924] 1947), the routinization (or institutionalization) of charisma was a fundamental aspect of its life cycle. He argued that charisma either fades or becomes institutionalized with the accomplishment of the charismatic leader's mission. In the latter case, he commented: "If [charisma] is not to remain a purely transitory phenomenon, but to take on the character of a permanent relationship forming a stable community, it is necessary for the character of charismatic authority to be radically changed. . . . It cannot remain stable, but becomes either traditionalized or rationalized or both" (Weber, [1924] 1947, p. 364). Despite the importance Weber attached to this aspect of charisma, little empirical research has focused on the routinization process (see Clark, 1972; Kanter, 1972; Trice and Beyer, 1986). Clark (1972), for example, undertook a study of the histories of three distinct colleges, in which he examined the processes by which ideologies and "organizational sagas" of founding leaders were institutionalized. He discovered five "essential carrying mechanisms" (1970, p. 246) that ensured fulfillment of the organization's ideological roots. First was a core group of believers among powerful faculty who routinized the charisma of the leader in "collegial authority" (1972, p. 81). Second was a set of "unusual courses, noteworthy requirements, or special methods of teaching" that permitted program embodiment of the saga (1972, p. 181). Third was an outside set of believers, usually alumni, who provided a supporting social base. Fourth involved a student subculture that "steadily and dependably transfered the ideology from one generation to the other" (1972, p. 182). Fifth was saga imagery expressed by such means as catalogues, ceremonies, statues, and written histories. Through these five mechanisms the transmission and institutionalization of the founder's charisma and mission were ensured.

   In addition, Kanter (1972) in a study of utopian communities employed the term *institutionalized awe* to describe the process by which charisma was diffused throughout the organization. She found that charismatic awe was institutionalized through shared ideology, leadership, and power and that it provided an important mechanism for promoting member commitment to the community.

   Among organizational theorists, however, Harrison M.

Trice and Janice M. Beyer provided one of the more systematic analyses of charisma's routinization, and their work essentially represents the institutionalization perspective.

Trice and Beyer: The Routinization of Charisma. In a field study of two charismatic leaders, Trice and Beyer (1986) found that in one case charisma had routinized, and in the other it had not. Using data collected through participant observation, they concluded that five factors are largely responsible for successful institutionalization: (1) the development of an administrative apparatus apart from the charismatic leader that puts the leader's mission into practice; (2) the transfer of charisma through rites and ceremonies to other members of the organization; (3) the incorporation of the charismatic's message and mission into oral and written traditions; (4) the selection of a successor who resembles the charismatic founder and is committed to the founder's mission; and (5) a continued identification with and commitment to the charismatic's original mission. These factors were largely absent in the case in which routinization did not take place.

Trice and Beyer were helpful in expanding the focus of organizational theorists to consider the institutionalization processes behind charisma. They provided certain important insights into the mechanisms that ensure the successful routinization of charisma, and they drew attention to an aspect of charisma that has received little research attention.

Psychoanalytical Perspectives

In the study of charismatic political leaders, psychoanalytical theory has been applied widely (see, for example, Devereux, 1955; Hummel, 1975; and Schiffer 1973), especially in attempts to understand the psychological predispositions of followers. It has been hypothesized that conversion to a charismatic movement involves a regression on the followers' part to an infantile state: Extreme anxiety triggered by crisis, serious internal conflict, or a weakened sense of personal identity induces followers to regress and "demand a leader who conforms to infantile ideas of adult behavior'' (Devereux, 1955, p. 150). Through a process of identification, the charismatic leader then becomes a powerful surrogate parent. However, as Willner (1984) notes, a lack of clinical studies makes such claims difficult to validate and generalize.

The first psychoanalysts to consider charismatic leadership in management settings were Zaleznik and Kets de Vries (1975). In contrast to political psychoanalysts who focused on followers, Zaleznik and Kets de Vries devoted their attention to the leader, his or her developmental history, and his or her disposition. Drawing upon William James's notion of the "twice-born" leader, they created a typology of leadership—the "maximum man" (or charismatic leader) and the "minimum man" (or consensus leader).

Zaleznik and Kets de Vries: The Inner Workings of Charismatic Man. For Abraham Zaleznik and Manfred F. R. Kets de Vries (1975), maximum man leads by charisma, minimum man by consensus. Maximum man is the creative institution builder, whereas minimum man represents the modern manager; "usually, the maximum men start great businesses but leave their future in the hands of minimum men, who function until crises occur" (Zaleznik and Kets de Vries, 1975, p. 237). In relationships with others, maximum man differs greatly from minimum man: "[Maximum man's relationship] is usually simple: He is their leader. At times he may be recognized practically on sight because of the glow of confidence his inner light gives him. He is charismatic; people are drawn to him by the power of his convictions and visions of reality. His presence inspires both dread and fascination; he evokes mystical reactions. The maximum man is a great innovator, but not always a good leader—he will have little use for subordinates who have different opinions—and his extremely high self-esteem may create problems. . . . The minimum man is concerned with the opinion of his peers. He would rather have egalitarian relations with men as brothers than be in the socially distant position of a father figure. He does not, therefore, lead public opinion, but follows it" (Zaleznik and Kets de Vries, 1975, pp. 237–241).

Zaleznik and Kets de Vries described the charismatic leader as a man of tremendous self-confidence and conviction. People are drawn to his strength and vision. The influence process rests on his captivating style of presentation, the power of his own self-image, and the grandiosity of his dreams. For followers, the maximum man assumes the quality of an idealized parent: "The 'inner light' of the charismatic leader [is] a kind of internal audience . . . with which maximum man has a continuous dialogue, . . . and one has the feeling, observing him, of watching a dramatization . . . as we listen to the charismatic leader we are on the inside and have lost the separation between self and other that characterizes rational thought. Intellect and emotion are no longer distinct. Somewhere within us, the images of parents as protectors and love objects come to the surface in a collapse of time, a merging of past and present. . . . Now the charismatic leader exerts his influence" (Zaleznik and Kets de Vries, 1975, p. 247).

Zaleznik and Kets de Vries took their analysis a step further by tracing the roots of charismatic personalities to an early childhood bond with one or both parents. They argued that charismatic leaders are the "chosen ones" in childhood; they are perceived as special, as favored. This attention leads to a strong sense of self-esteem that ultimately distinguishes these individuals from consensus leaders who lack such strong internal images of themselves: "As the lack of these images produces minimum man's dependence on others, so their strong presence in the maximum man diminishes his dependence, making him self-sufficient" (Zaleznik and Kets de Vries, 1975, p. 242). Out of these images, the charismatic leader develops a personality that is more creative, personal, and individual than that of a traditional manager. Organizationally, this strong sense of independence from others leads the charismatic leader to be an innovator, an institution builder.

For Zaleznik and Kets de Vries, the locus of charismatic leadership resides largely in the leader's personality. His or her personal qualities are the source of his or her influence, so his or her power is not dependent on outside forces. However, by implicitly highlighting transference as a critical element of the influence process, Zaleznik and Kets de Vries do imply an underlying relational dynamic. In Chapter Eight, Kets de Vries expands on the power and dynamics of transference and the dangers it presents for both the charismatic leader and his or her followership.

Conclusion

While this review provides a historical backdrop to our thinking on charismatic leadership, readers will discover that the next nine chapters attest to a significant deepening of our understanding of these leaders in management settings. More empirical evidence is beginning to appear and is giving new shape to existing theories. Ideas are being modified or deepened, such as in the study of strategic vision. Certain theorists are moving beyond simple formulations involving static attributes (which have characterized much of the existing research) to more complex theories explaining interrelationships and underlying processes. In addition, the negative consequences of charisma are being explored for the first time as is a growing awareness of contextual influences.

References

Avolio, B. J., and Bass, B. M. "Transformational Leadership, Charisma and Beyond." Working paper, School of Management, State University of New York, Binghamton, 1985.

Avolio, B. J., Waldman, D. A., Einstein, W. O., and Bass, B. M. "Transformational Leadership and Organizational Effectiveness." Unpublished manuscript, School of Management, State University of New York, Binghamton, 1985.

Bass, B. M. *Stogdill's Handbook of Leadership.* New York: Free Press, 1981.

Bass, B. M. *Leadership and Performance Beyond Expectations.* New York: Free Press, 1985.

Bass, B. M., Waldman, D. A., Avolio, B. J., and Bebb, M. "Transformational Leadership and the Falling Dominoes Effect." *Group and Organization Studies,* 1987, *12* (1), 73–87.

Berger, P. L. "Charisma and Religious Innovation: The Social

Location of the Israelite Prophecy." *American Sociological Review*, 1963, *28*, 940-950.

Berlew, D. E. "Leadership and Organizational Excitement." *California Management Review*, 1974, *17* (2), 21-30.

Blake, R. R., and Mouton, J. S. *The Managerial Grid.* Houston, Tex.: Gulf, 1964.

Blau, P. "Critical Remarks on Weber's Theory of Authority." *American Political Science Review*, 1963, *57* (2), 305-315.

Burns, J. M. *Leadership.* New York: Harper & Row, 1978.

Chinoy, E. *Society.* New York: Random House, 1961.

Clark, B. R. *The Distinctive College: Antioch, Reed, and Swarthmore.* Chicago: Aldine, 1970.

Clark, B. R. "The Organizational Saga in Higher Education." *Administrative Science Quarterly*, 1972, *17*, 178-184.

Conger, J. A. "Charismatic Leadership in Business: An Exploratory Study." Unpublished doctoral dissertation, School of Business Administration, Harvard University, 1985.

Conger, J. A., and Kanungo, R. N. "Towards a Behavioral Theory of Charismatic Leadership in Organizational Settings." *Academy of Management Review*, 1987, *12*, 637-647.

Devereux, G. "Charismatic Leadership and Crisis." In W. Muensterberger and S. Axelrod (eds.), *Psychoanalysis and the Social Sciences.* New York: International University Press, 1955.

Dow, T. E., Jr. "The Theory of Charisma." *Sociological Quarterly*, 1969, *10*, 306-318.

Eisenstadt, S. N. (ed.). *Max Weber: On Charisma and Institution Building.* Chicago: University of Chicago Press, 1968.

Etzioni, A. *A Comparative Analysis of Complex Organizations.* New York: Free Press, 1961.

Evans, M. G. "The Effects of Supervisory Behavior on the Path-Goal Relationship." *Organizational Behavior and Human Performance*, 1970, *5*, 277-298.

Friedland, W. H. "For a Sociological Concept of Charisma." *Social Forces*, 1964, *43* (1), 18-26.

Friedrich, C. J. "Political Leadership and the Problem of the Charismatic Power," *The Journal of Politics*, 1961, *23*, 3-24.

Hater, J. J., and Bass, B. M. "Superiors' Evaluations and Subordinates' Perceptions of Transformational and Transactional Leadership." Working paper, School of Management, State University of New York, Binghamton, 1986.

Hersey, P., and Blanchard, K. H. *Management of Organizational Behavior.* (4th ed.) Englewood Cliffs, N.J.: Prentice-Hall, 1977.

House, R. J. "A Path-Goal Theory of Leadership Effectiveness." *Administrative Science Quarterly,* 1971, *16,* 321–338.

House, R. J. "A 1976 Theory of Charismatic Leadership." In J. G. Hunt and L. L. Larson (eds.), *Leadership: The Cutting Edge.* Carbondale: Southern Illinois University Press, 1977.

House, R. J. "Research Contrasting the Behavior and Effect of Reputed Charismatic Versus Reputed Noncharismatic Leaders." Paper presented at annual meeting of the Administrative Science Association of Canada, Montreal, Apr. 1985.

House, R. J. "Führungs Theoriencharismatische Führung" [Exchange and Charismatic Theories of Leadership]. In A. Kaiser, G. Reber, and W. Wunderer (eds.), *Handwörterbuch der Führung* [Handbook of Leadership]. Stuttgart: C. E. Poeschel Verleg, 1987.

House, R. J., and Baetz, M. L. "Leadership: Some Empirical Generalizations and New Research Directions." *Research in Organizational Behavior,* 1979, *1,* 399–401.

House, R. J., and Mitchell, T. R. "Path-Goal Theory of Leadership." *Journal of Contemporary Business,* 1974, *3* (4), 81–97.

House, R. J., and Singh, J. V. "Organizational Behavior: Some New Directions for I/O Psychology." *Annual Review of Psychology,* 1987, *38,* 669–718.

Howell, J. M. "A Laboratory Study of Charismatic Leadership." Paper presented at annual meeting of the Academy of Management, San Diego, Calif., Aug. 1985.

Hummel, R. P. "Psychology of Charismatic Followers." *Psychological Reports,* 1975, *37,* 759–770.

Kanter, R. M. *Commitment and Community.* Cambridge, Mass.: Harvard University Press, 1972.

Katz, D., and Kahn, R. L. *The Social Psychology of Organizations.* New York: Wiley, 1978.

Loewenstein, K. *Max Weber's Political Ideas in the Perspective of Our Time.* Amherst: University of Massachusetts Press, 1966.

McClelland, D. C. *Power: The Inner Experience.* New York: Irvington, 1975.

Marcus, J. T. "Transcendence and Charisma." *The Western Political Quarterly,* 1961, *14,* 236–241.

Pereira, D. F. *Factors Associated with Transformational Leadership in an Indian Engineering Firm.* Unpublished paper, Lawson & Toubro Ltd., Bombay, India, 1987.

Roberts, N. C. "Transforming Leadership: Sources, Process, Consequences." Paper presented at annual meeting of the Academy of Management, Boston, Aug. 1984.

Runciman, W. G. (ed.). *Weber: Selections in Translation.* Cambridge, Eng.: Cambridge University Press, 1978.

Schein, E. *Organizational Psychology.* (3rd ed.) Englewood Cliffs, N.J.: Prentice-Hall, 1980.

Schiffer, I. *Charisma: A Psychoanalytic Look at Mass Society.* Toronto: University of Toronto Press, 1973.

Smith, B. J. "An Initial Test of a Theory of Charismatic Leadership Based on the Response of Subordinates." Unpublished doctoral dissertation, Faculty of Management, University of Toronto, 1982.

Trice, H. M., and Beyer, J. M. "Charisma and Its Routinization in Two Social Movement Organizations." *Research in Organizational Behavior,* 1986, *8,* 113–164.

Waldman, D. A., Bass, B. M., and Einstein, W. O. "Effort, Performance, and Transformational Leadership in Industrial and Military Service." Working paper no. 85–80. School of Management, State University of New York, Binghamton, 1985.

Weber, M. *The Theory of Social and Economic Organization.* (A. M. Henderson and T. Parsons, trans.; T. Parsons, ed.) New York: Free Press, 1947. (Originally published 1924.)

Willner, A. R. *The Spellbinders: Charismatic Political Leadership.* New Haven, Conn.: Yale University Press, 1984.

Wolpe, H. "A Critical Analysis of Some Aspects of Charisma." *Sociological Review,* 1968, *6,* 305–318.

Yukl, G. A., and Van Fleet, D. D. "Cross-Situational, Multi-Method Research on Military Leader Effectiveness." *Organizational Behavior and Human Performance,* 1982, *30,* 87–108.

Zaleznik, A., and Kets de Vries, M.F.R. *Power and the Corporate Mind.* Boston: Houghton Mifflin, 1975.

2

Evolving Perspectives on Charismatic Leadership

Bernard M. Bass

Charismatic leadership is seen in extremely highly esteemed persons (Weber, [1924] 1947). Such individuals exude confidence, dominance, a sense of purpose, and the ability to articulate the goals and ideas for which followers are already prepared psychologically (Fromm, 1941; House, 1977). The response of followers is likewise extreme. It is both cognitive and emotional, as well as devoted and unquestioning. Charismatic leaders have extraordinary influence over their followers, who become mobilized with moral inspiration and purpose. The followers experience a magnetic attention that transcends their usual experience. They become zealots and leaders in their own right (Burns, 1978; Trice and Beyer, 1986).

Although principal attention has been paid to charismatic leaders in the religious and political arenas, they also appear in organizational and military settings (Handy, 1976). Based on his observations of such successful leaders, Lawler (1984, p. 327) concluded that leadership occurs "through a combination of factors that can be captured by words like *vision, communication, symbols,* and *charisma.*" Such leaders are more concerned with doing the right things than with doing things right.

Charismatic leaders often emerge in times of crisis as prospective saviors who by their magical endowments will fulfill

Note: Parts of this chapter are adapted from Chapter 12 of *Bass and Stogdill Handbook of Leadership* (3rd ed.), forthcoming from Free Press (New York).

the unmet emotional needs of their completely trusting, overly dependent, and submissive followers. If successful, charismatic leaders bring about radical transformations in society.

Burns (1978) prefers to speak about *heroic* leadership, believing that *charisma* has been overworked in usage. In Burns's view, the highly esteemed individual is a hero. There is "belief in (heroic) leaders because of their personage alone, aside from their tested capacities, experience, or stand on issues; faith in the leaders' capacity to overcome obstacles and crises; readiness to grant to leaders the powers to handle crises; mass support for such leaders expressed directly—through votes, applause, letters, shaking hands—rather than through intermediaries or institutions. Heroic leadership is not simply a quality or entity possessed by someone; it is a type of relationship between leader and led. A crucial aspect of this relationship is the absence of conflict" (p. 244). The heroic, transcending leader excites and transforms previously dormant followers into active ones. He or she heightens motivation and instills in followers a sense of purpose and missionary zeal. Ultimately, followers become proselytizers acting as leaders as a consequence of their own raised awareness.

Etzioni (1961) and Hollander (1978) believe that charisma-like leadership can be a property of one's position (providing celebrity status) as well as of one's person. For example, an American president has a lot of luster, some of which may be lost after he or she leaves office. As an "office charismatic," such a leader may attain celebrity status by virtue of the strong public image afforded the holder of a valued role. In contrast, the personal charismatic is regarded extremely highly by virtue of the extent to which others have faith in him or her as a person. For instance, a charismatic avatar can attract people to his or her person because of his or her sacrificial renunciation of all worldly power and possessions. These two types of charismatic leaders may or may not be regarded in the same way, and their roles may overlap. Personal charismatics may have positions with high or low status (for example, a personal charismatic can occupy the highly valued office of president).

Etzioni (1961) notes that although charismatic office frequently has to be achieved, "office charisma" is ascribed: Regardless of his or her ability or performance, every incumbent obtains it with the office. Charisma can attach to any high social status, achieved or inherited, as can be seen in aristocratic offices (witness the public reaction to a visit by or the marriage of the Prince of Wales).

Although Weber felt that the personal charismatic creates a charismatic office to be filled by a noncharismatic successor, Etzioni (1961) points out there is nothing to preclude the personal charisma of a Roosevelt, for example, revealing itself more forcefully as the incumbent following uncharismatic predecessors in the same office (such as Harding, Coolidge, and Hoover). There also seems to be nothing necessarily precluding one charismatic succeeding another.

Publicly celebrated charismatics may display little charisma in their private lives: "Top executives, heads of state, and kings, who have charisma in the eyes of the public . . . may have little or [none] in the eyes of [their] private secretaries, valets, and cabinet ministers" (Etzioni, 1961, p. 316). Visibility and name recognition provided by television and media events have been essential for political election.

We cannot ignore the vicarious effect on mass audiences of the superstar who can only be an image and a name with which to identify. For instance, enlistment rates can increase substantially after a popular star appears in a war movie. "To most people . . . political figures . . . are just like box-office attractions in the field of entertainment—this despite the fact that many politicians are often bearers of ideals and ideologies. . . . We embrace the images . . . popular actors, actresses, and musicians who, above and beyond their talents, have been given charismatic status despite—or perhaps because of—certain flaws in their character or theatrical skills" (Schiffer, 1983, p. 9). Psychological projection and identification play important roles in the processes of this charismatic influence at a distance.

Weber's Concept of Charisma and Its Legacy

Weber's ([1922] 1963) introduction of the concept of charisma into social science was an adaptation from theology. In theology, charisma means endowment with the gift of divine grace. In Weber's model, a charismatic leader is viewed as a mystical, narcissistic, and personally magnetic savior. He also viewed charisma as a phenomenon that arose in times of crisis.

Weber ([1924] 1947) applied the concept to understanding the development and maintenance of complex organizations, in which the gift of extraordinariness is bestowed on a person by colleagues and subordinates instead of by God. Trice and Beyer (1986) show Weber's conceptualization of charisma to include five components: a person with extraordinary gifts; a crisis; a radical solution to the crisis; followers attracted to the exceptional person, believing that they are linked through him or her to transcendent powers; and validation of the person's gifts and transcendence in repeated experiences of success.

According to Weber, charismatic leaders inspire the creation of organizations that subsequently become traditionally or bureaucratically managed. After such routinization of the organization, charismatic offices can arise, as in the case of the pope or a hereditary chief. In most complex organizations, managerial bureaucrats then take charge. The charismatics formulate the basic purposes and principles by which these bureaucratic administrators are to live.

Weber's conceptualization of charisma has been used as an explanatory concept in sociology, political science, and psychoanalysis. However, his original concept has been modified, expounded upon, and extended in numerous sociological, political science, and psychoanalytical treatises (see, for example, Schiffer, 1983; Schweitzer, 1984; Willner, 1968). Weber's lead was also followed by a number of organizational theorists, who found charisma in complex organizations among holders of organizational offices, particularly at higher levels (Blau and Scott, 1962; Etzioni, 1961; Friedland, 1964). Such charismatics were likely to be at the center of institutional structures with the power to radically transform their organizations (Berger, 1963).

Certain theorists favor a more restricted view of charisma. Friedrich (1961), for instance, limits charisma to inspirational leadership that entails charismatics having a call from God for their mission. Others, such as Bradley (1984), argue that the intense cohesiveness of the group is what results in endowing leaders with charismatic qualities. Dow (1969) places the emphasis on the exceptional individual and his or her ideas rather than on the social or political scene. Trice and Beyer (1986), in contrast, feel that all five Weberian components must be present before they can accept a condition as charismatic. They reject labeling any leadership as charismatic merely because it is inspiring or dynamic. They feel that Berlew's (1974) three characteristics of charismatic leadership (confidence building, shared vision, and creating valued opportunities) are "rather incomplete and pale in comparison to Weber's conception of charisma" (Trice and Beyer, 1986, p. 122). They dismiss Salaman (1977) as discussing personalized, autocratic leadership, not charisma. According to Trice and Beyer, although George Washington was worshipped as a charismatic because he embodied the values of his society (Schwartz, 1983), he was not charismatic because he and his situation lacked some of the other Weberian features.

Just as in efforts to define the concept of leadership (Bass, 1960), we are confronted with absolutists insisting that theirs is the only proper way to define charisma. Such insistence may restrict the operational and explanatory utility of the construct. The meaning of charisma does not have to remain fixed with Weber and his interpreters. Some of the variance in the charismatic phenomenon is due to the exceptional individual, some to the exceptional situation, and some to the interaction of the exceptional individual and the exceptional situation. There are large numbers of exceptional people. They may form a sizable subset near the end of a distribution. In all walks of life and at all organizational levels, we are likely to encounter charismatic and charismatic-like interactions between confident, gifted leaders with seemingly radical solutions to critical problems whose followers say they are unquestioningly and magnetically attracted to their leaders (Smith, 1982; Bass, Waldman, Avolio, and Bebb, 1987).

For the purposes of this chapter, we will regard the Weberian requirements and those of some revisionists as sufficient but not essential in each instance. For example, continued unquestioning acceptance of the leader is not an absolutely essential consequence of charismatic leadership: "Followers can be under the spell of a leader and can accept him as supremely authoritative without necessarily agreeing with him on all occasions or refraining from argument with him. In the highly argumentative atmosphere of a modern radical party, for example, a leader can be both charismatic and contested on specific points, as Lenin often was by his close followers. Indeed, he can even manifest some of his charisma in the inspired way in which he conquers dissent by the sheer power of his political discourse. Immense persuasiveness in argument may, in other words, be one of the extraordinary qualities by virtue of which a leader acquires charisma in his followers' eyes'' (Tucker, 1970, p. 4). Furthermore, the charismatic relationship can appear in the absence of a crisis. For instance, imagine a dynamic leader of a financial services organization with devoted unquestioning followers. As Boal and Bryson (1987) argue, visionary charismatics need no crisis.

As the use of the concept has been extended beyond sociology and political science to psychoanalysis and psychology, increasing attention has been focused on the followers' needs to identify with the leader and on the endurance of the charismatic rather than on the institutionalization or routinization that, according to Weber, was to follow. In addition, the charismatic leader may inspire opposition or even hatred in those who strongly favor the old order of things (Tucker, 1970). This argues strongly for dyadic rather than group analyses of charismatic leader-follower relationships. One can see the subordinates of a single charismatic supervisor divided in the extent to which they love, fear, or hate him or her. The very behaviors and qualities that transport supporters into extremes of admiration of the charismatic may send opponents into extremes of animosity (Bass, 1985b).

Charismatic leaders vary greatly in their pragmatism, flexibility, and opportunism. Different charismatic leaders display quite different styles to achieve their impact. On the one hand, Charles de Gaulle was always more concerned with being right than with achieving immediate results. He spoke of his ''contempt for contingencies,'' and his attitude was unbending (Hoffman and Hoffman, 1970). Other inflexible charismatics of our time include Khadaffi and Khomeini. On the other hand, John F. Kennedy and Franklin D. Roosevelt avoided speaking out and risking political battles they felt they might lose. Lenin also was a practical activist and a pragmatic organizer (Tucker, 1970). Finally, the move toward routinization of leader-follower relations may be initiated by charismatic leaders rather than by those following them, as suggested by Weber. Tito of Yugoslavia was a good case in point. Moreover, successors Augustus, Stalin, and Nehru served to continue the routinization already begun by the charismatic Caesar, Lenin, and Gandhi, respectively, and had many, if not all, of the charismatic qualities of their predecessors. Were not the successors just as charismatic even though complete, strong bureaucracies emerged under their leadership?

Distinguishing Characteristics of Charismatic Leadership

Of the elements associated with the charismatic relationship, two seem most essential. First, although not as rare as some would have it, there is a pattern of requisite abilities, interests, and personal traits that is common to most charismatic leaders. Second, there is a strong desire by followers to identify with the leader. Charismatic leaders have strong referent power over followers. Even if concise and radical solutions to crises are not present, belief by followers in their missions' outcomes results from faith in charismatic leaders. The effect of this emotion-driven charismatic relationship endures through a more rational routinization process.

Requisite Abilities, Interests, and Personal Traits of the Charismatic Leader

Charismatic leaders generally exhibit such attributes as extraordinary emotional expressiveness, self-confidence, self-determination, and freedom from internal conflict, among others. They are likely to have a strong conviction in the righteousness of their own beliefs (House, 1977). Biographies, case studies, anecdotal material, and empirical research provide the available evidence.

Expressive Behavior. Friedman, Prince, Riggio, and Di-Matteo (1980) suggest that charismatic leadership manifests itself in nonverbal emotional expressiveness. Expressive persons can use nonverbal cues "to move, inspire or captivate others" (p. 333). Such expressiveness can be assessed by a test developed by the authors, the self-reporting Affective Communication Test. Items on the validated test include dramatic flair and experience in acting and in politics. Females generally score higher on the test in emotional expressiveness, just as they tend to be seen as more charismatic than comparable males (Avolio and Bass, 1987).

For Bensman and Givant (1975) and Willner (1968), charismatic leaders project a powerful, confident, dynamic presence. Their tone of voice is engaging and captivating. Their facial expressions are animated, yet they remain relaxed (Friedman and Riggio, 1981). Eye contact is direct. People often comment on the magnetic attraction of their eyes (Willner, 1968). Riggio (1986) shows that extroverted and charismatic females are facially expressive, which leads to their being evaluated more favorably than their nonexpressive counterparts. Expressive cues include fluid, outward-directed cues, such as speaking rate and fluency; outward-directed gestural fluency and smiles; and cues of body emphasis along with contact with the body and inward gestures.

Self-Confidence. Charismatic leaders display complete confidence in the correctness of their positions and in their capabilities (Hoffman and Hoffman, 1970). They project this in their public image. Even when personally discouraged and facing failure, they are unlikely to make public such feelings (Tucker, 1968). Such high self-esteem helps charismatics avoid defensiveness in dealing with conflicting interpersonal situations. It also helps maintain their subordinates' confidence in them (Hill, 1976). Charismatics tend to project onto like-minded loyal followers their continuing confident opinions of themselves (Bass, 1985b). Charismatic leaders are great actors. They are always "on stage." They are always conveying to their followers their extreme self-confidence and convictions so that they become larger than life. They must be able to present themselves as miracle workers likely to succeed where others would fail (House, 1977).

Self-Determination. For Weber ([1924] 1947), charisma was a personal attribute of some leaders whose purposes, powers, and extraordinary determination set them apart from ordinary people. Nietzsche's ([1883] 1974) superman had some of the same character: inner direction, originality, self-determination, sense of duty, and responsibility for this unique self. For Nietzsche, ordinary men conformed to the expectations of others, but supermen could free themselves from the expected. They were a point of contact with the future, creating new values and goals. Supermen were highly self-oriented narcissists. Weber's charismatics could also be mystical ascetics, concerned with themselves rather than involved with others and interested in promoting ideas for their own sake rather than for material gain.

Insight. Charismatic leaders can arouse as well as articulate feelings and needs among followers. These leaders also can provide solutions to problems. Charismatics have insight into the needs, values, and hopes of followers (McClelland, 1975) and the ability to build on them through dramatic and persuasive words and actions. They have the ability to "both conceive and articulate goals that lift people out of their petty preoccupations." Such leaders can unite people to seek objectives "worthy of their best efforts" (Gardner, 1961). Charismatics can say things publicly that followers feel privately but cannot express (Yukl, 1981).

Freedom from Internal Conflict. The ability of charismatic leaders to "see around corners" stems from their relative freedom from the internal conflict that ordinary mortals are likely to experience between their emotions, impressions, feelings, and associations (Freud's id) and their strong, controlling conscience (superego). Freedom from the id-superego conflict makes for strong ego ideals and assurance of what the leader values as good, right, and important. Convinced of the goodness, rightness, and importance of his or her own point of view, the charismatic leader is likely to be forthright and candid in reprimanding subordinates. He or she can maintain a clear conscience if he or she feels that someone must be replaced (Keichel, 1983). In contrast, the ordinary manager may be continuously victimized by self-doubts and personal traumas in such circumstances, regardless of extensive career success (Levinson and others, 1978).

Eloquence. Because we are now in the era of speech writers, we can no longer readily attribute the emotional flair of expressive language to the leaders who deliver speeches. However, eloquence is still an important asset for charismatic leaders. For instance, it is known that highly charismatic Mario Cuomo writes his own colorful, incisive, inspiring speeches, such as the famous speech he gave at the 1984 Democratic convention. He can respond extemporaneously on television to telephone questions in the same dynamic way. This use of language helped him win a record landslide gubernatorial reelection in 1986.

Activity and Energy Level. According to a three-year survey conducted by the Group for the Advancement of Psychiatry (1974), high energy level, optimism, fatherliness, and capacity to inspire loyalty were cited as necessary qualities in filling 100 vacant medical school chairs in psychiatry. In another example (Maranell, 1970), in a study of previously collected opinions of political historians, charismatic presidents were seen as being more active and taking significantly stronger actions than noncharismatic presidents. They were also judged more highly esteemed and able to accomplish more in their administrations. High activity levels coupled with strong self-confidence, determination, ego ideals, and a sense of mission were seen to lie behind the success of chief executive officers turning around their organizations. Peters and Waterman (1982) noted that successful CEOs consistently support and hammer away at a theme, usually over a period of years. In this way, they orchestrate a shift of attention throughout management.

Followers' Desire and Need to Identify with the Charismatic Leader

Weber ([1924] 1947) wrote about the follower's "devotion to the specific and exceptional sanctity, heroism, or exemplary character of an individual charismatic person and of the normative patterns or order revealed or ordained by him'' (p. 328). And Willner (1968) describes an intense emotional attraction to the charismatic for followers, above and beyond ordinary esteem, affection, admiration, and trust, involving "devotion, awe, reverence, and blind faith" (p. 6); there is unqualified belief in the "man and his mission about what is, what should be, and what should not be done" (p. 9). It is an absolute emotional and cognitive identification with the leader.

For Madsen and Snow (1983), charismatic leadership may depend as much on the "magnetizability" of the followers as on the magnetism of the leader. Followers' magnetizability takes different forms. For example, in prison for two decades, murderer Charles Manson still has a devoted following of personality misfits living near California's Russian River. The "Moonies," who are ardently devoted to their charismatic Reverend Moon, showed more feelings of helplessness, cynicism, and distrust of political action and less confidence in their own sexual identities, their own values, and the future than did a sample of college students (Lodahl, 1982). A review by Galanter (1982) concluded that those in psychological distress are prone to join a charismatic leader's coterie. Freemesser and Kaplan (1976) observed that those joining a charismatic religious cult had lower self-esteem than did a comparable set of others. In the case of Malcolm X, Corsino (1982) argued that his charismatic leadership was due in part to the intellectual, moral, and emotional predispositions of his followers, who could identify with his experiences and who projected their own frustrations with white society onto him. After a content analysis of statements made by followers about Stevenson and Eisenhower in the 1952 election campaign, Davies (1954) concluded that those who attributed special endorsements to the leader (in contrast to those who did not) had a higher intolerance for indecision and crisis, used rigid categories of good and evil, and felt that other people were more in agreement with them than was actually so.

Different underlying dynamics associating the followers' identification with their leader have been suggested by several scholars. Freud (1922) accounted for the follower's identification with the charismatic leader and the follower's total commitment by suggesting that it was a way to resolve the conflict between the follower's ego and his or her superego. Downton (1973) agrees, suggesting that we resolve the conflict between our self-image and what we wish to be by substituting the leader as the embodiment of our ego ideal. The leader is idealized and becomes the model of behavior to be emulated.

Erikson (1968) perceived identity confusion growing out of a failure to mature in adolescence and young adulthood and a failure to develop a strong ego ideal due to oppressive, weak, or absent parents. Lack of such an ideal to guide one's behavior and interpersonal relationships arouses uneasiness and a sense of drift. Downton (1973) feels that identifying with the charismatic leader is a way of coping with such identity confusion as well as with the conflict between ego and ego ideal. As a consequence, the charismatic leader benefits the follower by providing him or her with new goals and a positive identity and thus enhancing the follower's self-esteem. The charismatic leader gives the follower a second chance to attain maturity. For example, identification of young women with Mother Teresa can give such women an enhanced self-image and make them agents of contribution to a worthy cause. Identification with a maniacal murderer, such as Charles Manson, can likewise enhance self-image, but through a most unworthy cause.

This identification process engenders in followers strong responses of affection and a generalized influence of the leader beyond the immediate situation and beyond the ordinary exchange of compliance for promises of reward or threats of punishment. The vicarious satisfaction obtained from basking in the glory of the charismatic may be the same for the starstruck as doing God's work is for the pious. Admiration of the charismatic leader and the desire to identify with and emulate him or her are powerful influences on followers.

House (1977) describes the dynamic process involved as follows: Self-confident in their own competence, convinced of the rightness of their own beliefs and ideals, and strong in the need for power, charismatic leaders are highly motivated to influence their followers. Their self-confidence and strong convictions increase their followers' trust in the leaders' judgments. Charismatics engage in impression management to bolster their image of competence, thereby increasing subordinate compliance and faith in them. The charismatic leaders relate the work and mission of their group to strongly held values, ideals, and aspirations shared by the members of their organization's culture. In organizational settings, they vividly portray for their subordinates an attractive vision of the possible outcomes of their efforts. This provides subordinates with more meaning for their work, and it arouses their enthusiasm, excitement, emotional involvement, and commitment to group objectives. Roles are defined in ideological terms that appeal to the subordinates. Charismatic leaders use themselves as examples for subordinates to follow.

In some instances, a lack of talent may make popular but untalented charismatic figures easier for their uncritical followers to identify with and to gain vicarious satisfaction from for their own frustrated ambitions (Schiffer, 1983). Unlike Freud's (1922) Moses-like charismatic leader, who oriented followers toward personal and moral growth and toward a transcendental purpose and mission, the pseudocharismatic totemic leader operates as an idol made easy to identify with at a superficial level by his or her catering to followers' whims and fantasies. Token identity and perfunctory rituals satisfy the followers' needs for belonging (Faucheux, 1984). Followers deny what they do not like in the leader and enhance what they do like. They regress to childlike images of a faultless leader, which replace realistic appraisal (Schiffer, 1983). Even when their faults are recognized, as in the case of Ronald Reagan, supporters see in their leaders illustrations of their greater humanity and find it easier to forgive them for having their own shortcomings. (Similarly, when evaluating their superiors, subordinates often rate prototypes they carry around in their heads of a generalized leader rather than their actual superiors.) Reactions to charismatic leaders are likely to obey similar psychometric principles. For example, Bass and Avolio (1987) obtained a correlation of .83 between subordinates' behavioral descriptions of the charismatic leadership of their superiors and the subordinates' ratings of the prototypical leader using the Lord, Foti, and Phillips (1982) prototypicality scale. Correlations of prototypicality with other leadership styles were much lower. Prototypicality correlations fell to .61 with contingent reward and .38 with practicing management-by-exception.

The charismatic leader reduces resistance to attitude change in followers and inhibitions of their responses by arousing emotional responses toward him or her and a sense of excitement and adventure. But the cost of such emotional responding may be impaired follower judgment if there is uncritical acceptance of the leader.

The mystical and fantasy aspects of charisma—and their costs—need to be considered more fully. Charismatics are not merely self-confident, determined, and convinced of their own beliefs: They may believe that they have supernatural missions and purposes. For instance, Martin Luther King really had a waking dream of what he was to accomplish. And followers do not merely have favorable perceptions of their leaders: For them, the charismatic leaders may be larger than life. They can act like mesmerists. Followers' critical judgments may be suspended. The sense of reality of the charismatic leaders and their followers can be distorted by such psychodynamic mechanisms as projection, regression, and disassociation. Followers' own processes and needs can be projected onto the charismatic leader. The leader may become the catalyst for the followers' rationalizations.

> John F. Kennedy ushered in a new Camelot complete with his Queen Guinevere and knights ready to do battle in Cuba, Berlin, and Vietnam with the villainous foes of freedom, the Cuban devils and Soviet dragons. The depth of the public depression resulting from Kennedy's assassination can only be explained by the strong, emotional idolization of the image of Kennedy as dragon slayer, savior, and creator of a new life on earth for the disadvantaged. In reality, he was an astute politician who changed a fictitious Soviet superiority in missiles—the so-called missile gap—into the beginning of a new

arms race led by the United States. He did not lead
but was led into supporting the civil rights movement. His statesman-like qualities grew with his experience in office. But for the mass of the U.S.
public, his image was that of the youthful world
leader who was lifting the U.S. out of the stodgy
Eisenhower years with the focus of a future of U.S.
leadership among the nations of the world and in
space [Bass, 1985b, pp. 56–57].

Although, as mentioned earlier, Freemesser and Kaplan (1976)
found that youths joining a charismatic cult were lower in self-
esteem than a comparison sample, their self-esteem was raised
in six to twelve months by membership in the cult.

Avolio and Bass (1987) have attempted to fine tune this
interactive process in terms of the follower's own cognitive process using Smith and Ellsworth's (1985) cognitive dimensions
that account for how emotions differ from each other. The novelty
to the follower of the leader's message will increase the follower's
attention to it. Uncertainty of the follower in the current situation also will increase the follower's attention to the leader's
message.

The charismatic leader makes concrete a vision that the
follower views as worthy of his or her effort. This raises the
follower's excitement and increases his or her motivation. But
Downton (1973) sees that people who seek to identify with the
leader but who are at a distance from him or her may become
only passingly committed—aroused but not taking action to conform to the leader's initiatives. If they are free to act and not
constrained by other commitments or lack of opportunity, such
individuals may become committed even to leaders at a distance.
Downton describes this as a transformational rather than a transactional process, further noting its greater likelihood of taking
effect: "In the formation of a charismatic commitment, the opportunity for action is apt to be greater than strictly transactional relationships because the follower who identifies with a
leader can transform his behavioral pattern without necessarily
exchanging tangible goods with the leader" (p. 230).

Tension is reduced within the follower who strongly identifies with a charismatic leader. Since the leader has become a
substitute for the follower's ego ideal, continuing, uncritical acceptance of the leader's initiatives is a way of bringing the ego
into line with the ego ideal. In the case of identity confusion,
when the follower has been unable to "find him- or herself,"
the follower's intolerance of criticism of the leader counteracts
problems of identity destabilization. Protecting the idealized
identity of the leader is assumed by the follower as a defense.
Any criticism of the leader is a challenge to the follower defend-
ing the image, since it is in identifying with that image that the
follower develops a sense of who he or she is and what he or
she wants to become.

Antecedents and Aftermath of Charisma

Antecedents

Crises and Their Solutions. Some explanations of the charismatic relationship emphasize social crisis as the root cause of
its emergence. The charismatic appears in times of crisis to save
society from great distress. This salvation from distress engenders
"special emotional intensity of the charismatic response. . . .
Followers respond to the charismatic leader with passionate
loyalty because the [promise of] salvation . . . that he appears
to embody represents the fulfillment of urgently felt needs"
(Tucker, 1970, p. 81).

Among the five sociopolitical factors that accounted for
half the variance in the degree to which charismatic leadership
was attributed to thirty-four twentieth-century heads of state,
Cell (1974) isolated such factors as national social crisis and
disruptive youth. It is not only acute crisis that brings out the
charismatic leader: Charismatic leadership also arises when a
crisis is chronic, such as when the ultimate values of a culture
are being undermined (Hummel, 1973). Charisma carries with
it a challenge to the old order, a break with continuity, a sense
of risky adventure, continual movement, ferment, and change
(Bass, 1985b). The empowered leaders can continue to influence

these feelings to maintain their positions, but they need to provide new, usually radical solutions to the crisis or relate it "to a higher purpose that has intrinsic validity" for the followers (Boal and Bryson, 1987). The charismatic leader can also promote unlearning and the search for new actions. In highly ambiguous situations, such new solutions may be chosen precipitately (Hedberg, 1981).

Individuals who experience crisis and feel a loss of control over their environment generally are more ready than others to accept the authority of a charismatic leader (Devereux, 1955). People become "charisma hungry" due to the decline of old values and rituals, shocks to the culture, growing fears, anxieties, and identity crises. Mahatma Gandhi satisfied such hunger by giving his people a new collective identity and new rituals (Erikson, 1969). Hitler rose as a savior in Germany in response to the disappointments of military defeat and social, political, and economic distress. Despite final victory in World War I, Mussolini's rise to power in 1922 illustrated the same distress theme in Italy (Fermi, 1966). In the United States, Martin Luther King and Jesse Jackson stirred disadvantaged blacks into believing that by their own personal efforts combined with collective action they could reshape American society to advance their place in it, ultimately for the benefit of all Americans.

Organizational cultures in transition provide opportunities for charismatic leaders to appear in industry. Charisma arises when traditional authority and legal, rational, and bureaucratic means cannot meet the organization's need for leadership. Old, highly structured, successful organizations are unlikely to need such leadership. Charismatic leaders are more likely to appear in failing organizations or in newly emerging ones that are struggling to survive. In such organizations, charismatic leaders can create "radicalization" from within rather than through a challenge from outside the organization (Berger, 1963). Charismatic leaders create new cultures for their supporters by creating new meanings and beliefs for them.

The rise of chronic structural unemployment may give rise to new types of charismatic labor leaders. The change from smokestack industry to service and high-technology industries may presage the appearance of new charismatic industrial leaders (Bass, 1985b). But industrial change is driven by opportunity as well as threat. The opportunities present in changing market demands and technological developments can bring forth charismatic leadership of consequence and result in necessary organizational changes.

Charisma Without Crisis. Boal and Bryson (1987) suggest that charismatic effects can emerge not only under crisis conditions but also under noncrisis conditions as a consequence of the charismatic's vision and the articulation of that vision creating a sense of need for action by the followers. The "visionary charismatic" begins with ideological fervor and then moves on to action, unlike the "crisis charismatic," who begins with solutions to crises and then develops ideological justifications for those solutions.

Whether resulting from crisis or an ideology, charismatic leaders' solutions can move in opposite directions. The dedicated follower of one charismatic can be uplifted and moved to a new and better life; the dedicated follower of another can be moved to murder or suicide. Charismatic leadership can be beneficial, or it can be deleterious to society and to organizational life. This will depend on whether the follower's needs are authentic or contrived and whether the leader has prosocial or antisocial goals.

According to Tsurumi (1982), it is also important to note that charismatics appear in societies that have traditions of support for them and expectations about their emergence. Thus, for example, charismatic prophets and messiahs could arise in ancient Israel because they fit with a long prophetic tradition. They were being awaited. In the absence of such tradition, as in ancient China, the emergence of such charismatics was much less possible. Moreover, the followers must share certain norms in order for the charismatic leader to resort to particular influence tactics. For instance, sinfulness is a shared norm in the Judeo-Christian world; thus, the Western charismatic leader can stimulate guilt among his or her followers. The importance of "face" is a shared norm in the Orient; the Oriental charismatic leader can focus on shame. An important aspect accompanying the introduction of quality control circles into Japan was Charles Protzman's emphasis on the need for a charismatic manager to "secure the faith and respect of those under him by his being an example of high purpose, courage, honor, and independence." This conformed with the Japanese tradition of leaders as men of exemplary moral courage and self-sacrifice.

The Aftermath

Routinization. History is replete with charismatic leaders whose revolutionary changes have endured: "The known world was remade socially, culturally and politically by Alexander the Great in his own brief career. Simón Bolívar's efforts had lasting political effects on much of Latin America. Mohammed's works transformed societies stretching from North Africa to Indonesia and left lasting effects on cultures from Spain to Central Asia" (Bass, 1985b, p. 41). But charismatic leaders are hard acts to follow. Institutional practices and the cultural imperatives built by charismatic leaders must replace them after they are gone.

So what makes for these lasting effects of the charismatic leader? Weber ([1924] 1947) saw routinization as the cause. Focused on expression and emotions, the relationship between the charismatic leader and the led is basically unstable. It must be routinized by the development of organizational rules and arrangements if it is to achieve stability (Weber, [1924] 1947). Such routinization of the charismatic leader's mission can occur in several ways: First, unless a charismatic leader is replaced by an equally charismatic successor, an administrative apparatus may be created, along with rites and ceremonies, to provide continuity of message and mission. For example, the charismatic revolutionary hero Bonaparte became the Emperor Napoleon, with a new court, new legal codes, a new educational system, and a new administration. Mao Tse-tung, the permanent revolutionary, was succeeded by Deng Xiaoping, the administrator, providing more of a steady state for China's development. Tito of Yugoslavia planned carefully for succession after his death but was not optimistic that any associate could accumulate the personal authority that his own charisma had given Tito (Drachkovitch, 1964). Actually, the structures remain in place in Yugoslavia, but the excitement and commitment to them appear to be gone. Second, oral and written traditions may emerge to ensure the endurance of the charismatic's effects. Third, continuity may be provided by key groups of believers, and by distinctive practices and imagery in the form of visual art, ceremonies, and stories.

In a study of Alcoholics Anonymous and the National Council on Alcoholism, both founded by charismatic leaders (in 1935 and 1946, respectively), Trice and Beyer (1986) found that routinization occurred with: (1) the development of an administrative apparatus that puts the charismatic's program into practice, (2) the transfer of charisma to others in the organization through rites and ceremonies, (3) the incorporation of the charismatic's message and mission into organizational traditions, and (4) the selection of a successor who resembles the charismatic founder, with sufficient esteem to achieve the charismatic's level of personal influence.

Charisma May Emerge from Routinization. The office may make the leader. Apart from "office charisma," the demands of the office—effectively met—may greatly elevate the esteem of the office holder. For instance, profligate Prince Hal developed into charismatic Henry V in response to the demands of kingship. In this case, charisma grew from administrative routine. Such an interesting reverse effect was demonstrated by Scott (1978). Rather than supporting Weber's thesis that charismatic authority eventually leads to routinization, Scott found that routinization, as evidenced by years of tenure in a bureaucratic office, contributes to one's charismatic authority. In a random sample of Kentucky school superintendents, stratified by tenure, Scott found a correlation of .52 between charismatic authority and tenure. It was not until their thirteenth year of tenure that the superintendents' charismatic authority was rated consistently high. A peak of charismatic authority was reached after thirteen years of tenure and continued through the twenty-first year of tenure before declining slightly for superintendents nearing retirement.

Using Mao Tse-tung as an example, Chang (1982) argues that the emergence of a charismatic leader is a long-term process of interaction between leader and followers and their collective ability to accumulate political power. Charismatic leadership such as Mao's was legitimatized, reinforced, and maintained through institutional efforts. And institutionalization did not bring routinization, as Weber maintained. Thus, we need to allow for varying possible relations among the charismatic leader, his or her immediate colleagues, and the public, which may result in more personalized leadership rather than routinization over time.

The Distribution of Charisma. Charismatic leader-follower relations are widely found in political life as well as complex organizations, appearing not only "in extravagant forms and fleeting moments, but in an abiding, if combustible, aspect of social life that occasionally bursts into open flame" (Geertz, 1977, p. 151). Charismatic relationships have been reported in such diverse organizations as suburban school systems, communes, utopian communities, colleges, Alcoholics Anonymous, the National Council on Alcoholism, the Chippewa tribe, a maternity home, a British manufacturing firm, Tanganyikan labor unions, and royal families, among others.

In agreement with the earlier findings of Shils (1965), Dow (1969), and Oberg (1972), Bass (1985b) found in empirical surveys that charisma is widely distributed as an interpersonal relationship and is not limited only to world-class leaders or to those who found movements or head organizations. "[Charisma] shows up with . . . Lee Iacocca at Chrysler convincing workers, suppliers, congressmen, and customers that Chrysler could be turned around and doing it; the young Robert Hutchins recasting the prestigious University of Chicago in his own image; Hyman Rickover, taking on the whole Navy Department with an idea, the nuclear submarine, whose time had come. . . . [M]uch of what the Iacoccas, Hutchins, and Rickovers can do from the top of the organizations can occur in varying amounts and degrees all through complex organizations. Such charismatic effects can be studied and found or developed in supervisors at all levels of the complex organization" (Bass, 1985b).

Charisma, in turn, is a component—the most general and important component—of the larger concept of transformational leadership. In this regard, it is to be found to a considerable degree in industrial, educational, governmental, and military leaders at all organizational levels, although admittedly it is more salient and visible at the top than at the bottom or middle levels. Many survey respondents describe their military or industrial superior as someone who makes everyone enthusiastic about assignments, inspires loyalty to the organization, commands respect from everyone, has a special gift for seeing what is really important, has a sense of mission, and excites subordinates. Some of these subordinates have complete faith in their charismatic leader and feel good being in his or her presence. They are proud to be associated with the charismatic leader and trust his or her capacity to overcome any obstacle. The charismatic leader serves as a symbol of success and accomplishment for followers.

Charismatics may be more likely to appear in political and religious movements than in business or industry (Katz and Kahn, 1978), but they do also appear at various levels among business executives, educational administrators, military officers, and industrial managers. For Zaleznik (1983), charisma distinguishes the ordinary manager from the true leader in organizational settings. The leader attracts intense feelings of love (and sometimes hate) from his or her subordinates. They want to identify with him or her. Feelings about ordinary managers are bland, but relations are smoother and more steady. Like most intimate relationships, the relations between the charismatic leader and his or her followers tend to be more turbulent. Such "commando leaders" emerge to accomplish challenging and exhilarating tasks that need to be undertaken in an organization. Although they are highly effective, they may be "glamorous nuisances" (Handy, 1976).

Katz and Kahn (1978) argue that the charismatic relation-

ship is strengthened to the degree that the leader distances him-
or herself from followers. This fits with Hollander's (1978) in-
ference that charismatic leadership is less likely to emerge in
complex organizations because the close contact of superiors and
subordinates prevents the maintenance of the magical properties of charisma. But many charismatic leaders, such as Lenin
and Lyndon Johnson, have immediate subordinates who worship them throughout their lives with intense devotion. Social
distance between leader and follower is not essential for the
maintenance of the charismatic relationship.

Yukl (1981) attributes the presumed scarcity of charismatic leaders in business and industry to a lack of managers
with the necessary skills. Berlew (1974) feels that many managers
have the skills but do not recognize the opportunities available.
Bass (1985b) suggests that such managers might not be willing
to risk standing out so visibly among their peers in organizations, believing that conformity is more important for success.
Nevertheless, charismatics can be found throughout complex
organizations, as is evidenced by their effects on their followers,
including: followers' trust in the correctness of the leader's
beliefs, similarity of followers' beliefs to those of the leader, unquestioning acceptance of the leader, followers' affection for the
leader, followers' willing obedience to the leader, emotional involvement of followers in the mission of the organization, heightened performance goals of followers, and belief by followers that
they are able to contribute to the success of the group's mission
(House, 1977).

Utility of Charismatic
Leadership in Complex Organizations

Weber ([1924] 1947) noted that charismatic leadership
substituted as a way to provide order and direction in complex
organizations that were neither bureaucratized nor operated according to traditions. In the 1980s, in order to meet the challenges of rapidly changing work force, markets, and technologies, there is increasing effort in productive organizations to
avoid bureaucratic and traditional rigidities by resorting to ad

hoc groups, temporary systems, and organicity (Robbins, 1983). Elaborate formal coordination and planning are being replaced by teamwork and devoted, intense efforts by organization members. Increasingly, leader-subordinate relationships are displaying more charismatic characteristics (Quinn and Cameron, 1983).

Etzioni (1961) suggests that more charismatic-like leadership is needed in organizations to induce subordinates to accept guidance in expressive matters and in making value judgments and decisions about purpose. Less of such leadership is needed to achieve agreement about instrumental means, which usually are based on facts and rationales. More charisma is needed also if compliance depends on moral involvement, and less if it depends on material reward or on the avoidance of penalties. For Etzioni, the lower ranks are instrumental performers, decisions about means are relegated to middle levels, and charismatic concerns for ends should be restricted to the top levels. For him, in service and production bureaucracies, lower-level charismatic leadership would be dysfunctional: "Development of charisma on levels other than the top is not only unnecessary but is likely to undermine the rational processes required to maximize organizational effectiveness" (Etzioni, 1961, p. 317).

But Etzioni sees that where decisions about ends remain important—such as for priests, shop stewards, and military combat officers who are low in the hierarchy of their organizations—charismatic leadership still has utility. Empirical support can be found in Bass's (1985b) findings that surveyed subordinates saw significantly greater amounts of charismatic leadership among United States Army combat officers than among combat support officers. Nevertheless, Etzioni's argument about business and industrial organizations depends on limiting decisions about values, objectives, goals, and missions to the top when in fact participation in aspects of such decisions can be encouraged at all levels. Therefore, it is not surprising to find that subordinates in lower organizational ranks who describe their immediate supervisors as charismatic also see their units and their organizations as more productive than others of their kind (Waldman, Bass, and Einstein, 1985). And the opinions about the lower- and middle-level charismatic leaders' effectiveness are shared by their superiors (Hater and Bass, forthcoming).

Research on Charismatic Leadership

There is a paucity of empirical research on charisma. Trice and Beyer (1986) were able to list nine sociological and anthropological studies of charisma as of 1977, which they regarded as relevant, but House (1977) was unable to unearth any controlled empirical efforts to investigate the phenomenon as of 1976. This may be a reason why Lawler (1984) complained that despite thousands of empirical studies of leadership, this empirical literature offered little guidance to serious practitioners of the art.

At least two reasons may underlie the paucity (until recently) of laboratory and field experiments and surveys to study charismatic leadership. First, many, if not most, scholars assumed charisma to be a rare attribute limited to a few extraordinary leaders. Second, bringing charisma into the laboratory or validly measuring it with adequate methodological rigor was seen as impossible. Both of these assumptions have proved to be mistaken, as will be seen in the following review of some recent studies.

A Laboratory Experiment. Although some doubted the possibility of bringing the charismatic phenomenon into the laboratory, Howell (1985) succeeded in doing so. In her first laboratory experiment on charisma, Howell compared the effects on subordinates of three types of leaders: charismatic, structuring, and considerate leaders. The leaders' roles were played by one of two actresses, each of whom trained for thirty hours. They were given an in-depth description of their roles and a demonstration of the behaviors, emotional states, body language, facial expressions, and paralinguistic cues they were to use in the experiment. They viewed videotapes of actual managers portraying the different leadership styles. The actresses also extensively practiced reading the scripts. Videotapes of the actresses enacting the three styles after training were rated by 203 judges. This manipulation check attested to the validity of the actresses' performance.

When playing the charismatic:

> the leader articulated an overarching goal, communicated high performance expectations and exhibited confidence in participants' ability to meet these expectations, and empathized with the needs of participants. . . . The highly charismatic leader also projected a powerful, confident, and dynamic presence and had a captivating, engaging voice tone. . . . Nonverbally, the charismatic leader alternated between pacing and sitting on the edge of her desk, leaned toward the participant, maintained direct eye contact, and had a relaxed posture and animated facial expression. . . . The structuring leader . . . explained the nature of the task, provided detailed directions, emphasized the quantity of work to be accomplished within the specified time period, maintained definite standards of work performance, and answered any task-related questions. . . . Nonverbally, the structuring leader sat on the edge of her desk, maintained intermittent eye contact, and had neutral facial expressions and a moderate level of speech intonation. . . . The considerate . . . leader engaged in participative two-way conversations, emphasized the comfort, well-being, and satisfaction of participants, and reassured and relaxed participants. The highly considerate leader was also friendly and approachable and had a warm voice tone. Nonverbally, the considerate leader sat on the edge of her desk, leaned toward participants, maintained direct eye contact, and had a relaxed posture and friendly facial expression [Howell, 1985, p. 8].

The laboratory task was an in-basket exercise requiring the completion of fifteen memos in forty-five minutes, followed by an optional task of completing five memos in fifteen minutes (which most participants actually did). Two co-workers who were confederates of the experimenter plus the participant made up the task group. The confederate co-workers (also trained) either encouraged the participant (high-productivity condition) or discouraged the participant (low-productivity condition). A total of 144 undergraduates were allocated to the six experimental treatments—24 participants per treatment—combining each type of leadership with high- or low-productivity norms.

The most important finding was that only the charismatic leader was able to generate high-productivity when confederate co-workers tried to discourage the participant. The leader that initiated structure did almost as well, but only if co-workers encouraged high-productivity. The structuring leader generated even less productivity than did the considerate leader when co-workers were discouraging and set low-productivity norms. In addition, in contrast to participants working under the leadership that initiated structure or was considerate, participants working under a charismatic leader had higher task performance in terms of the number of courses of action suggested, greater task satisfaction, lower role conflict, and greater satisfaction with the leader. Also, the qualitative task performance of individuals with a charismatic leader was better than was that of individuals with a considerate leader.

Surveys and Interviews. A charismatic leadership scale of ten items dealing with both the leader's behavior and the follower's reactions was developed by Bass (1985b). He began with Burns's definition of a transformational leader, who raises followers' level of consciousness about the importance and value of designated outcomes and ways of reaching them; gets the followers to transcend their own self-interests for the sake of the team, organization, or larger policy; and raises their need level on Maslow's 1954 hierarchy from lower-level concerns about safety and security to higher-level needs for achievement and self-actualization. Seventy senior executives (all male) were able to describe at least one such transformational leader they had known in their careers. Their descriptive statements, along with other statements about transactional leadership (featuring an exchange of rewards for the follower for compliance), were sorted by eleven graduate students into transformational and transactional categories. In another study, seventy-three statements about which the judges could agree were administered to 177 senior army officers. They were asked to describe their most recent superior using a five-point scale of frequency from 0 (the behavior is displayed *not at all*) to 4 (the behavior is displayed frequently, if not always).

A factor analysis revealed the following items to load highly on a "charismatic leadership" factor:

Item 1: "I have complete faith in him/her," factor loading .87

Item 2: "Is a model for me to follow," factor loading .86

Item 3: "Makes me proud to be associated with him," factor loading .85

Item 4: "Encourages understanding of points of view of other members," factor loading .81

Item 5: "Has a special gift of seeing what it is that is really important for me to consider," factor loading .71

Item 6: "Has a sense of mission which he/she transmits to me," factor loading .71

Sixty-six percent of the covariance of all the 143 items can be accounted for by this first factor of charismatic leadership (Bass, 1985b). Hater and Bass (forthcoming) achieved similar results when they refactored the 70-item questionnaire completed by subordinates describing their immediate management superiors. Subsequently, a 10-item scale of such items was included with Multifactor Leadership Questionnaire–Revised Form 5 (MLQ-5). High reliabilities (.85 and above) were routinely reported for large industrial samples of subordinates describing their superiors. Hater and Bass showed that twenty-eight managers identified by their superiors as "top performers" in an express package shipping firm earned a significantly higher charismatic leadership score from their subordinates than did a random sample of twenty-six managers.

For a sample of managers in an Indian engineering firm and an American sample from high-tech companies, Waldman and Bass (1986) reported correlations of .72 and .81 between subordinates' ratings of the charisma of their leaders and the effectiveness of their leadership. This was in contrast to the correlations between rated effectiveness and degree of contingent rewarding (r = .48) and management-by-exception (r = .06) practiced by the manager. To specify the effects more clearly, Waldman, Bass, and Einstein (1985) computed a hierarchical regression analysis of transactional and transformational leadership on self-reported effort and performance measures for two samples of United States Army officers and one sample of industrial managers. By first entering the two transactional leadership scores for contingent reward and management-by-exception into the regression equation and then following with the entry of the interrelated transformational leadership scales (including three factors: charismatic leadership, intellectual stimulation, and individualized consideration), they demonstrated that transformational leadership had an incremental effect over and above transactional leadership. The incremental increases ranged from 9 to 48 percent for the different samples and outcomes predicted. Highly significant incremental effects of transformational leadership were also obtained by Bass (1985b), Gibbons (1986), and Seltzer and Bass (1987).

In a survey of employees in Silicon Valley electronics firms, O'Reilly (1984) found that the credibility of top management—as judged on the basis of their dynamism, trustworthiness, and expertise—was significantly enhanced if the CEO was regarded as charismatic. Employee commitment was similarly elevated.

Leaders who scored high on the charismatic scale were also seen to encourage self-actualization among subordinates, as measured by the Bradford and Cohen (1984) scales. Correlations between the charismatic and the Bradford-Cohen scales ranged from .43 to .65 (Seltzer and Bass, 1987). Consistent with this, charismatic leadership correlated highly with the transformational leadership measures of individualized consideration and with its strong component of orientation toward subordinate development. Charismatic leadership and intellectual stimulation are also highly correlated (Bass, 1985b). The latter is a transformational component that overlaps charismatic leadership to a considerable degree, although the distinction has some conceptual merit (Bass, 1985b).

Biographical and Historical Analyses. House (1977, 1985, 1987) bases the definition of charismatic leadership on its effects on followers. A charismatic leader induces a high degree of loyalty, commitment, and devotion to the leader; identification with the leader and the leader's mission; emulation of the leader's values, goals, and behavior; inspiration; a sense of self-esteem from relationships with the leader and his or her mission; and an exceptionally high degree of trust in the leader and the correctness of the leader's belief. In his study described in Chapter Four, House's results reveal that the cabinet members of charismatic presidents expressed more positive affect toward them than did the cabinet members of noncharismatic presidents. Needs for achievement and for power were higher among the charismatics than among the noncharismatics.

The same pattern of correlations emerged when the Multifactor Leadership Questionnaire was used by sets of undergraduates to describe the leadership of sixty-nine world-class leaders—political, military, and industrial—after the undergraduates had read biographical material about them. The students completed the seventy-item forms as if they were immediate assistants of the world-class leader they were describing. Those leaders seen as having greater charisma were also described as being much more satisfying and effective as leaders than leaders who were rated lower in charisma but higher in transactional factors, such as contingent reward and management-by-exception. Highest in charismatic score were such figures as Martin Luther King, Mahatma Gandhi, and John F. Kennedy. World-class leaders rated lowest in charisma included President Gerald Ford, Henry Ford II, and J. Edgar Hoover (Bass, Avolio, and Goodheim, 1987).

A Simulated Business Game. The pattern of correlations was the same when the MLQ-5 was used by colleagues to rate the presidents of twenty-seven "companies." Each firm was composed of nine M.B.A. students competing in a semester-long complex business game with two other such firms. Although the business game ran for twelve weeks, it simulated eight quarters of performance. The success of the presidents and their firms was announced at the end of each of the eight quarters. Leadership ratings of each team's president were collected at the end of the eighth quarter. Although each company began with equivalent assets, those companies led by presidents rated high in charismatic leadership also performed better on objective indexes of success, such as return on investment, stock prices, and market share. Results were the same when videotapes of the company meetings were used by independent raters to complete the MLQ-5 describing the presidents. Presidents judged high in charisma by the raters of the videotapes were in agreement with the presidents' colleagues (Avolio, Waldman, and Einstein, 1986).

Conclusion

Although our review of conceptual and empirical studies began with Weber, it advocated an evolving conception of charismatic leadership. Furthermore, it was assumed that those perceived as charismatic leaders by their colleagues do not necessarily meet all the criteria of Weber's original formulation. Finally, recent empirical studies on charismatic leadership dispel the notion that charisma cannot be objectively studied and measured using available social science methodology.

References

Avolio, B. J., and Bass, B. M. "Charisma and Beyond." In J. G. Hunt (ed.), *Emerging Leadership Vistas.* Boston: Lexington, 1987.

Avolio, B. J., Waldman, D. A., and Einstein, W. O. "Beating the Competition: Transforming Leadership at the Bottom-line." Working Paper no. 86-121, School of Management, State University of New York, Binghamton, 1986.

Barlow, J. A. "Mass Line Leadership and Thought Reform in China." *American Psychologist,* 1981, *36,* 300–309.

Bass, B. M. *Leadership, Psychology and Organizational Behavior.* New York: Harper & Row, 1960.

Bass, B. M. "Leadership: Good, Better, Best." *Organizational Dynamics,* 1985a, *13* (3), 26–40.

Bass, B. M. *Leadership and Performance Beyond Expectations.* New York: Free Press, 1985b.

Bass, B. M. *Producing More New Model Leadership.* Working paper no. 86-113, School of Management, State University of New York, Binghamton, 1987.

Bass, B. M., and Avolio, B. J. *Biases in Transformational Leadership Ratings.* Working Paper no. 87-124, School of Management, State University of New York, Binghamton, 1987.

Bass, B. M., Avolio, B. J., and Goodheim, L. "A Retrospective Survey Analysis of World-Class Leadership." *Journal of Management,* 1987, *13,* 7–19.

Bass, B. M., Waldman, D. A., Avolio, B. J., and Bebb, M. "Transformational Leadership and the Falling Dominoes Effect." *Group and Organization Studies,* 1987, *12* (1), 73–87.

Bensman, J., and Givant, M. "Charisma and Modernity: The Use and Abuse of a Concept." *Social Research,* 1975, *42,* 570–614.

Berger, P. L. "Charisma and Religious Innovation: The Social Location of the Israelite Prophecy." *American Sociological Review,* 1963, *28,* 940–950.

Berlew, D. E. "Leadership and Organizational Excitement." In D. A. Kolb, I. M. Rubin, and J. M. McIntyre (eds.), *Organizational Psychology.* Englewood Cliffs, N.J.: Prentice-Hall, 1974.

Blau, P. M., and Scott, W. R. *Formal Organizations.* San Francisco: Chandler, 1962.

Boal, K. B., and Bryson, J. M. "Charismatic Leadership: A Phenomenological and Structural Approach." In J. G. Hunt (ed.), *Emerging Leadership Vistas.* Boston: Lexington, 1987.

Bradford, D. L., and Cohen, A. R. "The Postheroic Leader." *Training and Development Journal,* 1984, *38* (1), 40–49.

Bradley, R. T. *Charisma and Social Structure: A Relational Analysis of Power and Communion in Communes.* Unpublished working manuscript, Department of Sociology, University of Minnesota, 1984.

Burns, J. M. *Leadership.* New York: Harper & Row, 1978.

Cell, C. P. "Charismatic Heads of State: The Social Context." *Behavioral Science Research,* 1974, *4,* 255–304.

Chang, M. "A Re-Examination of Weber's Theory of Charismatic Authority: The Case of Mao Tse-tung and the Chinese Communist Party." Paper presented at the annual conference of the North Central Sociological Association, Chicago, 1982.

Corsino, L. "Malcolm X and the Black Muslim Movement: A Social Psychology of Charisma." *Psychohistory Review,* 1982, *10,* 165–184.

Davies, J. C. "Charisma in the 1952 Campaign." *American Political Science Review,* 1954, *48,* 1083–1102.

Demause, L. *Foundations of Psychohistory.* New York: Creative Roots, 1982.

Devereux, G. "Charismatic Leadership and Crisis." In W. Muensterberger and S. Axelrod (eds.), *Psychoanalysis and the Social Sciences.* New York: International University Press, 1955.

Dow, T. "The Theory of Charisma." *Sociological Quarterly,* 1969, *10,* 306–318.

Downton, J. V. *Rebel Leadership: Commitment and Charisma in the Revolutionary Process.* New York: Free Press, 1973.

Drachkovitch, M. M. "Succession and the Charismatic Leader in Yugoslavia." *Journal of International Affairs,* 1964, *18* (1), 54–66.

Erikson, E. *Identity, Youth, and Crisis.* New York: Norton, 1968.

Erikson, E. *Gandhi's Truth.* New York: Norton, 1969.

Etzioni, A. *A Comparative Analysis of Complex Organizations.* New York: Free Press, 1961.

Faucheux, C. "Leadership, Power and Influence Within Social Systems." Paper presented at symposium: The Functioning of Executive Power. Case Western Reserve University, Cleveland, Ohio, Oct. 1984.

Fermi, L. *Mussolini.* Chicago: University of Chicago Press, 1966.

Freemesser, G. F., and Kaplan, H. B. "Self-Attitudes and Deviant Behavior: The Case of the Charismatic Religious Movement." *Journal of Youth and Adolescence,* 1976, *5* (1), 1–9.

Freud, S. *Group Psychology and the Analysis of Ego.* London: International Psychoanalytical Press, 1922.

Friedland, W. H. "For a Sociological Concept of Charisma." *Social Forces,* 1964, *43* (1), 18–26.

Friedman, H. S., Prince, L. M., Riggio, R. E., and DiMatteo, M. R. "Understanding and Assessing Nonverbal Expressiveness: The Affective Communication Test." *Journal of Personality and Social Psychology,* 1980, *39,* 331–351.

Friedman, H. S., and Riggio, R. E. "Effect of Individual Differences in Nonverbal Expressiveness on Transmission of Emotion." *Journal of Nonverbal Behavior,* 1981, *6,* 96–104.

Friedrich, C. "Political Leadership and the Problem of Charismatic Power." *Journal of Politics,* 1961, *23,* 19.

Fromm, E. *Escape from Freedom.* New York: Farrar and Rinehart, 1941.

Galanter, M. "Charismatic Religious Sects and Psychiatry: An Overview." *American Journal of Psychiatry,* 1982, *139* (2), 1539–1548.

Gardner, J. W. *Excellence: Can We Be Equal and Excellent Too?* New York: Harper & Row, 1961.

Geertz, C. "Centers, Kings and Charisma: Reflections on the Symbolics of Power." In J. Ben-David and T. N. Clark (eds.), *Culture and Its Creators: Essays in Honor of Edward Shils.* Chicago: University of Chicago Press, 1977.

Gibbons, T. C. *Revisiting the Question of Born Vs. Made: Toward a Theory of Development of Transformational Leaders.* Unpublished doctoral dissertation, Fielding Institute, Santa Barbara, Calif., 1986.

Group for the Advancement of Psychiatry (GAP). "Problems of Psychiatric Leadership." *GAP Report,* 1974, *8,* 925–946.

Handy, C. D. *Understanding Organization.* New York: Penguin Books, 1976.

Hater, J. J., and Bass, B. M. "Supervisors' Evaluations and Subordinates' Perceptions of Transformational and Transactional Leadership." *Journal of Applied Psychology,* forthcoming.

Hedberg, B. "How Organizations Learn and Unlearn." In P. C. Nystrom and W. H. Starbuck (eds.), *Handbook of Organizational Design.* Vol. 1. London: Oxford University Press, 1981.

Hill, N. "Self-Esteem: The Key to Effective Leadership." *Administrative Management,* 1976, *31* (8), 24.

Hoffman, S., and Hoffman, I. "The Will to Grandeur: de Gaulle as Political Artist." In D. A. Rustow (ed.), *Philosophers and Kings: Studies in Leadership.* New York: Braziller, 1970.

Hollander, E. P. *Leadership Dynamics.* New York: Free Press, 1978.

House, R. J. "A 1976 Theory of Charismatic Leadership." In J. G. Hunt and L. L. Larson (eds.), *Leadership: The Cutting Edge.* Carbondale: Southern Illinois University Press, 1977.

House, R. J. "Research Contrasting the Behavior and Effect of Reputed Charismatic Versus Reputed Noncharismatic Leaders." Paper presented at annual meeting of Administrative Science Association of Canada, Montreal, Apr. 1985.

House, R. J., and Singh, J. V. "Organizational Behavior: Some New Directions for I/O Psychology." *Annual Review of Psychology,* 1987, *38,* 669–718.

Howell, J. M. "A Laboratory Study of Charismatic Leadership." Working Paper no. 85-35, School of Business Administration, University of Western Ontario, London, Canada, 1985.

Hummel, R. P. "Charisma in Politics: Psycho-Social Causes of Revolution as Preconditions of Charismatic Outbreaks Within the Framework of Weber's Epistemology." Unpublished thesis, New York University, 1973.

Kamerman, J. B. "A 'Scrutinization' of Charisma: Charismatic Authority and Control in the Work of the Symphony Orchestra Conductor." Paper presented at the annual Eastern Sociological Society conference, 1981.

Katz, D., and Kahn, R. L. *The Social Psychology of Organizations.* New York: Wiley, 1978.

Keichel, W., III. "Wanted: Corporate Leaders." *Fortune,* May 30, 1983, pp. 135–140.

Lawler, E. E., III. "Leadership in Participative Organizations." In J. G. Hunt, D. Hosking, C. A. Schriesheim, and R. Stewart (eds.), *Leaders and Managers: International Perspectives on Managerial Behavior and Leadership.* Elmsford, N.Y.: Pergamon Press, 1984.

Levinson, D. J., and others. *The Seasons of a Man's Life.* New York: Knopf, 1978.

Levinson, H., and Rosenthal, S. *CEO: Corporate Leadership in Action.* New York: Basic Books, 1984.

Lodahl, A. "Crisis in Values and the Success of the Unification Church." Unpublished bachelor of arts thesis in sociology, Cornell University, 1982.

Lord, R. G., Foti, R. J., and Phillips, J. S. "A Theory of Leadership Categorization." In J. G. Hunt, U. Sekaran, and C. Schriesheim (eds.), *Leadership: Beyond Establishment Views.* Carbondale: Southern Illinois University Press, 1982.

McCall, M. W., Jr., and Lombardo, M. M. *Off the Track: Why and How Successful Executives Get Derailed.* Technical Report no. 21. Greensboro, N.C.: Center for Creative Leadership, 1983.

McClelland, D. C. *Power: The Inner Experience.* New York: Irvington, 1975.

Madsen, D., and Snow, P. G. "The Dispersion of Charisma." *Comparative Political Studies,* 1983, *16* (3), 337–362.

Maranell, G. M. "The Evaluation of Presidents: An Extension of the Schlesinger Polls." *Journal of American History,* 1970, *57*, 104–113.

Mitscherlich, A. "Changing Patterns of Authority: A Psychiatric Interpretation." In L. J. Edinger (ed.), *Political Leadership in Industrialized Societies.* New York: Wiley, 1967.

Newman, R. G. "Thoughts on Superstars of Charisma: Pipers in Our Midst." *American Journal of Orthopsychiatry,* 1983, *53*, 201–208.

Nietzsche, F. "Thus Spoke Zarathustra." In O. Levy (ed.), *The Complete Works of Friedrich Nietzsche.* New York: Gordon Press, 1974. (Originally published 1883.)

Oberg, W. "Charisma, Commitment, and Contemporary Organization Theory." *Business Topics,* 1972, *20*, 18–32.

O'Reilly, C. "Charisma as Communication: The Impact of Top Management Credibility and Philosophy on Employee Involvement." Paper presented at annual meeting of the Academy of Management, Boston, Aug. 1984.

Peters, T. J., and Waterman, R. H., Jr. *In Search of Excellence.* New York: Harper & Row, 1982.

Quinn, R. E., and Cameron, K. "Organizational Life Cycles and Shifting Criteria of Effectiveness: Some Preliminary Evidence." *Management Science,* 1983, *29*, 33–51.

Riggio, R. E. "Impression Formation: The Role of Expressive Behavior." *Journal of Personality and Social Psychology,* 1986, *50,* 421–427.

Robbins, S. P. "The Theory Z Organization from a Power-Control Perspective." *California Management Review,* 1983, *25,* 67–75.

Salaman, G. "A Historical Discontinuity: From Charisma to Routinization." *Human Relations,* 1977, *30* (4), 373–388.

Sashkin, M., and Fulmer, R. M. "Toward an Organizational Leadership Theory." Paper presented at Biennial Leadership Symposium, Texas Tech University, July 1985.

Schiffer, I. *Charisma: A Psychoanalytic Look at Mass Society.* Toronto: University of Toronto Press, 1983.

Schwartz, B. "George Washington and the Whig Conception of Heroic Leadership." *American Sociological Review,* 1983, *48,* 18–33.

Schweitzer, A. *The Age of Charisma.* Chicago: Nelson-Hall, 1984.

Scott, L. K. "Charismatic Authority in the Rational Organization." *Educational Administration Quarterly,* 1978, *14* (2), 43–62.

Seltzer, J., and Bass, B. M. "Leadership Is More than Initiation and Consideration." Paper presented at meeting of the American Psychological Association, New York, Aug. 1987.

Seltzer, J., Numerof, R. E., and Bass, B. M. "Transformational Leadership: Is It a Source of More or Less Burnout and Stress?" Paper presented at meeting of the Academy of Management, New Orleans, Aug. 1987.

Shils, E. A. "Charisma, Order, and Status." *American Sociological Review,* 1965, *30, 199–213.*

Smith, B. J. "An Initial Test of a Theory of Charismatic Leadership Based on the Responses of Subordinates." Unpublished doctoral dissertation, Faculty of Management, University of Toronto, 1982.

Smith, C. A., and Ellsworth, P. C. "Patterns of Cognitive Appraisal in Emotion." *Journal of Personality and Social Psychology,* 1985, *48,* 813–838.

Trice, H. M., and Beyer, J. M. "Charisma and Its Routinization in Two Social Movement Organizations." *Research in Organizational Behavior,* 1986, *8,* 113–164.

Tsurumi, R. R. "American Origins of Japanese Productivity: The Hawthorne Experiment Rejected." *Pacific Basin Quarterly,* 1982, *7,* 14–15.

Tucker, R. C. "The Theory of Charismatic Leadership." *Daedalus,* 1968, *97,* 731–756.

Tucker, R. C. "The Theory of Charismatic Leadership." In D. A. Rustow (ed.), *Philosophers and Kings: Studies in Leadership.* New York: Braziller, 1970.

Tucker, R. C. *Politics as Leadership.* Columbia: University of Missouri Press, 1981.

Waldman, D. A., and Bass, B. M. "Adding to Leader and Follower Transactions: The Augmenting Effect of Transformational Leadership." Working Paper no. 86-109, School of Management, State University of New York, Binghamton, 1986.

Waldman, D. A., Bass, B. M., and Einstein, W. O. *Effort, Performance and Transformational Leadership in Industrial and Military Service.* Working paper no. 85-80, School of Management, State University of New York, Binghamton, 1985.

Weber, M. *The Theory of Social and Economic Organization.* (A. M. Henderson and T. Parsons, trans.; T. Parsons, ed.) New York: Free Press, 1947. (Originally published 1924.)

Weber, M. *The Sociology of Religion.* Boston: Beacon Press, 1963. (Originally published 1922.)

Willner, A. R. *Charismatic Political Leadership: A Theory.* Princeton, N.J.: Center for International Studies, Princeton University, 1968.

Yukl, G. A. *Leadership in Organizations.* Englewood Cliffs, N.J.: Prentice-Hall, 1981.

Zaleznik, A. "The Leadership Gap." *Washington Quarterly,* 1983, *6* (1), 32–39.

3

Behavioral Dimensions of Charismatic Leadership

Jay A. Conger
Rabindra N. Kanungo

Charismatic leadership is a very rich and complex social phenomenon, and its manifestation among different kinds of leaders and its overpowering effects on followers have lent it an elusive and mystical character. Yet, in spite of its complexity, its effects are widely recognized. For example, it is not uncommon to hear members of an organization describe a leader as charismatic or attribute their motivation to a leader's charisma. It would seem that most of us carry in our heads a naive theory of what charisma really is. However, a more precise and scientific understanding of charisma remains to be developed. Social scientists have shied away from studying charisma's seemingly mysterious and impressionistic qualities. As research has moved toward greater methodological rigor and control, behavioral scientists have been attracted to phenomena that they could quantify and test under controllable conditions. They have moved away from the more subjectively complex topics that are difficult to quantify or replicate in laboratory or field experiments. Charisma's complexity has led to its neglect as a subject worthy of scientific study.

If we are to develop a deeper understanding of this complex phenomenon, it is important that we begin to strip this impression of mysticism from charisma. Charismatic leadership, like any other type of leadership, should be considered an observable behavioral process that can be described and analyzed in terms of a formal model. With this in mind, we will describe a conceptual framework that will assist researchers and practitioners in coming to grips with this elusive phenomenon.

The model we present builds on the idea that charismatic leadership is an attribution based on followers' perceptions of their leader's behavior. For example, most social psychological theories consider leadership to be a by-product of interaction between members of a group (Yukl, 1981). As members work together to attain group objectives, they begin to realize their status in the group as either a leader or a follower. This realization is based on observations of the influence process within the group helping members to determine their status. The individual who exerts maximum influence over other members is perceived to be playing the leader role. Leadership is then consensually validated when the membership recognizes and identifies the leader on the basis of their interaction with that person. In other words, leadership qualities are attributed to an individual when group members accept and submit to that individual's influence.

Charismatic leadership is no exception to this process. Thus, charisma must be viewed as an attribution made by followers. The roles played by a person make that individual (in the eyes of followers) not only a task leader or a social leader and a participative or directive leader but also a charismatic or noncharismatic leader. The leader's observed behavior can be interpreted by his or her followers as expressions of charismatic qualities. Such qualities are seen as part of the leader's inner disposition or personal style of interacting with followers. These dispositional attributes are inferred from the leader's observed behavior in the same way as other styles of leadership that have been identified previously (Blake and Mouton, 1964; Fiedler, 1967; Hersey and Blanchard, 1977). In this sense, charisma can be considered an additional inferred dimension of leadership behavior. As such, it should be subjected to the same empirical and behavioral analysis as participative, task, or social dimensions of leadership.

The Behavioral Dimensions of Charisma

If a follower's attribution of charisma depends on the observed behavior of the leader, what are the behavioral components responsible for such an attribution? Can these components be identified and operationalized so that we may understand the nature of charisma among organizational leaders? In the following sections, we describe what we hypothesize to be the essential and distinguishable behavioral components of charismatic leadership. We also hypothesize that these behaviors are interrelated and that the presence and intensity of these characteristics are expressed in varying degrees among different charismatic leaders.

To begin, we can best frame and distinguish these components by examining leadership as a process that involves moving organizational members from an existing present state toward some future state. This dynamic might also be described as a movement away from the status quo toward the achievement of desired longer-term goals.

This process can be conceptualized into three specific stages (see Figure 1). In the initial stage, the leader must evaluate the existing situation or status quo. Before devising appropriate organizational goals, he or she must assess what resources are available and what constraints stand in the way of realizing future goals. As well, the leader must assess the needs and level of satisfaction experienced by followers. This evaluation leads to a second stage: the actual formulation and conveyance of goals. Finally, in stage three, the leader demonstrates how these goals can be achieved by the organization. It is along these three stages that we can identify behavioral components unique to charismatic leaders.

A caveat is in order. In reality, these stages do not follow such a simple linear flow. Instead, most organizations face ever changing environments, and their leadership must constantly be revising existing goals and tactics in response to unexpected opportunities or other environmental changes. This model, however, nicely simplifies this dynamic process and allows us to more effectively contrast the differences between charismatic

Figure 1. The Charismatic Leadership Influence Process.

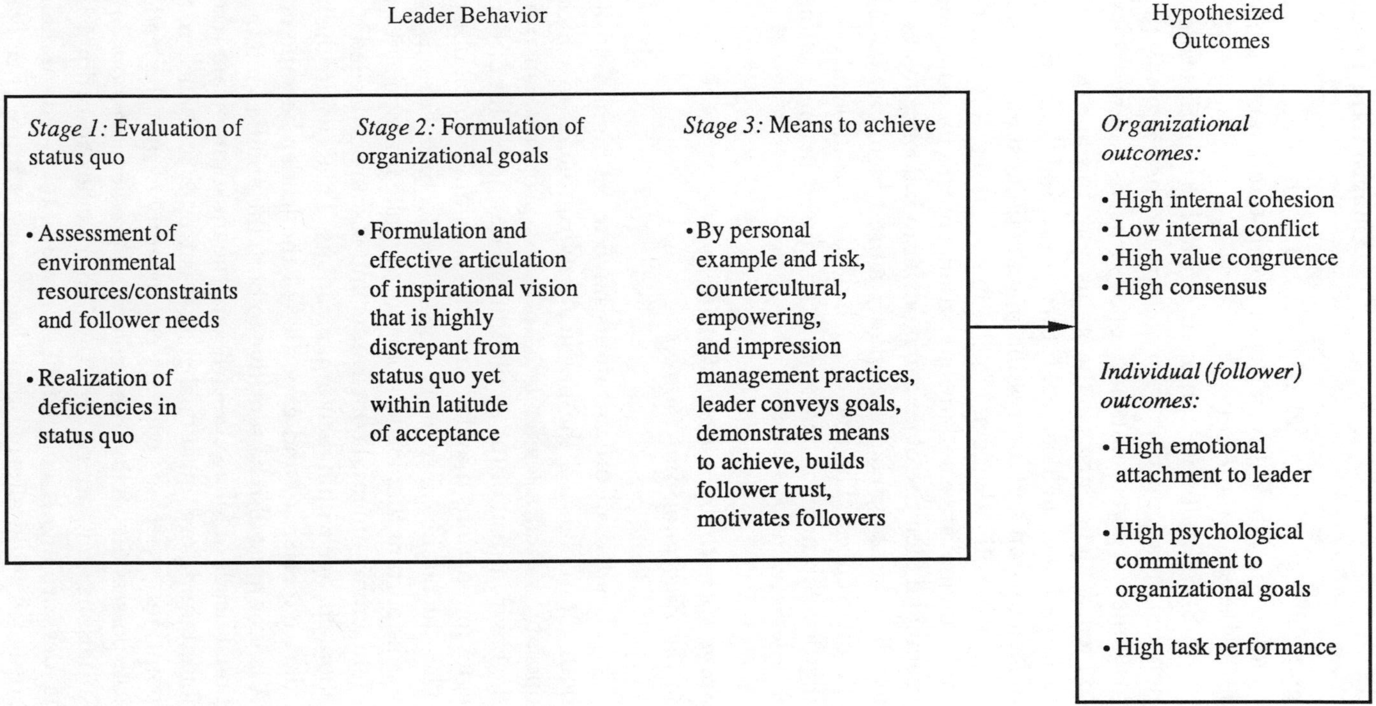

Leader Behavior

Hypothesized Outcomes

Stage 1: Evaluation of status quo

- Assessment of environmental resources/constraints and follower needs

- Realization of deficiencies in status quo

Stage 2: Formulation of organizational goals

- Formulation and effective articulation of inspirational vision that is highly discrepant from status quo yet within latitude of acceptance

Stage 3: Means to achieve

- By personal example and risk, countercultural, empowering, and impression management practices, leader conveys goals, demonstrates means to achieve, builds follower trust, motivates followers

Organizational outcomes:

- High internal cohesion
- Low internal conflict
- High value congruence
- High consensus

Individual (follower) outcomes:

- High emotional attachment to leader

- High psychological commitment to organizational goals

- High task performance

and noncharismatic leadership. As such, the reader should keep in mind that, in reality, a leader is constantly moving back and forth between these stages.

Specifically, we can distinguish charismatic leaders from noncharismatic leaders in stage one by their sensitivity to environmental constraints and follower needs and by their ability to identify deficiencies in the status quo. In stage two, it is their formulation of an idealized future vision and their extensive use of articulation and impression management skills that set them apart from other leaders. Finally, in stage three, it is their deployment of innovative and unconventional means for achieving their vision and their use of personal power to influence followers that are distinguishing characteristics. Figure 1 highlights these essential differences. The role of each of these behavioral criteria in the development of charisma is discussed in the sections that follow.

Stage One: Charisma and Sensitivity to the Environmental Context

Leaders of organizations have to be highly sensitive to both the social and the physical environments in which they operate. When a leader fails to assess properly constraints in the environment or the availability of resources, his or her strategies and actions may fail to achieve organizational objectives. Then he or she, in turn, is labeled ineffective. For this reason, it is important that leaders be able to make realistic assessments of the environmental constraints and resources needed to bring about change within their organizations. This is where the knowledge, experience, and expertise of the leader become critical. A leader must also be sensitive to both the abilities and the emotional needs of followers—who are the most important resources for attaining organizational goals. As Kenny and Zacarro (1983) point out, "persons who are consistently cast in the leadership role possess the ability to perceive and predict variations in group situations and pattern their own approaches accordingly. Such leaders are highly competent in reading the needs of their constituencies and altering their behaviors to more effectively respond to these needs" (p. 683).

Such assessments, while not a distinguishing feature of charismatic leaders, are nonetheless particularly important for these leaders because they often assume high risks by advocating radical changes. Their assessment of environmental resources and constraints then becomes extremely important before planning courses of action. Thus, instead of launching a course of action as soon as a vision is formulated, a leader's environmental assessment may dictate that he or she prepare the ground and wait for an appropriate time and place, and/or the availability of resources. It is presumed that many a time charisma has faded due to a lack of sensitivity for the environmental context.

In the assessment stage, what distinguishes charismatic from noncharismatic leaders is the charismatic leaders' ability to recognize deficiencies in the present system. In other words, they actively search out existing or potential shortcomings in the status quo. For example, the failure of a firm to exploit new technologies or new markets might be highlighted as a strategic or tactical opportunity by a charismatic. In other words, deficiencies in a firm's strategic objectives are more readily detected by the charismatic leader. Likewise, a charismatic entrepreneur might more readily perceive marketplace needs and transform them into opportunities for new products or services. In addition, internal organizational deficiencies may be perceived by the charismatic leader as platforms for advocating radical change.

Thus, any context that triggers a need for a major change and/or presents unexploited market opportunities is relevant for the emergence of a charismatic leader. In some cases, contextual factors are so overwhelmingly in favor of a change that leaders take advantage of them by advocating radical changes for the system. For example, when an organization is dysfunctional or when it faces crisis, leaders may find it to their advantage to advocate radical changes, thereby increasing the probability of fostering a charismatic image for themselves.

During periods of relative tranquillity, charismatic leaders may play a major role in fostering the need for change by creating deficiencies or exaggerating existing minor ones. They may also anticipate future changes and induce supportive conditions. In any case, context must be viewed as a precipitating factor, sometimes facilitating the emergence of certain behaviors in a leader that form the basis of his or her charisma. As Willner (1984) points out with regard to political leadership, "preconditions of exogenous social crisis and psychic distress are conducive to the emergence of charismatic political leadership, but they are not necessary. . . . If we extend the notion of crisis to include those largely generated by the actions of the leader, greater weight can be attached to crisis as an explanatory factor" (p. 52).

Because of their emphasis on deficiencies in the system and their high levels of intolerance for them, charismatic leaders are always seen as organizational reformers or entrepreneurs. In other words, they act as agents of innovative and radical change. However, the attribution of charisma is dependent not on the outcome of change but simply on the actions taken to bring about change or reform.

From the perspective of managing and fostering change, charismatic leaders then must be distinguished from administrators and other leaders (Zaleznik, 1977). Administrators generally act as caretakers who are responsible for the maintenance of the status quo. They influence others through the power of their positions as sanctioned by the organization. As such, they have little interest in significant organizational change. Noncharismatic leaders, as opposed to administrators, can be seen as change agents who may direct or nudge their followers toward established and more traditional goals. While they may advocate change, it is usually incremental and within the bounds of the status quo. Charismatic leaders, however, seek radical reforms for the achievement of their idealized goals and transform their followers (instead of directing or nudging them). Charisma, then, can never be perceived either in an administrator (caretaker) role or in a leadership role designed only to nudge the system.

Stage Two: Charisma and the Future Vision

Formulating the Vision. After assessing the environment, a leader will formulate goals for achieving the organization's objectives. Charismatic leaders can be distinguished from others by the nature of their goals and by the manner in which they articulate them. As the literature suggests, charismatic leaders are often characterized by a sense of strategic vision (Bass, 1985; Berlew, 1974; Conger, 1985; Dow, 1969; House, 1977; Marcus, 1961; Willner, 1984; Zaleznik and Kets de Vries, 1975). Here the word *vision* refers to some idealized goal that the leader wants the organization to achieve in the future. We hypothesize that the nature, formulation, articulation, and means for achievement of this goal proposed by the charismatic leader can be distinguished from those advocated by other types of leaders.

The more idealized or utopian the future goal advocated by the leader, the more discrepant it becomes in relation to the status quo. And the greater the discrepancy of the goal from the status quo, the more likely is the attribution that the leader has extraordinary vision, not just an ordinary goal. Moreover, by presenting a very discrepant and idealized goal to followers, a leader provides a sense of challenge and a motivating force for change. If we turn to the attitude change literature, it is suggested that a maximum discrepant position within the latitude of acceptance puts the greatest amount of pressure on followers to change their attitudes (Hovland and Pritzker, 1957; Petty and Cacioppo, 1981). Since the idealized goal represents a perspective shared by the followers and promises to meet their hopes and aspirations, it tends to be within this latitude of acceptance in spite of its extreme discrepancy. Leaders then become charismatic as they succeed in changing their followers' attitudes to accept their advocated vision. We argue that leaders are charismatic when their vision represents an embodiment of a perspective shared by followers in an idealized form.

What are the attributes of charismatic leaders that make them successful advocates of their discrepant vision? Research on persuasive communication suggests that in order to be a successful advocate, one needs to be a credible communicator and that credibility comes from projecting an image of being a likable, trustworthy, and knowledgeable person (Hovland, Janis, and Kelley, 1953; Sears, Freedman, and Peplau, 1985).

It is the shared perspective of the vision and its potential for satisfying followers' needs that make leaders "likable" persons. Both the perceived similarity and the need satisfaction potential of the leaders form the basis of their attraction (Byrne, 1977; Rubin, 1973). However, the idealized (and therefore discrepant) vision also makes the leaders adorable persons deserving of respect and worthy of identification and imitation by the followers. It is this idealized aspect of the vision that makes them charismatic. Charismatic leaders are not just similar others who are generally liked (as popular consensus-seeking leaders) but similar others who are also distinct because of their idealized vision.

Articulating the Vision. In order to be charismatic, leaders not only need to have visions and plans for achieving them, but they must also be able to articulate their visions and strategies for action in effective ways so as to influence their followers. Here articulation involves two separate processes: articulation of the context and articulation of the leader's motivation to lead. First, charismatic leaders must effectively articulate for followers the following scenarios representing the context: the nature of the status quo and its shortcomings, their future vision, how, when realized, the future vision will remove existing deficiencies and provide fulfillment of the hopes of followers, and their plans of action for realizing their vision.

In articulating the context, the charismatic's verbal messages construct reality in such a way that only the positive features of the future vision and the negative features of the status quo are emphasized. The status quo is often presented as intolerable, and the vision is presented, in clear specific terms, as the most attractive and attainable alternative. In articulating these elements for subordinates, the leader often constructs several scenarios representing the status quo, the goal for the future, the needed changes, and the ease or difficulty of achieving the goal depending on available resources and constraints. In his or her scenarios, the charismatic leader attempts to create among followers a disenchantment or discontentment with the status quo, a strong identification with the future goal, and a compelling desire to be led in the direction of the goal in spite of environmental hurdles. This process of influencing the followers is very similar to the path-goal approach to leadership behavior advocated by many theorists (for example, see House, 1971).

Besides verbally describing the status quo, the future goal, and the means to achieve the future goal, charismatic leaders must also articulate their own motivation for leading their followers. Using expressive modes of action, both verbal and nonverbal, they manifest their convictions, self-confidence, and dedication to materialize what they advocate. In the use of rhetoric, words are selected to reflect their assertiveness, confidence, expertise, and concern for followers' needs. These same qualities may also be expressed through their dress, their appearance, and their body language. Charismatic leaders' use of rhetoric, high energy, persistence, unconventional and risky behavior, heroic deeds, and personal sacrifices all serve to articulate their high motivation and enthusiasm, which then become contagious among their followers. These behaviors form part of a charismatic leader's impression management.

Stage Three: Achieving the Vision

In the final stage of the leadership process, effective leaders build in followers a sense of trust in their abilities and clearly demonstrate the tactics and behaviors required to achieve the organization's goals. The charismatic leader does this by building trust through personal example and risk taking and through unconventional expertise. It is critical that followers develop a trust in the leader's vision. Generally, leaders are perceived as trustworthy when they advocate their position in a disinterested manner and demonstrate a concern for followers' needs rather than their own self-interest (Walster, Aronson, and Abrahams, 1966). However, in order to be charismatic, leaders must make these qualities appear extraordinary. They must transform their concern for followers' needs into a total dedication and commitment to the common cause they share with followers and express them in a disinterested and selfless manner. They must engage in exemplary acts that are perceived by followers as involving great personal risk, cost, and energy (Friedland, 1964). In this case, personal risk might include the possible loss of per-

sonal finances, the possibility of being fired or demoted, and
the potential loss of formal or informal status, power, authority,
and credibility. Examples of such behaviors entailing risk include Lee Iacocca's reduction of his salary to one dollar in his
first year at Chrysler (Iacocca and Novak, 1984) and John
DeLorean's confrontations with General Motors's senior management (Martin and Siehl, 1983). The higher the manifest personal cost or sacrifice for the common goal, the greater is the
trustworthiness of a leader. The more leaders are able to demonstrate that they are indefatigable workers prepared to take on
high personal risks or incur high personal costs in order to achieve
their shared vision, the more they reflect charisma in the sense
of being worthy of complete trust.

Finally, charismatic leaders must appear to be
knowledgeable and experts in their areas of influence. Some
degree of demonstrated expertise, such as reflected in successes
in the past, may be a necessary condition for the attribution
of charisma (Weber, [1924] 1947)—for example, Iacocca's responsibility for the Ford Mustang. Furthermore, it is hypothesized that the attribution of charisma is generally influenced by
the expertise of leaders in two areas. First, charismatic leaders
use their expertise in demonstrating the inadequacy of the traditional technology, rules, and regulations of the status quo as
a means of achieving the shared vision (Weber, [1924] 1947).
Second, charismatic leaders show an expertise in devising effective but unconventional strategies and plans of action (Conger,
1985). Leaders are perceived as charismatic when they demonstrate expertise in transcending the existing order through the
use of unconventional or countercultural means. Iacocca's use
of government-backed loans, money-back guarantees on cars,
union representation on the board, and advertisements featuring
himself are examples of unconventional strategic actions in the
automobile industry.

The attribution of charisma to leaders also depends on
followers' perceptions of their leaders' "revolutionary" and
"countercultural" qualities (Berger, 1963; Conger, 1985; Dow,
1969; Friedland, 1964; Marcus, 1961). The countercultural
qualities of leaders are partly manifested in their discrepant
idealized visions. But more important, charismatic leaders

must engage in unconventional, countercultural, and therefore innovative behavior while leading their followers toward the realization of their visions. Martin and Siehl (1983) demonstrated this in their analysis of John DeLorean's countercultural behavior at General Motors. Charismatic leaders are not consensual leaders but active innovators and entrepreneurs. Their plans and strategies for achieving desired changes and their exemplary acts of heroism involving personal risks or self-sacrificing behaviors have to be novel and unconventional. Their uncommon behavior, when successful, evokes in their followers emotional responses of surprise and admiration. Such uncommon behavior also leads to a dispositional attribution of charisma (or the possession of superhuman abilities).

Personal Power and Charisma

A leader's influence over followers can stem from different bases of power, as suggested by French and Raven (1959). Charismatic influence, however, stems from the leader's personal idiosyncratic power (referent and expert powers) rather than from their position power (legal, coercive, and reward powers), which is determined by organizational rules and regulations. Participative leaders also may use personal power as the basis of their influence. Their personal power, however, is derived from consensus seeking. In addition, some organizational leaders may use personal power through their benevolent but directive behavior. But charismatic leaders are different from both consensual and directive leaders in the use of their personal power. The sources of charismatic leaders' personal power are manifest in their elitist idealized vision, their entrepreneurial advocacy for radical changes, and their depth of knowledge and expertise. In charismatic leaders, all these personal qualities appear extraordinary to followers, and these extraordinary qualities form the basis of both their personal power and their charisma.

Charisma as a Constellation of Behaviors

Through the leadership or influence process model just discussed, we have identified a number of behavioral components that distinguish charismatic from noncharismatic leaders. These components are listed in Table 1. Although each component when manifested in a leader's behavior can contribute to a follower's attribution of charisma to the leader, we consider all of these components interrelated because they often appear in a given leader in the form of a constellation rather than in isolation. It is this constellation of behavior components that distinguishes charismatic leaders from other leaders.

Certain features of the components listed in Table 1 are critical for the perception of charisma in a leader. It is quite probable that effective and noncharismatic leaders will sometimes exhibit one or more of the behavioral components we have identified. However, the likelihood of followers attributing charisma to a leader will depend on three major features of these components: the number of these components manifested in a leader's behavior, the level of intensity of each component as expressed in a leader's behavior, and the level of saliency or importance of individual components as determined by the existing situation or organizational context.

As the number of behavioral components manifested in a leader's behavior increases, the likelihood of a follower's attribution of charisma to the leader also increases. Thus, a leader who is only skillful at detecting deficiencies in the status quo is less likely to be seen as charismatic than is one who not only detects deficiencies but also formulates future visions, articulates them, and devises unconventional means for achieving them.

Besides the total number of manifested behavioral components, leaders may differ in the magnitude (and/or frequency) of a given behavioral component they exhibit. The higher the manifest intensity or frequency of a behavior, the more likely it is to reflect charisma. Thus, leaders who engage in advocating highly discrepant and idealized visions and use highly unconventional means to achieve these visions are more likely to be perceived as charismatic. Likewise, leaders who express high personal commitment to an objective, who take high personal risk, and who use intense articulation techniques are more likely to be perceived as charismatic.

Finally, followers are more likely to attribute charisma to a leader when they perceive his or her behavior to be contex-

Table 1. Distinguishing Attributes
of Charismatic and Noncharismatic Leaders.

	Noncharismatic Leaders	Charismatic Leaders
Relation to status quo	Essentially agrees with status quo and strives to maintain it	Essentially opposed to status quo and strives to change it
Future goals	Goals not too discrepant from status quo	Idealized vision that is highly discrepant from status quo
Likableness	Shared perspective makes him or her likable	Shared perspective and idealized vision make him or her likable and an honorable hero worthy of identification and imitation
Trustworthiness	Disinterested advocacy in persuasion attempts	Passionate advocacy by incurring great personal risk and cost
Expertise	Expert in using available means to achieve goals within the framework of the existing order	Expert in using unconventional means to transcend the existing order
Behavior	Conventional, conforming to existing norms	Unconventional or counternormative
Environmental sensitivity	Low need for environmental sensitivity to maintain status quo	High need for environmental sensitivity for changing the status quo
Articulation	Weak articulation of goals and motivation to lead	Strong and/or inspirational articulation of future vision and motivation to lead
Power base	Position power and personal power (based on reward and/or expert power; and liking for a friend who is a similar other)	Personal power (based on expert power; respect and admiration for a unique hero)
Leader-Follower relationship	Egalitarian, consensus seeking, or directive; nudges or orders people to share his or her views	Elitist, entrepreneurial, and exemplary; transforms people to share the radical changes advocated

tually appropriate and/or in congruence with their own values. Thus, in a traditional organizational culture that subscribes to conservative modes of behavior among employees and the use of conventional means to achieve organizational objectives, leaders who engage in excessive unconventional behavior may be viewed more as deviants than as charismatic figures. Similarly, a leader whose vision fails to incorporate important values and lacks relevance for the organizational context is unlikely to be perceived as charismatic. Certain behavioral components are more critical and effective sources of charisma in some organizational or cultural contexts, but not in others. For example, in some contexts, unconventionality may be less valued as an attribute of charisma than articulation skills, and in other contexts it may be more valued. The constellation of behaviors and their relative importance as determinants of charisma will differ from one organization to another or from one cultural (or national) context to another. Thus, in order to develop a charismatic influence, a leader must have an understanding of the appropriateness or importance of the various behavioral components for a given context.

Implications for Research and Practice

In order to demystify the notion of charisma, we have presented a model that describes a set of behavioral components that form the basis of an attribution of charisma to leaders. On the basis of this model, we proposed in an earlier article a set of tentative hypotheses for future testing (Conger and Kanungo, 1987). This set of testable hypotheses is reproduced in Table 2. Evidence in the literature supports the general framework we have suggested here, but the specific predictions listed in Table 2 remain to be tested. The development and validation of several new scales may be necessary to capture the phenomenon of charismatic leadership within organizations. Such measurement devices would lead to testing the validity of this model.

Table 2. Some Testable Hypotheses on Charismatic Leadership.

Hypotheses on Charisma and Context

1. Charismatic leaders, in order to foster or retain their charisma, engage in realistic assessments of the environmental resources and constraints involving their visions. They put their innovative strategies into action when they find the environmental resource-constraint ratio is favorable to them.
2. Contextual factors that cause potential followers to be disenchanted with the prevailing social order, or which cause followers to experience psychological distress, although not a necessary condition for the emergence of charismatic leaders, facilitate such emergence.

Table 2. Some Testable Hypotheses on Charismatic Leadership, Cont'd.

3. Under conditions of relative social tranquility and lack of potential follower psychological distress, the induction of an organizational context by a leader that fosters or supports an attribution of charisma will facilitate the emergence of that leader as a charismatic leader.
4. Charismatic leaders act as reformers or agents of radical changes, and their charisma fades when they act as administrators (caretaker role) or managers (nudging role).

Hypotheses on Charisma and Vision Formulation and Articulation

1. Leaders are charismatic when their vision represents an embodiment of a perspective shared by followers in an idealized form that is highly discrepant from the status quo yet within a latitude of acceptance.
2. Charismatic leaders articulate the status quo as negative or intolerable and the future vision as the most attractive and attainable alternative.
3. Charismatic leaders articulate their motivation to lead through assertive behavior and expression of self-confidence, expertise, unconventionality, and concern for followers' needs.

Hypotheses on Charisma and Achieving the Vision

1. Charismatic leaders take on high personal risks (or incur high costs) and engage in self-sacrificing activities to achieve a shared vision.
2. Charismatic leaders demonstrate expertise in transcending the existing order through the use of unconventional or extraordinary means.
3. Charismatic leaders engage in behaviors that are novel, unconventional, and counternormative, and as such, involve high personal risk or high probability of harming their own self-interest.

Hypotheses on Charisma and Personal Power

1. Charismatic leaders' influence on their followers stems from the use of their personal idiosyncratic power (expert and referent) rather than the use of their position power (legal, coercive, and reward) within the organization.
2. Charismatic leaders exert idiosyncratic personal power over their followers through elitist, entrepreneurial, and exemplary behavior rather than through consensus-seeking and directive behavior.

In the framework we are proposing, understanding charismatic leadership involves two steps. We have viewed charisma as representing two sides of the same coin: a set of dispositional attributions by followers and a set of leaders' manifest behavior. The two sides are linked in the sense that the leader's behaviors form the basis of followers' attributions. A comprehensive understanding of the charismatic influence process will involve both the identification of the various components of leaders' behavior and assessment of how the components affect the perceptions and attributions of followers.

In order to validate the behavioral model we have proposed, two steps in the research process are necessary. First, our proposed behavioral and dispositional attributes of charismatic leaders require independent empirical confirmation. For convergent validity purposes, a behavioral attribute checklist or questionnaire could be developed that would employ the attributes we have described as well as those cited in the literature for other leadership forms. A group of test subjects would then be asked to identify leaders whom they perceive as charismatic and as noncharismatic. Respondents would be instructed to describe the distinguishing attributes of the charismatic and noncharismatic forms using the checklist. With this format, it would be possible to test whether an attribution of charisma is associated with the behavioral components we are describing. It would also be important to test these behavioral dimensions across various contexts and cultures to determine situational variations.

A recent study (Butala, 1987) designed to test the convergent validity of the charismatic leadership construct provides encouraging evidence in support of our model. In this study, a sample of 105 M.B.A. students were first asked to name two familiar effective leaders, one whom they considered charismatic and one noncharismatic. Following this, the students were then asked to describe these leaders using a checklist of 300 adjectives (Gough, 1952). Comparison of frequency counts of adjectives attributed to the charismatic and the noncharismatic leaders provided support for many of the distinguishing characteristics suggested in our model. For instance, charismatic leaders were perceived to be daring, reckless, energetic, enterprising, unconventional, rebellious, and emotional. In contrast, noncharismatics were seen to be conventional, conservative, reflective, serious, timid, organized, and aloof. Qualities such as patient, realistic, clear thinking, intelligent, and clever were seen in both types of leaders with equal frequency. These results require further confirmation.

The second step in the research process requires tests of discriminant validity of the charismatic leadership construct. This can be done by designing studies to demonstrate that some dependent variables (such as followers' trust) are related to charisma differently than other leadership constructs. These dependent variables are listed in Figure 1 under the organizational and individual outcomes of the leadership process. This type of research will establish the unique effects of charismatic leadership on organizational and individual (follower) outcomes.

The model also has direct implications for management. Specifically, if the behavioral components of charismatic leadership can be isolated, it may be possible to develop in managers several of the model's attributes. Films and cases employing critical incidents demonstrating the characteristics we are considering, as well as behavioral exercises, could be used to train managers. Also, assuming that charismatic leadership is important for organizational reform, companies may wish to select managers on the basis of the characteristics we have identified. The assumption is that individuals appropriate for reformer roles may be those with the dispositional characteristics described in this chapter (for example, managers who tend to have discrepant views). Certain tests, such as those already developed to test sensitivity to the environment (Kenny and Zacarro, 1983), could be administered to potential managerial candidates. The need for such training and selection procedures is likely to be particularly important in developing countries, where greater levels of organizational change are necessary to adopt new technologies and transform traditional ways of operating.

Conclusion

In this chapter, we have outlined an influence process model of leadership. In each stage of the influence process we have identified a set of behavioral components that are critical for the attribution of charisma to a leader. In doing so, we have argued that charismatic leadership be viewed as another critical dimension of leadership behavior with important effects on organizational and followers' outcomes. Furthermore, we have presented a set of testable hypotheses derived from our model. It is our hope that future research will be directed toward testing and refining the model.

References

Bass, B. M. *Leadership and Performance Beyond Expectations.* New York: Free Press, 1985.

Berger, P. L. "Charisma and Religious Innovation: The Social Location of the Israelite Prophecy." *American Sociological Review,* 1963, *28,* 940–950.

Berlew, D. E. "Leadership and Organizational Excitement." *California Management Review,* 1974, *17* (2), 21–30.

Blake, R. R., and Mouton, J. S. *The Managerial Grid.* Houston: Gulf, 1964.

Blau, P. "Critical Remarks on Weber's Theory of Authority." *American Political Science Review,* 1963, *57* (2), 305–315.

Butala, B. "Charismatic Leadership: A Behavioral Study." Unpublished manuscript, Department of Psychology, McGill University, Montreal, 1987.

Byrne, D. *The Attraction Paradigm.* New York: Academic Press, 1977.

Conger, J. A. "Charismatic Leadership in Business: An Exploratory Study." Unpublished doctoral dissertation, School of Business Administration, Harvard University, 1985.

Conger, J. A., and Kanungo, R. N. "Towards a Behavioral Theory of Charismatic Leadership in Organizational Settings." *Academy of Management Review,* 1987, *12,* 637–647.

Dow, T. E., Jr. "The Theory of Charisma." *Sociological Quarterly,* 1969, *10,* 306–318.

Fiedler, F. F. *A Theory of Leadership Effectiveness.* New York: McGraw-Hill, 1967.

French, J. R., Jr., and Raven, B. H. "The Bases of Social Power." In D. Cartwright (ed.), *Studies of Social Power.* Ann Arbor: University of Michigan Press, 1959.

Friedland, W. H. "For a Sociological Concept of Charisma." *Social Forces,* 1964, *43* (1), 18–26.

Gough, H. G. *The Adjective Check List.* Palo Alto, Calif.: Consulting Psychologist Press, 1952.

Hersey, P., and Blanchard, K. H. *Management of Organizational Behavior.* (4th ed.) Englewood Cliffs, N.J.: Prentice-Hall, 1977.

House, R. J. "A Path-Goal Theory of Leadership Effectiveness." *Administrative Science Quarterly,* 1971, *16,* 321–332.

House, R. J. "A 1976 Theory of Charismatic Leadership." In

J. G. Hunt and L. L. Larson (eds.), *Leadership: The Cutting Edge.* Carbondale: Southern Illinois University Press, 1977.

Hovland, C. I., Janis, I. L., and Kelley, H. H. *Communication and Persuasion.* New Haven, Conn.: Yale University Press, 1953.

Hovland, C. I., and Pritzker, H. A. "Extent of Opinion Change as a Function of Amount of Change Advocated." *Journal of Abnormal Psychology,* 1957, *54,* 257–261.

Iacocca, L., and Novak, W. *Iacocca: An Autobiography.* New York: Bantam Books, 1984.

Katz, D., and Kahn, R. L. *The Social Psychology of Organizations.* New York: Wiley, 1978.

Kenny, D. A., and Zacarro, S. J. "An Estimate of Variance Due to Traits in Leadership." *Journal of Applied Psychology,* 1983, *68,* 678–685.

Marcus, J. T. "Transcendence and Charisma." *The Western Political Quarterly,* 1961, *14,* 236–241.

Martin, J., and Siehl, C. "Organizational Culture and Counter-culture: An Uneasy Symbiosis." *Organizational Dynamics,* 1983, *12,* 52–64.

Petty, R. E., and Cacioppo, J. T. *Attitudes and Persuasion: Classic and Contemporary Approaches.* Dubuque, Iowa: Brown, 1981.

Rubin, Z. *Liking and Loving: An Invitation to Social Psychology.* New York: Holt, Rinehart & Winston, 1973.

Sears, D. O., Freedman, L., and Peplau, L. A. *Social Psychology.* (5th ed.) Englewood Cliffs, N.J.: Prentice-Hall, 1985.

Walster, E., Aronson, D., and Abrahams, D. "On Increasing the Persuasiveness of a Low-Prestige Communicator." *Journal of Experimental Social Psychology,* 1966, *2,* 325–342.

Weber, M. *The Theory of Social and Economic Organization.* (A. M. Henderson and T. Parsons, trans.; T. Parsons, ed.) New York: Free Press, 1947. (Originally published 1924.)

Willner, A. R. *The Spellbinders: Charismatic Political Leadership.* New Haven, Conn.: Yale University Press, 1984.

Yukl, G. A. *Leadership in Organizations.* Englewood Cliffs, N.J.: Prentice-Hall, 1981.

Zaleznik, A. "Managers and Leaders: Are They Different?" *Harvard Business Review,* 1977, *15* (3), 67–78.

Zaleznik, A., and Kets de Vries, M. *Power and the Corporate Mind.* Boston: Houghton Mifflin, 1975.

4

Charismatic and Noncharismatic Leaders: Differences in Behavior and Effectiveness

Robert J. House
James Woycke
Eugene M. Fodor

Research on leadership in the 1960s and early 1970s was predominantly concerned with identifying leader behaviors that had a significant impact on follower attitudes, behavior, and performance. During this period, a major portion of this research was conceived within a transactional or exchange framework of leader/follower relationships. Research in the late 1970s and 1980s, however, included not only tests and extensions of transactional theories but also an emphasis on a new class of theories referred to as charismatic or transformational theories of leadership.

In this chapter, we contrast transactional and charismatic or transformational theories of leadership. We then briefly review prior research and evidence on charismatic and transformational theory. This evidence is primarily concerned with determining the kinds of leader behavior that contribute to charismatic or transformational leader effectiveness. Our review demonstrates that there is a substantial convergence of findings that provides a rather clear picture of the behavior involved in effective charismatic and transformational leadership. Finally, we present a study designed to test predictions of theories concerning the effects and behavior of charismatic compared with noncharismatic United States presidents.

Theories of Leader Behavior

Transactional Theories. This class of leadership theories is founded on the idea that leader/follower relationships are based on a series of exchanges or implicit bargains between leaders and followers (Evans, 1970; Hollander, 1964; House, 1971; House and Mitchell, 1974; Graen and Cashman, 1975; Graen and Scandura, 1987). The general notion that runs through this class of theories is that when the job and the environment of the follower fail to provide the necessary motivation, direction, and satisfaction, the leader, through his or her behavior, will be effective by compensating for the deficiencies.

The leader provides for subordinates "that which is missing" but which is required for them to perform effectively and achieve their goals. In this manner, the leader compensates for, or overcomes, obstacles and deficiencies in the followers' environment. What is missing is determined by the environment, the task, and the competence and motivation of followers. It is the role of the leader to complement that which "is missing" to enhance followers' motivation, satisfaction, and performance. It is also the role of the leader to enhance follower competence through coaching and support and by making available to followers opportunities for growth and development in the form of challenging tasks and opportunities to work under conditions of autonomy.

Two such transactional theories have been subjected to rather extensive testing: the Path-Goal Theory of Leadership (Evans, 1970; House, 1971; House and Mitchell, 1974) and the Vertical Dyadic Theory of Role Making (Graen and Cashman, 1975; Graen and Scandura, 1987). Both have received considerable empirical support (see Indvik, 1986, regarding the path-goal theory and Graen and Scandura, 1987, regarding the vertical dyadic theory).

These theories call attention to the importance of situational factors that moderate the effects of a leader's behavior. They also call attention to dyadic relationships between superiors and subordinates and suggest that these relationships need to be measured along with more aggregate measures (such as group members' average perceptions of the leader) in order to predict the effects of leader behavior on individuals. In general, these compensatory theories emphasize the need for managers to diagnose what is missing and take action to facilitate followers' performance. Transactional theories have been successful in predicting variance in subordinate satisfaction, turnover, motivation, role ambiguity, and performance, as these variables normally vary.

Charismatic or Transformational Theories. In contrast to transactional theories, charismatic or transformational theories of leadership predict performance beyond expectations—that is, where substantial and voluntary efforts over and above the call of duty are made by followers. Further, these theories predict emotional attachment to the leader on the part of followers, as well as emotional and motivational arousal of the followers as a consequence of the leader's behavior.

In contrast to transactional theories, which focus on the effects of leader behaviors on follower cognitions, motivation, and performance, charismatic or transformational leadership theories take as their dependent variables followers' emotional responses to work-related stimuli, as well as their values, self-esteem, trust and confidence in the leader, and motivation to perform above and beyond the call of duty. Further, in contrast to transactional leadership theories that describe leaders in terms of task- and person-oriented behavior, these newer theories describe leaders in terms of articulating and focusing a vision and mission; creating and maintaining a positive image in the minds of followers, peers, and superiors; exhibiting a high degree of confidence in themselves and their beliefs; setting challenging goals for followers; providing a personal example for followers to emulate; showing confidence in and respect for followers; behaving in a manner that reinforces the vision and mission of the leader; and possessing a high degree of linguistic ability and nonverbal expressiveness. Theoretical perspectives of this kind have been advanced by Berlew (1974), House (1977), Burns (1978), Bennis and Nanus (1985), and Bass (1985) and by the authors of three chapters in this book: Conger and Kanungo (Chapter Three), Howell (Chapter Seven), and Sashkin (Chapter Five). All of these perspectives describe charismatic or transformational leaders as individuals who provide for their followers a vision of the future that promises a better and more meaningful way of life.

The difference between transactional theories and transformational or charismatic theories of leadership behavior lies in the components of the subordinate's motivation that are affected by the leader's behavior and in the specific behaviors of the leader that affect components of the subordinate's motivation. Transactional leaders have their primary effects on follower cognitions and abilities. Charismatic leaders have their major effects on the emotions and self-esteem of followers—the affective motivational variables rather than the cognitive variables.

To put the position succinctly, despite some danger of oversimplification, transactional theories describe actions of leaders that result in work behavior becoming more instrumental in followers reaching their *existing* goals while at the same time contributing to the goals of the organization. In contrast, charismatic or transformational theories address the actions of leaders that result in subordinates *changing* their values, goals, needs, and aspirations. This is somewhat of an oversimplification, since certain charismatic leader behaviors may also have instrumental effects. While Conger (Chapter One) and Bass (Chapter Two) review many of the empirical studies of charismatic leadership, we will briefly report on studies that have not been described in detail and that directly link the effects of charismatic and transformational leader behavior to specific follower outcomes, such as motivation and productivity.

Smith (1982), for example, found that thirty leaders who had reputations for being charismatic had significantly different effects on followers than did thirty effective but noncharismatic leaders. Followers of reputed charismatic leaders were found to be more self-assured, experienced more meaningfulness in their work, reported more back-up from their leaders, reported working longer hours, reported higher trust in their leaders, saw their leaders as more dynamic, and had higher performance ratings than did the followers of the noncharismatic but effective leaders.

Using the followers' questionnaire responses, Smith conducted and cross-validated a discriminant function analysis. This analysis classified followers into two groups. Eighty-one percent of the followers who reported to charismatic leaders were clustered together and 66.7 percent of the followers of the noncharismatic leaders were clustered together, yielding an overall hit rate of 80 percent (p = $<.0009$).

Additional support for this class of theories is provided by a laboratory experiment conducted by Howell and Frost (forthcoming) and by a field study of four military samples conducted by Yukl and Van Fleet (1982). Howell and Frost compared the effects of charismatic leader behavior on followers with the effects of directive and considerate leader behavior under experimentally induced high- and low-productivity norm conditions. The findings showed that charismatic leader behavior, as specified by prior theory (House, 1977), had a stronger and more positive influence on the performance, satisfaction, and adjustment of followers than did directive and considerate leader behavior.

A multiple analysis of variance in follower role conflict, role ambiguity, satisfaction, and adjustment to the leader demonstrated that the leader behavior treatment accounted for 96 percent of the variance in these dependent variables. It is most interesting that only the charismatic leader behavior was able to overcome the negative effects of the low-productivity norm condition. Those working under charismatic leaders had higher general satisfaction, higher specific task satisfaction, and less role conflict than did individuals working under structuring or considerate leaders. Under the latter two conditions, the negative effects of the low-productivity norm treatment persisted.

Another empirical study relevant to charismatic theory is presented by Yukl and Van Fleet (1982). These authors found in four separate military samples that "inspirational leadership" was significantly related to leader effectiveness and high levels of follower motivation. These findings held under combat, non-combat, and simulated combat conditions. Thus, studies of char-ismatic (or inspirational) leaders demonstrated that the behaviors specified by prior theory (House, 1977) rather consistently have the effects predicted by that theory.

A second theory of the same genre is the transformational leadership theory advanced by James MacGregor Burns (1978). According to Burns, transformational leadership occurs "when one or more persons *engage* with others in such a way that leaders and followers raise one another to higher levels of motivation and morality" (p. 20). Accordingly, transformational leaders address themselves to followers' "wants, needs, and other mo-tivations, as well as their own and, thus, they serve as an *inde-pendent force in changing the make-up of followers' motive base through gratifying their motives*" (p. 20).

As reported in Chapter Three, Bass and his associates have conducted a substantial amount of research testing hypoth-eses derived from Burns's theory of transformational leadership. These studies have yielded an impressive set of empirical find-ings. Specifically, leaders who are rated by subordinates to be transformational as compared with other leaders have been found to:

- receive high performance ratings from superiors (Bass, 1985; Hater and Bass, forthcoming)
- be rated more frequently by superiors as top performers (Hater and Bass, 1986)
- be rated more frequently by superiors as having potential for advancement (Avolio and Bass, 1985) or as having ex-cellent ability to manage (Hater and Bass, forthcoming)
- be classified more frequently by independent experts as trans-formational leaders (Bass, 1985)
- be more frequently classified as "great or world-class lead-ers" by biographers and historians (Bass, 1985)
- have higher-performing teams in a management simulation exercise (Avolio, Waldman, and Einstein, forthcoming)

- take greater strategic risks in the same management simulation (Avolio and Bass, 1985)
- have surbordinates who report greater satisfaction and more or "extra" work effort (Bass, 1985; Hater and Bass, forthcoming; Pereira, 1987) and greater organizational and unit effectiveness (Pereira, 1987)
- have subordinates who also demonstrate transformational leader behaviors (Bass, Waldman, Avolio, and Bebb, 1987)
- have higher-performing work groups (Hater and Bass, forthcoming)

These findings are impressive because the correlations between transformational leader behavior, followers' performance, and satisfaction are significantly higher under transformational leaders than under transactional leaders, because the correlations between transformational leader behaviors and ratings by followers and superiors are consistently above .5 and often as high as .7, and because they have been corroborated in India as well as in the United States (Pereira, 1987).

These findings indicate that leaders who engage in the theoretical charismatic or transformational leader behaviors do indeed produce the predicted charismatic effects and are viewed as more effective leaders by their superiors and followers than are transactional leaders. Further, the correlations between charismatic leader behavior and follower satisfaction and performance are consistently high compared with prior field studies' findings concerning other leader behavior.

The theories and supporting evidence presented in this section inform us of the kinds of behaviors that differentiate charismatic from noncharismatic leaders. Specifically, as stated previously, charismatic leaders articulate a mission or vision in ideological terms, demonstrate a high degree of self-confidence and a high degree of involvement in the mission, set a personal example for followers to emulate, create and maintain a positive image in the minds of followers, peers, and superiors, communicate high performance expectations to followers and confidence in followers' ability to meet such expectations, behave in a manner that reinforces the vision and the mission of the leader, show individualized consideration toward followers, and provide intellectual stimulation to followers. While laboratory and field evidence supports these conclusions, there have been no studies to date designed to test charismatic or transformational theories with respect to political leaders responsible for the management of government organizations. In the following section, we describe such a study and its implications for management practice.

A Study of United States Presidents

The study reported here was designed to test the following hypotheses: (1) The biographies of cabinet members reporting to charismatic United States presidents include more incidents of positive affective relations with the presidents and more positive affective reactions to their positions than do those of cabinet members reporting to noncharismatic United States presidents. (2) The biographies of cabinet members reporting to charismatic United States presidents include more incidents of charismatic behaviors on the part of the presidents than do biographies of noncharismatic presidents.

Method

Classification of Presidents. Nine well-reputed political historians, each with broad expertise in American history, received a questionnaire asking them to classify American presidents as charismatic, noncharismatic, neither charismatic nor noncharismatic, or uncertain (no opinion), using the following guideline: "Charisma is defined as the ability to exercise diffuse and intensive influence over the normative or ideological orientations of others (Etzioni, 1961). As a result, we can identify charismatic leaders by their effects on their followers such that followers of charismatic leaders: (a) have a high degree of loyalty, commitment, and devotion to the leader; (b) identify with the leader and the mission of the leader; (c) emulate his or her values, goals, and behavior; (d) see the leader as a source of inspiration; (e) derive a sense of high self-esteem from their relationship with the leader and his or her mission; and (f) have an exceptionally high degree of trust in the leader and the correctness of his or her beliefs.'' The historians were asked to classify the leaders with respect to their relationship to cabinet members rather than their relationship to United States voters, because our primary interest in this study was organizational leadership rather than mass or political leadership. Presidents who had served less than two full years in office were not included in the sample.

Seven presidents met the criterion for classification as charismatic leaders; that is, at least eight of the nine historians agreed that these presidents should so be designated. Six presidents met the criterion (eight or more historians agreeing) to qualify as noncharismatic leaders. The historians rated as charismatic Jefferson, Jackson, Lincoln, Theodore Roosevelt, Franklin Roosevelt, Kennedy, and Reagan. They classified as noncharismatic Coolidge, Harding, Arthur, Buchanan, Pierce, and Tyler.

In addition to the charismatic and noncharismatic presidents referred to above, three additional presidents were included in this study. These were Truman, Cleveland, and Polk, who declined renomination and died shortly after leaving office. Eight of the political historians agreed that these three presidents were neither charismatic nor noncharismatic. However, all three are consistently rated in polls of political historians as either "great" or "near great" (Murray and Blessing, 1983). These three presidents provide a comparison group of effective but noncharismatic presidents. Thus, the final sample includes seven charismatic presidents, six noncharismatic presidents, and three presidents who are viewed by political historians as great or near great but who were rated neither charismatic nor noncharismatic. We refer to these three groups as effective charismatics, effective noncharismatics, and ineffective noncharismatics in the remainder of this chapter. We assign these normative labels on the basis of historians' ratings of presidential greatness plus the fact that six of the seven charismatic presidents were reelected, whereas none of the noncharismatic presidents was reelected. The one charismatic president who was not elected to a second term was Kennedy, who was assassinated in his first term.

Biographical Data. In the next part of the study, the biographies of two or more cabinet members reporting to each president were content analyzed to determine whether there was evidence that (1) charismatic presidents engaged more frequently in behaviors that theoretically differentiate charismatic from noncharismatic leaders, and (2) charismatic presidents had a significantly more positive effect on their cabinet members than did noncharismatic presidents. The content analysis was applied to descriptions of the cabinet members' experiences in the first term of the presidents' administrations only, because no noncharismatic president served more than one term (defined as more than two years of any normal four-year term). President Reagan was not included in this analysis because there were no biographies of his cabinet members written at the time of the study.

To measure the effects of presidents on follower affective states, passages of the biographies of cabinet members that described interactions between the presidents and the cabinet members were coded. These interactions were coded as indicating positive effects of the presidents on the affective states of the secretaries if there was evidence of positive attitudes toward the president, willingness to accept his mission, enthusiasm for the mission, and generally positive attitudes concerning the cabinet member's role in the administration.

To measure the behavior of the presidents, passages were coded that indicated the presidents' expression of self-confidence, high performance expectations of followers, confidence in followers' abilities and performance, strong ideological goals, and individualized consideration for followers.

The use of scholarly biographies for this purpose is a well-accepted practice in social science studies (see Bass, Avolio, and Goodheim, 1987; Bass and Farrow, 1977; Simonton, 1986; Winter, 1987; Woodward, 1974). Cabinet secretaries are well-suited to reflect charismatic effects, because often they have not been associated with the president, they may be unknown to him, and they may have been chosen for party-political reasons (some were rival contenders for the presidential nomination). The best recent one-volume scholarly biography of each cabinet secretary was selected on the basis of references in *The Harvard Guide to American History* (Freidel, 1974) and the *Biographical Directory of the United States Executive Branch, 1774–1977* (Sobel, 1977). Biographies published since 1977 were identified in the University of Toronto library and confirmed on the basis of reviews in the *American Historical Review* and the *Journal of American History.* All cabinet secretaries (except postmasters general) about whom a scholarly biography or monograph had been written were included in the study. Further, we specifically included secretaries of state from each administration.

Only multivolume biographies were available for cabinet secretaries Caleb Cushing, Henry A. Wallace, and Robert Kennedy. In these cases, we used either the volume dealing with the first term or, when the first-term material spanned more than one volume, the complete index. Three secretaries—Thomas F. Bayard, Frank B. Kellogg, and Henry C. Wallace—were represented by scholarly monographs. Two secretaries—Frederick T. Frelinghuysen and Philander C. Knox—were represented by doctoral dissertations.

Biographies were scanned for relevant passages containing substantive remarks (author statements or direct quotations) pertaining to the relationship between the president and the secretary. Mundane or routine remarks were excluded. Passages were selected by scanning the chapter or chapters dealing with the relationship during the first term, provided that such material did not exceed fifty pages. If the chapter or chapters dealing with the first term exceeded fifty pages, we used the index to identify passages. If a relationship was illustrated by fewer than three extracts from any one source, that material was dropped. If more than fifteen extracts were obtained, the number was randomly reduced to fifteen. This selective process is a conservative one in that it increases the number of passages for those low on the criterion variables and reduces the number for those high on the criterion variables.

All passages in the indexes of the biographies referring to the president were transcribed onto index cards. Using House's (1977) theory as a guide, descriptions of each behavior and each effect thought to describe charisma were developed. A set of leadership passages separate from those to be used in the study was developed so that the operationalization of the behaviors and effects could be clarified. Two independent individuals coded these practice passages, discussed their ratings, and then clarified the descriptions where necessary. Four iterations of rating and discussion were completed before it was felt that there was an unambiguous operationalization of each behavior and each effect. The final coding of these practice passages became the key on which the subjects were trained.

Recruitment: Testing and Training of Coders. Undergraduate students were recruited and given a reading test to ensure that their reading comprehension was adequate for the material they would have to read. Students were trained on either behaviors or effects and were randomly assigned to each. Using the precoded practice material and the descriptions of the behaviors and effects, the students were trained so that they understood and were able to code the passages accurately. The students who were trained to code behaviors were 73 to 88 percent accurate. The students trained to code effects were 78 to 83 percent accurate. (Accuracy means they agreed with the key.) Students' accuracy was checked after every seventy-five experimental passages they coded, and the same level of accuracy was found to be maintained.

Table 1 presents the number of biographies and passages for each classification of leader. The behavior of the presidents and the affective responses of the cabinet members described in these passages were coded separately by two coders, one who coded behaviors and one who coded effects. The identities of the cabinet members were disguised so that the coders could not determine the names of the cabinet members to which the passages applied. Further, the coders were unaware of the hypotheses of the study.

Table 1. Number of Biographies Analyzed and Passages Coded.

	Effective Charismatics	Effective Non-charismatics	Ineffective Non-charismatics
Number of biographies	19	9	12
Number of passages describing affective states	180	50	59
Number of passages describing behaviors	139	56	46

Results

Biographical Analyses. Table 2 presents the results of the biographical content analysis concerning affective responses of cabinet members. This table reports the mean number of passages describing positive effects of the leaders per biography, per leader. The difference between effective charismatics and effective noncharismatics was significant at the .04 level ($F = 6.77$). These passages reflect positive attitudes toward the president, trust in and obedience to the president, willingness to accept the president's mission, enthusiasm for the mission, and generally positive statements concerning the cabinet member's role in the administration.

These findings are significant for two reasons. First, they serve as a check on the validity of the classification procedure. They confirm that those presidents classified as charismatic by historians are also described by biographers as having charismatic effects on cabinet members. Thus, the findings provide an independent check on the procedure used to classify charismatic and noncharismatic leaders. Second, these findings further confirm the theoretical definition of charismatic leaders as leaders who have significant effects on the affective state of their followers, thus providing support for hypothesis one.

Table 3 presents the results of the biographical content analysis concerning the frequency of charismatic behaviors by the presidents reported in the biographies.

A test of the difference between the behaviors of effective

Table 2. Analysis of Variance Comparing Mean Frequency of
Affective Responses Reported per Cabinet Member Biography.

	Effective Charismatics (N = 6)	Effective Non-charismatics (N = 3)	Ineffective Non-charismatics (N = 6)
Mean	9.01	5.56	4.42
S.D.	3.47	3.40	2.60

Note: F for effective charismatics versus ineffective noncharismatics = 6.77, $p < .04$.

charismatics and ineffective noncharismatics demonstrated a significant difference in the mean charismatic behaviors per biography for these two groups ($F = 7.42$; $p < .04$), thus providing support for hypothesis two. The specific behaviors that differentiate effective charismatics from ineffective noncharismatics are the leaders' display of self-confidence, high performance expectations of followers, confidence in followers' abilities and performance, strong ideological goals, and individualized consideration for followers.

Relationship to Previously Published Data. In addition to the test of the hypotheses reported above, we can also relate our presidential classifications to data published in the political science literature. There have been several surveys of political historians concerning presidential greatness. The results of the more prominent surveys are displayed in Table 4. In four of these surveys, the respondents were asked to indicate, for each

Table 3. Analysis of Variance Comparing Mean Frequency of
Charismatic Leader Behavior per Cabinet Member Biography.

	Effective Charismatics	Effective Non-charismatics	Ineffective Non-charismatics
Mean	7.54	6.22	3.06
S.D.	2.99	6.73	2.76

Note: F for effective charismatics versus ineffective noncharismatics = 7.42, $p < .04$.

Table 4. Ratings of Presidential Performance in Five Surveys of Political Scientists.

Porter 1981 (N = 41)		Schlesinger 1962 (N = 75)		Schlesinger 1948 (N = 55)	
Lincoln* Washington* F. Roosevelt* Jefferson* T. Roosevelt*	Great	Lincoln* Washington F. Roosevelt* Wilson Jefferson*	Great	Lincoln* Washington F. Roosevelt* Wilson Jefferson*	Great
Wilson Jackson* Truman** Polk** J. Adams L. Johnson	Near great	Jackson* T. Roosevelt* Polk** Truman** J. Adams Cleveland**	Near great	Jackson* T. Roosevelt* Cleveland** J. Adams Polk**	Near great
Eisenhower Madison Kennedy Cleveland** McKinley Monroe J. Q. Adams Van Buren Hayes Taft Hoover Carter Arthur*** B. Harrison Ford	Average	Madison J. Q. Adams Hayes McKinley Taft Van Buren Monroe Hoover B. Harrison Arthur*** Eisenhower A. Johnson	Average	J. Q. Adams Monroe Hayes Madison Van Buren Taft Arthur*** McKinley A. Johnson Hoover B. Harrison	Average
Taylor Tyler*** Fillmore Coolidge*** A. Johnson Grant Pierce***	Below average	Taylor Tyler*** Fillmore Coolidge*** Pierce*** Buchanan***	Below average	Tyler*** Coolidge*** Fillmore Taylor*** Buchanan*** Pierce***	Below average
Nixon*** Buchanan*** Harding***	Failure	Grant Harding***	Failure	Grant Harding***	Failure

* Effective charismatic
** Effective noncharismatic
*** Ineffective noncharismatic

Murray-Blessing 1982 (N = 846)		Mode	Mean	Chicago Tribune 1982 (N = 49)	
Lincoln*	Great	1	1.13	Lincoln*	Ten best
F. Roosevelt*		1	1.22	Washington*	
Washington		1	1.27	F. Roosevelt*	
Jefferson*		1	1.70	T. Roosevelt*	
T. Roosevelt	Near great	2	1.93	Jefferson*	
Wilson		2	2.07	Wilson	
Jackson*		2	2.32	Jackson*	
Truman**		2	2.45	Truman**	
J. Adams	Above average	3	2.85	Eisenhower	
L. Johnson		3	2.87	Polk**	
Eisenhower		3	2.99	McKinley	
Polk**		3	3.06	L. Johnson	
Kennedy*		3	3.13	Cleveland**	
Madison		3	3.30	Kennedy*	
Monroe		3	3.35	J. Adams } tie	
J. Q. Adams		3	3.42	Monroe }	
Cleveland**		3	3.43	Madison	
McKinley	Average	4	3.78	Van Buren	
Taft		4	3.87	J. Q. Adams	
Van Buren		4	3.97	Taft	
Hoover		4	4.03	Hoover	
Hayes		4	4.05	Hayes	
Arthur***		4	4.24	Ford	
Ford		4	4.32	Arthur***	
Carter		4	4.36	B. Harrison	
B. Harrison		4	4.40	Taylor	
Taylor	Below average	5	4.45	Carter	Ten worst
Tyler***		5	4.61	Tyler***	
Fillmore		5	4.64	Coolidge***	
Coolidge***		5	4.65	A. Johnson	
Pierce***		5	4.95	Fillmore	
A. Johnson	Failure	6	5.10	Grant	
Buchanan		6	5.15	Pierce***	
Nixon		6	5.18	Buchanan***	
Grant		6	5.25	Nixon	
Harding***		6	5.56	Harding***	

United States president, whether he or she viewed the president as great, near great, average, below average, or a failure. These ratings provide us with expert (political historian) opinions concerning presidential greatness. In these surveys, Lincoln, Franklin D. Roosevelt, and Jefferson were consistently rated as great. Jackson and Theodore Roosevelt were rated as great in two of these surveys and near great in the remaining two. While not rated as charismatic in our poll of political historians, Washington and Wilson also were consistently rated as great or near great in the polls of political historians.

The members of the effective noncharismatic group were consistently rated as near great, with the exception of the survey by Porter, reported in Murray and Blessing (1983), in which Cleveland was rated as average. The members of the noncharismatic sample were consistently rated as average or below. None of these presidents was rated as great or near great.

These findings suggest a strong relationship between charismatic leadership and presidential greatness. Further, considering another aspect of presidential performance, five of the six charismatic leaders were reelected. The one exception, Kennedy, was assassinated. In contrast, ineffective noncharismatic leaders consistently were not nominated by their parties for reelection, except for Harding, who died in office, and Coolidge, who declined to seek renomination.

It is possible to relate our classifications of presidents to political historians' opinions concerning several performance criteria of the presidency. Table 5 recasts data reported by Maranell (1970) into our classifications of presidents. These data are based on a poll of 846 political historians. From this table it is clear that charismatic presidents are rated as significantly higher than noncharismatics on general prestige, strength of action, presidential activeness, flexibility, accomplishment of their administrations, and the amount of information about the president available to respondents. Thus, it is clear that United States political historians are in substantial agreement with respect to their opinions concerning presidential performance.

These data show that charismatic presidents are given the majority of attention in the literature, as demonstrated by re-

Table 5. Ratings of Presidents by Political Historians.

	Charismatic	Neutral	Noncharismatic
General prestige	1.30[a]	0.50	− 1.22
Strength of action	1.39	0.60	− 0.90
Presidential activeness	1.34	0.68	− 0.95
Flexibility	1.23	0.13	0.21
Accomplishment of their administrations	1.30	0.58	− 0.91
Respondent's amount of information	1.25	0.35	− 0.92

[a]Index of number of standard deviations above or below the mean of all presidents.
Source: Maranell, 1970.

sponses of political historians, which indicates that more information is available about the charismatic presidents than about the noncharismatic presidents. This finding is further confirmed by our own finding that more biographies were available describing cabinet members of charismatic United States presidents than noncharismatic presidents.

These findings suggest a possible bias in the political historians' classification of presidents as charismatic or noncharismatic. It is likely that our expert classifiers are influenced by the results of prior polls concerning presidential greatness and by the fact that those presidents classified as charismatic were reelected or assassinated. If this is true, we may have a confounding of our independent variable—classification of presidents as charismatic or not—with ratings of presidential achievements. This could be due to a misattribution problem in which the attribution of charisma is made on the basis of the same data used to assess presidential performance. Further, it can be argued that all three sources of information (biographers, political historians who classified the presidents in the present study, and political historians polled in prior studies) may be generally informed by the same literature and therefore may all indirectly reflect a common source bias.

This explanation, while undoubtedly true to some extent, is considerably weakened by two observations. The first observation concerns the presidential classifications. Washington and

Wilson were consistently rated as great in all four polls of political historians and as above great in the Maranell poll. However, these presidents were not classified as charismatic in the present study. Further, a large number of presidents were rated as below average or as failures but were not classified as noncharismatic in the present study. Thus, presidential greatness or failure alone does not account for the political historians' attribution of charisma. Second, the charismatic presidents were described by biographers as engaging in more charismatic behaviors than the noncharismatic presidents. Since such behavior was *not* used as a criterion for presidential classification, the behavioral data can reasonably be regarded as independent of the classification process and thus can shed additional light on the nature of the charismatic phenomenon.

Organizational Implications

The above findings have several implications for organizational theory and practice.

Commitment to Organizational Goals. The first implication concerns the effect of charismatic leader behavior on follower commitment to the mission of the leader or the organization. The findings of Smith (1982), Bass and his associates as reviewed earlier in this chapter, and Howell and Frost (forthcoming), as well as the present study, all demonstrate that a high level of organizational commitment on the part of followers is associated with charismatic behavior of leaders. Thus, this kind of leader behavior provides a strong link between organizational goals and member commitment to such goals.

Early Detection of Charismatic Potential. The entire pattern of affective and behavioral data in the present study, as well as biographical ratings of presidential greatness and Maranell's (1970) findings with respect to attributes of presidential administrations, suggests a clear picture of charismatic leadership in the United States presidential office. Charismatic United States presidents are extremely active, assertive, and energetic, as are other charismatic leaders studied in prior investigation.

Further, their effects on the affective states of followers suggest that charismatic leaders are socially sensitive to the needs of their followers. These findings suggest that it is likely that individuals who have charismatic potential can be identified through psychological testing and observation of behavior in simulations, such as management games and assessment center exercises. Recall that Avolio and Bass (1985) found such leaders to behave differently from other leaders in a management game and that their teams performed more effectively than did teams led by noncharismatic leaders.

What should we make of these findings and speculations? We believe that at this time there is sufficient knowledge concerning leader personality to warrant the development and testing of selection procedures for identifying charismatic leadership potential. Clearly, selection validation studies are called for.

Conditions Requiring Charismatic Leadership. The findings from this and prior studies also suggest the conditions under which charismatic leadership is most likely to be required and effective. Our findings suggest that effective charismatic presidents were active, energetic, assertive, and socially sensitive individuals. Further recall that the cabinet members of charismatic presidents have expressed a high degree of commitment to the leader and his mission and a high degree of positive affect toward the leader and toward their position in his cabinet.

We speculate from these findings that charismatic leadership is required, or at least is more appropriate, in situations that require a combination of highly involved and active leadership plus emotional commitment and extraordinary effort by both leader and followers in pursuit of ideological goals. We speculate that situations that require these attributes are thus situations that require charismatic leadership. Under conditions requiring routine but reliable performance in the pursuit of pragmatic goals, charismatic leadership is not likely required and may even be dysfunctional.

Managerial Training and Development. The findings from prior studies have implications for managerial training, for role modeling and coaching by superiors, and for career counseling and planning. Bass, Waldman, Avolio, and Bebb (1987) demonstrated a role modeling effect of charismatic leaders. Specifically, followers of charismatic leaders were found to engage in behavior similar to that of their leaders. Evidence also suggests, although presently still somewhat tenuously, that charismatic leader behavior can be learned through training. Major evidence for the efficacy of charismatic training is Howell and Frost's (forthcoming) laboratory study of the effects of leader behavior. These researchers found that they were able to train selected individuals to engage in charismatic behavior as well as other kinds of leader behaviors.

If the Howell and Frost finding that charismatic leader behavior is trainable in a laboratory situation is found in future research to be generalizable to field settings, we would recommend such training efforts to develop such behavior. Clearly, a field test of the efficacy of charismatic leadership training in field settings is called for.

We would caution the reader, however, to expect the effects of such training to be conditional on the personality, ideological or goal commitment, and interpersonal skills of trainees. We would expect such training to be most effective for individuals who have shown a strong commitment to organizational goals, have demonstrated a high degree of involvement in their work, have high needs for achievement and power, and possess skills of linguistic and nonverbal expressiveness. Further, we would expect such training to be more effective under conditions requiring involved and active leadership, high levels of follower commitment, and follower effort beyond the call of duty.

Conclusion

Our study of United States presidents is intended to further our understanding of the elusive phenomenon referred to as charismatic or transformational leadership. We believe that we have shown in our review of prior theory and research evidence, in our review of political historians' opinion polls, and in our research on presidential biographical and motivational data that: (1) Reputed charismatic leaders have the affects hypothesized in theories of charismatic and transformational leadership. These affects distinguish charismatic from noncharismatic leaders. (2) Reported charismatic leaders engage in behaviors hypothesized in theories of charismatic and transformational leadership. These behaviors distinguish charismatic from noncharismatic leaders. These conclusions appear to be generalizable, at least in the North American culture, since they have been demonstrated in field, laboratory, and historical studies.

The above conclusions are derived from studies conducted in the Western world plus one study conducted in India. It will be interesting to follow the development of theory and research in this domain. We hope that cross-cultural research will inform us of the generalizability of these findings beyond the Western world and of the applicability of charismatic and transformational theory to leadership in complex organizations.

References

Avolio, B. J., and Bass, B. M. "Charisma and Beyond." Paper presented at the Academy of Management, San Diego, Aug. 1985.

Avolio, B. J., Waldman, D. A., and Einstein, W. O. "Transformational Leadership in a Management Game Simulation." *Group and Organized Studies,* forthcoming.

Bass, B. M. *Leadership and Performance Beyond Expectations.* New York: Free Press, 1985.

Bass, B. M., Avolio, B. J., and Goodheim, L. "Biography and the Assessment of Transformational Leadership at the World-Class Level." *Journal of Management,* 1987, *13* (1), 7–20.

Bass, B. M., and Farrow, D. L. "Quantitative Analysis of Biographies of Political Figures." *Journal of Psychology,* 1977, *97,* 281–296.

Bass, B. M., Waldman, D. A., Avolio, B. J., and Bebb, M. "Transformational Leadership and the Falling Dominoes Effect." *Group and Organization Studies,* 1987, *12* (1), 73–87.

Bennis, W., and Nanus, B. *Leaders: The Strategies for Taking Charge.* New York: Harper & Row, 1985.

Berlew, D. E. "Leadership and Organizational Excitement." *California Management Review,* 1974, *17* (2), 21–30.

Burns, J. M. *Leadership.* New York: Harper & Row, 1978.

Etzioni, A. *A Comparative Analysis of Complex Organizations.* New York: Free Press, 1961.

Evans, M. G. "The Effects of Supervisory Behavior on the Path-Goal Relationship." *Organizational Behavior and Human Performance,* 1970, *5,* 277–298.

Freidel, F. (ed.). *The Harvard Guide to American History.* Cambridge, Mass.: Harvard University Press, 1974.

Graen, G., and Cashman, J. F. "A Role-Making Model of Leadership in Formal Organizations: A Developmental Approach." In J. G. Hunt and L. L. Larson (eds.), *Leadership Frontiers.* Kent, Ohio: Kent State University Press, 1975.

Graen, G. B., and Scandura, T. A. "Toward a Psychology of Dyadic Organizing." In L. L. Cummings and B. M. Staw (eds.), *Research in Organizational Behavior.* Greenwich, Conn.: JAI Press, 1987.

Hater, J. J., and Bass, B. M. "Superiors' Evaluations and Subordinates' Perceptions of Transformational and Transactional Leadership." *Journal of Applied Psychology,* forthcoming.

Hollander, E. P. *Leaders, Groups, and Influence.* New York: Oxford University Press, 1964.

House, R. J. "Path-Goal Theory of Leader Effectiveness." *Administrative Science Quarterly,* 1971, *16,* 321–338.

House, R. J. "A 1976 Theory of Charismatic Leadership." In J. G. Hunt and L. L. Larson (eds.), *Leadership: The Cutting Edge.* Carbondale: Southern Illinois University Press, 1977.

House, R. J., and Mitchell, T. R. "Path-Goal Theory of Leadership." *Journal of Contemporary Business,* 1974, *5,* 81–94.

Howell, J. M., and Frost, P. "A Laboratory Study of Charismatic Leadership." *Organizational Behavior and Human Decision Processes,* forthcoming.

Indvik, J. "Path-Goal Theory of Leadership: A Meta-Analysis." *Proceedings,* Academy of Management, Chicago, 1986.

Maranell, G. M. "The Evaluation of Presidents: An Extension of the Schlesinger Polls." *Journal of American History,* 1970, *57,* 104–113.

Murray, R. K., and Blessing, T. H. "The Presidential Performance Study: A Progress Report." *Journal of American History,* 1983, *70,* 535–555.

Pereira, D. F. "Factors Associated with Transformational Leadership in an Indian Engineering Firm." Unpublished paper, Lawson & Toubro Ltd., Bombay, India, 1987.

Simonton, D. K. "Presidential Personality: Biographical Use of the Group Adjective Checklist." *Journal of Personality and Social Psychology,* 1986, *51* (1), 149–160.

Smith, B. J. "An Initial Test of a Theory of Charismatic Leadership Based on the Responses of Subordinates." Unpublished doctoral dissertation, University of Toronto, 1982.

Sobel, R. (ed.). *Biographical Directory of the United States Executive Branch, 1774–1977.* Westport, Conn.: Greenwood Press, 1977.

Winter, D. G. *The Power Motive.* New York: Free Press, 1973.

Winter, D. G. "Leader Appeal, Leader Performance, and the Motives Profile of Leaders and Followers: A Study of American Presidents and Elections." *Journal of Personality and Social Psychology,* 1987, *52* (1), 196–202.

Woodward, C. V. *Responses of the Presidents to Charges of Misconduct.* New York: Dell, 1974.

Yukl, G. A. *Leadership in Organizations.* Englewood Cliffs, N.J.: Prentice-Hall, 1981.

Yukl, G. A., and Van Fleet, D. D. "Cross Situational Multimethod Research on Military Leader Effectiveness." *Organizational Behavior and Human Performance,* 1982, *30,* 87–108.

5

The Visionary Leader

Marshall Sashkin

Top-level managers take on many roles. This has been documented through various observational and diary studies of executive behavior. One of the best-known of these is Mintzberg's (1973) intensive observational report of the activities of several chief executive officers, whose behaviors were sorted into ten emergent categories. One role, "leadership," if defined only a bit more broadly than did Mintzberg, seems to account for a large proportion of executive behavior and to include what many scholars see as its most important characteristics. Katz and Kahn (1978), for example, consider "origination"—the creation and development of organizational structures and policies—as the unique and identifying aspect of executive behavior.

Yet the study of leadership from an organizational perspective has been neglected in favor of a focus on low-level supervisors and mid-level managers (see Yukl, 1981, for an overview). While providing useful knowledge on supervision, this focus has produced relatively little insight on executive leadership. Such a focus has been almost entirely the province of Freudian and neo-Freudian interpretations, often centered on charisma and the psychodynamics of charismatic leadership (for example, see Pye, 1976; Schiffer, 1973; Zaleznik and Kets de Vries, 1975). The only others to explore organizational leadership appear to be sociologists, most of whom have concentrated on the mass-

Note: The views presented in this chapter are those of the author and do not represent the positions or policies of the Office of Educational Research and Improvement of the United States Department of Education.

122

movement effects of charismatic leaders, drawing on the original work of Weber ([1924] 1947; see, for example Burns, 1978, or Trice and Beyer, 1986). Only in the past decade has there been a renewed interest in the charismatic leader on the part of organizational psychologists, spurred by the early work of House (1977).

The need for effective leadership at the organizational level is clear and pressing throughout both the public and private sectors of modern societies. For example, in 1974, an incumbent chief executive of the American government was forced to resign—for the first time in the nation's history. In the private sector, we see large organizations subtly managed toward their decline (to borrow Hayes and Abernathy's [1980] classic phrase) or overtly exploited by corporate raiders whose names have become household words.

On the positive side, this book is an indication of exciting explorations now under way, whose aim is the understanding and improvement of leadership at the organizational level. This chapter aims to contribute to this effort.

The essential nature of organizational leadership can be stated clearly and briefly. Bennis and Nanus (1985) put it succinctly: "Managers do things right; leaders do the right things." Significant as this aphorism is, there remains the difficult task of understanding the dynamics of organizational leadership in a way that gives leverage and control over the phenomenon and its effects. I refer to the leadership described by Bennis and Nanus as visionary leadership, because leadership involves the creation of a vision on the part of the leader, a vision that is designed both to fit and to mold organizational conditions and requirements. Leaders who can create and then effectively enact such visions are designing their organizations' futures and are typically seen by organizational members and by outside observers as visionaries.

The theory proposed is the organizational side of a still broader approach put forth by Sashkin and Fulmer (1985, 1987). Our framework harks back to Kurt Lewin's dictum that behavior is a function of the person and the situation: $B = f(P,S)$. It is consistent with the more recent formulations of Bandura (1977), who argues that behavioral, personal, and situational factors all interact with one another to affect and, perhaps, determine one another. Thus, the real challenge is to connect the individual level, focused on the leader's characteristics and behaviors, with the organizational level of leadership actions and effects. This is done by examining the leader as an individual in terms of certain psychological variables and specific behaviors while at the same time keeping in focus the goal of the leader's intentions and actions: designing and implementing an organizational culture based on patterns of shared values, beliefs, and norms of behavior.

The present theory of visionary leadership considers not just the leader, not just the situation, and not just the leader's behavior; it incorporates all three interactively. Only by looking at each of these factors can we really understand the visionary leadership exemplified by Lee Iacocca (Chrysler), Tom Watson, Sr. (IBM), Ren McPherson (Dana), or Jack Welch (General Electric). These individuals share certain characteristics that are different from the personality traits identified by early leadership research. Moreover, the executives just named all have a deep awareness of key situational factors that dictate which leadership approach and actions are required at any given time. Finally, these individuals know, instinctively if not intellectually, what behaviors are required for effective visionary leadership, and all can enact these behaviors effectively.

Visionary leadership has three critical elements. First, visionary leaders possess certain personality prerequisites and cognitive skills needed to engage in the activity of creating a vision. The prerequisites concern the leader's need for power (McClelland, 1975) and approach to its use (Burke, 1986; Howell in Chapter Seven). Cognitive skills refer to the leader's level of cognitive development (Jaques, 1986). The second element of visionary leadership calls for leaders to understand the key content dimensions of an organizational vision, the elements that must be included in a vision in order for that vision to direct the organization into its future. These critical aspects relate to certain functions that define the organization's culture (Parsons, 1960; Sashkin, 1987). The third element of visionary leadership is the leader's ability to articulate the vision. This means communicating the vision to organizational members in ways that are compelling, that make them want to "buy into" the leader's vision and make it happen. To do this, leaders must have specific behavioral skills (Bennis, 1984; Sashkin, 1984a). These skills are used to implement policies and programs that reflect and operationalize the leader's organizational philosophy (Sashkin, 1985b). The remainder of the chapter explores these three elements of visionary leadership and considers their implications for leadership theory, for training, and for further research and development needs.

Visioning: Personality Prerequisites and Cognitive Skills

Two personal characteristics are required if a leader is to create an effective vision. The first characteristic is a personality orientation focused on obtaining power in order to empower others to carry out the vision, while the second characteristic involves a set of cognitive skills needed to develop the vision itself. Although it might seem that the first characteristic is tangential to the nature of "visioning" or developing a vision, it is truly an important factor: Without a focus on power and empowerment, the vision cannot be made real and is, therefore, of little practical interest. Indeed, there are some who believe that it is this focus on power and its use that is the central issue in visionary or transformational leadership.

The Need for Power and Its Use. Many years of research on human needs and motive patterns by David McClelland and his associates (see, for example, McClelland, 1955, 1958, 1975) have culminated in the argument that "power is the great motivator" of managerial performance and effectiveness (McClelland and Burnham, 1976). Expecting effective managers to show high need for achievement, McClelland and Burnham (1976) reported finding that exceptionally high achievement needs were more a hindrance than an asset. Managers with very high need for achievement (and average or low need for power) were often so committed to getting the job done that they did their employees' work themselves rather than working with and through employees.

Effective managers, in contrast, had a high need for power (typically combined with an average or above-average need for achievement). But even more interesting was that a high need for power was not sufficient for outstanding performance. Looking still closer, McClelland (1975; McClelland and Burnham, 1976) identified two basic ways in which the need for power was exhibited. Some managers wanted and used power because it was instrumental for obtaining personal gratifications (such as company cars, fancy office suites, or other "perks") and/or because they enjoyed dominating and humiliating other people. But such managers generally were not effective; in fact, they tended not only to be poor performers but to exhibit serious behavior disorders, such as alcoholism and drug abuse. Effective managers desired power just as much but differed in how they used it. They instead sought to attain goals that would benefit their employees and the organization as well as themselves.

Thus, it appeared that the most effective managers wanted to obtain and use power not solely for personal gain or to dominate others but to empower employees (Burke, 1986). McClelland (1975) calls this pattern of power need and application "socialized" power. More recently, he and Boyatzis showed that a pattern of moderate to high socialized power need, moderate to high need for achievement, and relatively low need for affiliation is characteristic of managers who have been successful over periods of fifteen years and more (McClelland and Boyatzis, 1982).

In Chapter Seven, Howell suggests two types of charismatic leadership based on the leader's need for power and how that need is played out. She argues that leaders who express their need for power through dominance (personalized power) achieve the status of a charismatic leader through a social influence process based on identification (Kelman, 1958). That is, followers identify with the leader, seeing themselves in the person of the leader. On the other hand, leaders whose motives are expressed through socialized power (McClelland, 1975) are hypothesized by Howell to use the social influence process that Kelman (1958) called "internalization," which results in a congruence of values and goals among the leader and his or her followers. Followers who have internalized the values and vision of the leader should appear neither dependent nor independent but should become more autonomous and self-directed in terms of activities aimed at implementing those values and making real the vision.

Howell's (1987) treatment of power is congruent in most respects with the present approach. The "socialized power" is a prerequisite orientation for the visionary leader. I will, however, emphasize that power is not the sole or the most central factor for understanding visionary leadership. There are others. I will address these other aspects by first examining the nature of the "visioning" process—that is, the cognitive process of creating a vision.

The Cognitive Skills of Visioning. Westley and Mintzberg, in Chapter Six, present some interesting new ideas about the ways effective and ineffective leaders go about creating and attaining visions. They argue that an ineffective leader (exemplified by Rene Levesque, former premier of Quebec and leader of the Parti Quebecois, whose vision was an autonomous state of Quebec) defines a very specific vision early on in the process of turning a vision into reality. But such a strategy, Westley and Mintzberg argue, is doomed from the start, because the vision is "eaten away" bit by bit as the leader engages in the normal and necessary activities of forming coalitions and building support through trade-offs and compromises; eventually, there is nothing left of the vision. This is in contrast to an effective leader, such as Lee Iacocca of Chrysler, whose approach to creating a vision is analogous to that of a sort of garbage collector with artistic genius. This type of leader looks for useful bits of "rubbish" as he or she makes his or her daily rounds, seizing on those with potential and building them into his or her vision as the essential content. Such leaders appear to operate on the principles defined by Lindblom (1959)—"muddling through" to succeed by dint of luck and skill. Their luck consists of finding an especially good or useful bit of "garbage," and their skill is in watching for opportunities and taking full advantage of those they find.

My own approach to "vision" is quite different from that of Westley and Mintzberg. I believe that the content of the leader's vision is anything but random, being determined by an acute (if often implicit or tacit) understanding of the essential nature of organizations and of the work of leadership. And the process by which leaders construct visions, in the present theory, is anything but a "random walk." While visionary leaders certainly take advantage of opportunities as they appear, such leaders are even more attuned to the construction of opportunities; they create the future as much as they adapt to it.

The specific concepts of vision and visioning I describe are based on the work of Elliott Jaques (1979, 1982, 1986). In his earlier work, Jaques (1979) found that individuals differed in terms of the time span over which they could think and plan effectively; such spans vary from weeks or months on the low to normal side to many years in some very rare individuals. He also observed that tasks could be defined in terms of their time spans, not just for a specific set of actions but for thinking about and planning the whole task. Again, there is considerable variation, from a matter of days or weeks to a matter of years. Finally, Jaques concluded that a match between the cognitive ability of the individual (in terms of its time span) and the time span of the task, in terms of the time span of discretion—the longest unsupervised time period—led to greater effectiveness, as well as to increased satisfaction both with the work and with one's pay.

In his more recent work, Jaques (1986) defined four cognitive skills that are applied in a developmental sequence over increasingly long time spans. These skills have been relabeled for simplicity and clarity (Sashkin, 1986a).

The first skill is *expressing the vision,* not verbally but through behavior. This involves behaving in ways that advance the vision step-by-step. Consider the case of a manufacturing firm whose chief executive wishes to create a plantwide operation that will involve employees in a "participative management" program. To make this vision a reality, the CEO must be able to perform the following steps: write a proposed set of policy actions that would create a plant-level worker involvement program; meet with the relevant parties—plant-level managers as well as workers—to develop a document detailing the new policy and program; meet with and arrange meetings of all plant-level managers and all employees to review and revise the program and to plan for its implementation; work with relevant managers to identify ways to track the program's effects and effectiveness; and oversee the monitoring of the program and work with relevant parties on any further modifications that are needed. Expressing the vision, then, calls for the leader to physically perform a sequence of actions that represent steps in making the vision real.

The second cognitive skill is *explaining the vision to others*—making the nature of the vision clear in terms of required actions and aims and doing so through clear oral and written communication. For example, unless the CEO can explain his or her vision to the program manager, constant uncertainty will arise as to the specific steps and the handling of problems and issues. Unless the CEO can explain the program to plant managers, their support for the vision will fade as the CEO loses touch with the day-to-day program details, as is inevitable for any chief executive. Explaining involves more than just restating the vision's nature or aim. The visionary leader must be able to describe how the actions required for the vision link together to attain the goals defined or implied by the vision.

The third skill is *extending the vision*—applying the sequence of activities involved in carrying out the vision to a variety of situations so that the vision can be implemented in several ways and places. To continue our example, the CEO will probably, at some point, wish to extend the vision to other parts of the organization. This might mean working with the program manager to revise the worker involvement plan and apply it to the headquarter's staff departments, as well as in the plant. Doing so will call for changes in the way the program is implemented and may even require alterations in the program itself. The expressed vision is an important frame of reference, but the effective visionary leader is able to adapt the vision to varied circumstances, as well as change situations to better fit with the vision.

The fourth and final cognitive skill involves *expanding the vision*—applying it not just in one limited way and not even in a variety of essentially similar ways, but applying it in many different ways, in a wide range of circumstances, and to a broader context. The CEO who has a vision of worker involvement at the plant level and who goes about implementing this vision in the manner outlined above may still fail to be an effective visionary leader. The effective visionary leader will have the conceptual skill needed to look at an overall plan for worker involvement in the organization. This means more than extending the program to another unit, department, or division. The visionary leader thinks through the spread of the worker involvement vision throughout the organization, considers different ways that the program might be spread (for example, unit by unit rather than division by division), and constructs ways of "revising" the entire organization to be more consistent with the new employee involvement system (rather than thinking only of revising the program to suit organizational conditions).

The four cognitive skills are applied in a repeating hierarchical sequence, with each higher-level skill applied over a longer time span and to a broader system level. As already noted, Jaques (1979, 1982) has shown that managerial work differs in time span at different hierarchical levels. A supervisor or foreman, at the first level, may need to think only in terms of days or weeks. Lower-level managers might prepare plans that extend over a period of months and perhaps to a year or more. At the middle levels of management, the work is timed in years, and leaders at the executive levels must think in spans of at least five years. True organizational leaders, the sort of visionary leaders this chapter describes, create and realize visions over periods of decades.

As a vision encompasses longer and longer time spans, more uncertain and perhaps unpredictable factors appear. Such factors must be dealt with interactively. That is, no step-by-step plan, no matter how well prepared, can take into account future "unknowns." The effective visionary leader realizes this. Rather than preparing step-by-step plans over periods of years, such leaders concentrate on designing and creating future conditions so as to reduce any unpredictable disruptive effects on their visions. At the same time, they leave longer-range plans sufficiently open so that empowered organization members can deal with contingencies that arise.

Jack Welch, CEO of General Electric (GE), is widely thought of as a visionary leader (see, for example, Bennis and Nanus, 1985; Hickman and Silva, 1984; Potts, 1984; Tichy and Devanna, 1986). Central to Welch's vision is his plan for GE to be first or second in every market in which the organization competes. When evidence suggests this is not possible, GE leaves that market—such as when the entire small appliance division was sold to Black and Decker. In contrast, to forestall market problems in the consumer electronics and communication field, Welch absorbed RCA, including the NBC radio and television networks. This had the effect of immediately eliminating some competition in the consumer electronics field and in some parts of the major home appliance market, in which RCA and GE had been rivals. More significantly, this strategy cleared a long-term path for GE in the information/telecommunications field. Without this purchase—the largest in American business history—it is doubtful that GE would be able to compete successfully in the information/telecommunications area a decade from now. As it now stands, GE has a new and strong potential, developed as part of Welch's vision, and is operating to create future conditions that will further facilitate that vision while modifying or eliminating future conditions that might hamper its realization.

It is rare to find CEOs like Jack Welch, who has the cognitive capacity to create a vision over a time span of decades and to do so in ways that design both the organization and the future conditions in which the organization exists and operates.

To this point, I have considered the personal characteristics of the visionary leader: the nature of the leader's cognitive abilities and whether the leader's motive pattern is such that it aids or hinders the effective use of the capacity to create a vision. Two other critical questions, one concerning the content of visions and the other dealing with the specific leadership actions needed to turn a vision into reality, will be discussed in the following sections.

The Nature of Vision

Key Content Dimensions

Visions vary infinitely in the specifics of their content, yet I believe it is possible to identify some underlying common themes that refer to the processes of organizational operation or functioning. That is, certain basic issues must be dealt with by any vision if it is to have a substantial impact on or "transform" an organization. I will define and describe three such underlying themes.

Dealing With Change: Theme One. Visions that work help the organization deal with change—change in the environment, in markets, and in product technology, for example. In the case of McDonald's, this element of the vision concerns an ongoing, never-ending search for new products, some of which succeed (for example, the McD.L.T.) and many of which fail to catch on and disappear (such as McRibs). For Frank Perdue, owner of Frank Perdue Chicken Farms, it is the incremental change produced by a continual search for quality improvements (through such innovations as specially designed chicken food and "yellower" skin). For Scandinavian Airlines Systems (SAS), change enters Jan Carlzon's vision in terms of a competitive edge achieved by taking hold of and using changing market forces and through empowering employees to take on and resolve problems (Carlzon, 1987).

Ideal Goals: Theme Two. Effective visions incorporate goals, not in the sense of clearly defined final ends but in terms of ideal conditions or processes. McDonald's managers and employees go to "Hamburger U" to be "socialized" to value above all else the goals of quality service, cleanliness, and value, along with the maintenance of required standards (including secret procedures and formulas) that ensure that the Big Mac one eats in Portland, Oregon, is identical to the Big Mac one eats in Portland, Maine.

Perdue's goal may seem obvious: the best-quality chicken in the industry. This is not, however, completely accurate, for the assumption that quality has no limits means that the search for higher quality is never ending. It is a process rather than a final state. Carlzon (1987) states that his goals for SAS center on passenger satisfaction—that is, on making passengers feel that they are being treated well as individuals. This may seem unexceptional, and Carlzon himself has said (as quoted by Bennis and Nanus, 1985), "That's been everybody's vision since the beginning of time in this industry." The difference with respect to SAS, he went on to say, is that "we executed!" Visionary leaders take goals that might seem obvious or trivial to a person outside the organization and make those goals appear and "feel" critically important to those inside the organization.

People Working Together: Theme Three. A final theme common to effective visions is a focus on people, both as organization members and as customers. Perhaps it is obvious that only through people can any vision be enacted and thus become real. Nonetheless, many elegant visions fail to provide roles for people, ways to involve people and give them responsibility, and methods for effectively coordinating and integrating their activities based on involvement rather than on structures or rules. Only when people are part of the vision in these ways can they take charge of the vision and make it their own. If, in contrast, a vision remains identified as the "property" of the leader and is never "owned" by the organization's members, it is not likely to be carried out effectively. People are involved in and committed to creating innovations and maintaining standards at McDonald's. They are deeply involved in finding and implementing ways to improve product quality at Perdue. And they are shown that they are highly regarded, in both word and deed, and empowered to treat customers similarly at SAS. In all of these cases, people are integral to the leader's vision. The effective management of change and the attainment of goals can only be achieved through the committed and coordinated activity of the organization's members.

A Theoretical Framework

Why have I selected the three themes just defined and why not some other, equally sensible set of factors? The answer is based on the classic sociological theory of Talcott Parsons (1937, 1951, 1960; Parsons, Bales, and Shils, 1953). Weber's ([1924] 1947) assertion that one cannot fully understand ends without understanding the means, and vice versa, was elaborated by Parsons in terms of an open system perspective (von Bertalanffy, 1950). That is, Parsons observed that the most basic characteristic of any system is the existence of a boundary that sets the system apart from its environment. This implies that any system must have an inside and an outside. The result is the four-box model shown in Figure 1, the "action framework." Parsons argued that to survive, any goal-directed or "action" system must deal with the four functions defined by the boxes of the action framework: adapting, attaining goals, coordinating activities (or "integrating"), and maintaining these patterns of action. All organizations must adapt to meet the demands of changing environments (theme one). By definition, all goal-directed systems must attain goals (theme two). Continued existence depends on ongoing continuous and continuing operations as carried out through the activities and patterns of human interaction of the organization's members (theme three). These events, actions, and patterns of interactive behavior must be coordinated, or "integrated" in Parsons's terminology.

The action framework shown in Figure 1 includes a fourth box, which does not obviously match up with any of the three themes I defined. This fourth function is, however, the most basic of all. It concerns the maintenance of the pattern of action in each of the other three functions. That is, this fourth function defines the boundaries of the other three and acts to maintain those perimeters, ensuring that organizational life is played out in a complex but consistent—and enduring—pattern. These patterns of action are maintained by a set of shared values, beliefs, and norms, constituting the essence of the organization's culture. Thus, the shared beliefs that make up the culture determine how the organization adapts to change, what sorts of changes are acceptable, and what adaptive actions are simply not allowable, no matter how useful they might prove. Pope John Paul II, for example, may soon be faced with an adaptive choice that goes back to basic values: Is it more important that

Figure 1. Parsons's Action Framework.

	Means	Ends
Outside	Adaptation: changing to meet new or changing environmental conditions	Goal attainment: activity related to the production and delivery of some output
Inside	Values: definitions of what is good or bad and basic beliefs shared by most members of the organization	Integration: formal and informal patterns of coordination— rules and norms

the church have celibate priests or that it have enough priests to perform the critical tasks of the church? The values behind performing a mass and other critical activities of the church are obvious; to the extent that these goals are not achieved, the organization will suffer—for example, in the loss of membership. The values behind priestly celibacy are less obvious but are both symbolic and pragmatic: Celibate priests are far more easy to incorporate into the church, in terms of effort and energy, since they are, in effect, "married" to the organization. What makes this choice especially difficult is the strong value of not changing and adapting, of maintaining the existing structural and functional patterns to the greatest extent possible.

In addition to regulating the way organizations adapt, this fourth pattern-maintaining function defines the goals the organization aims for and how these goals relate to client or customer desires. And this pattern of shared values and beliefs determines how the organization deals with its members and how they deal with one another in working together, coordinating and integrating their work activities.

I argue that the essential work of organizational leaders is defining, constructing, and gaining commitment to a set of shared values, beliefs, and norms about change, goals, and people working together—that is, defining, building, and involving people in the organization's culture. This is the primary task work of organizational leaders, and it is the reason that the three themes of change, goals, and people working together must be built into a leader's vision.

With final consideration to the Parsonian model, it is only appropriate to ask whether there is empirical evidence supporting the action framework and demonstrating a relationship to organizational performance. While it is obvious that an organization doing a poor job of adapting to change, attaining goals, and coordinating work activities and possessing a weak culture is not likely to be characterized by sustained high performance, there are few "hard" data to support this "self-evident" conclusion.

One recent study by Hoy and Ferguson (1985) involved the collection of data to judge whether each of the four functions was being performed effectively in a sample of schools. They found that when the four functions were being performed well, schools were more likely to be seen as effective by expert judges. Furthermore, the judges' ratings were consistent with objective performance measures, such as student achievement scores on standardized tests. Of course, the results of one small-scale study cannot be offered as strong proof for a theory. Still, it provides encouraging support for the notion that effective performance of the four functions defined by the action framework is associated with high levels of organizational effectiveness.

The Content of Vision

Having defined the issues dealt with in leaders' visions, one might still wonder whether common specific values and beliefs are characteristically present within the three themes contained in effective visions. I believe there is evidence to suggest that there are specific values and beliefs relating to each of the three functions of adapting, attaining goals, and working with people. For example, content common to the three basic themes is identified in a purely pragmatic, atheoretical analysis of high-performing organizations by Peters and Waterman (1982). They defined eight strategies characteristic of high-performing organizations. More recently, Peters (1984) condensed these eight strategies into three. Each of the three relates to one of the three themes (and, of course, to one of Parsons's functions):

Adapting Through Autonomous Action. The adaptive function is strengthened and supported by a value that says, in effect, "Take action, do *something!*" Many organizations today are faced with rapid environmental and technological change and must confront such change through effective adaptive responses. It is therefore critical that organization members be empowered to take sensible risks and to believe that even actions that are not fully successful are more desirable than no action at all.

Goal Attainment Through Achieving What Clients Want. The goal attainment function is supported by a value that recognizes client or customer wants as one of the organization's top priorities. In private-sector organizations, it is through satisfaction of clients' goals that the organization prospers, and this is analogously true for many public-sector organizations (except that it is often more difficult to obtain feedback from—or even to define—the clients; see Sashkin, 1986c). By focusing attention on major client wants and goals, the leader strengthens this value and thus strengthens organizational goal attainment.

Integration Through Coordinated Interpersonal Interaction. The integration function is strengthened by the value of concern for people and, even more specifically, the value of influence and participation (Sashkin, 1984b). Emphasis on these values facilitates the effective management of complex interdependencies that can only be coordinated through direct contact and "mutual adjustment" (Thompson, 1967).

Vision in Action:
Communicating and Operationalizing the Vision

Having suggested what it is about leaders that enables them to create visions and having identified themes and values that effective visions incorporate, I will now consider *how* visionary leaders go about implementing their visions. Burns (1978) suggests that leaders transform organizations through their personal charisma in combination with a long-range strategic vision. Bennis and Nanus (1985) expand on this, suggesting that leaders focus on key strategic issues, using a set of specific strategic approaches. Both Burns and Bennis and Nanus make sense, but neither is clear as to exactly how visionary leaders enact such strategies to carry out their visions through behavior. I suggest that they are expressed and explained through words and actions in three ways: strategic, tactical, and personal. I shall discuss in detail how visionary leaders communicate and operationalize their visions through strategic, tactical, and personal actions.

A Strategic Organizational Philosophy

At the strategic level, visionary leaders begin the process of enacting their visions by developing clear and concise statements of organizational philosophy, centered on the specific elements of their visions. Such organizational philosophies are relatively common among Japanese firms (Ouchi, 1981) and are by no means unheard of among American organizations. Such statements must be so clear that every person in the organization can provide a brief but accurate version, showing that the philosophy is understood by everyone, from the CEO to the janitor.

Returning for a moment to the example of GE's Jack Welch as a visionary leader, one observes a clear strategic philosophy in action (Potts, 1984). The *goal* of being first or second in any market in which the firm competes is a strong aspect of theme two (goals), incorporating the *value* of achieving a high proportion of market share as the specific goal. Innovation is an important aspect of GE's philosophy, which includes the adaptive function and theme one (change). Specifically, it is technological innovation that is explicitly valued at GE. Finally, the organizational philosophy emphasizes the value of organization members working together to create technological innovations and makes quite clear the importance of theme three (working with people). Not only is theme one (adaptive change) reinforced, but the explicit promise that innovation failures will not automatically be punished strengthens the importance placed on people. This is reinforced by the symbols GE uses in its advertising and slogans (advertising showing all the different people that make up GE and such slogans as, "We bring good things to life," which emphasize innovation, outcomes, and people). Although none of the above appears as a formal, written philosophy, all of these elements are easily observable in organization members' behaviors and can be verbalized by organizational members.

An organizational philosophy, whether contained in a formal, written document or expressed only in action, gives the visionary leader a strategic lever with which to directly design and change organizational culture (Sashkin, 1985a) and thus transform the organization. Sashkin (1985b) has detailed an explicit, step-by-step process for creating an organizational philosophy or "mind set."

Even when it is contained in a written document, an organizational philosophy should be only a very brief summary of the leader's vision. This serves, of course, as one way of communicating that vision, clearly identifying its underlying values and providing a sketch of the desired organizational culture. The clearer the philosophy, the more potentially useful it can be. It will have greater potential if it speaks to all three organizational functions and defines values that give support to each of the three functions defined by the action framework (the fourth function, of course, represents the philosophy and its values). Finally, the utility of an organizational philosophy is enhanced if most or all top managers are involved in developing it.

No matter how clear, straightforward, and inclusive the statement of philosophy is, it means nothing unless it is coupled with actions. Many fine-sounding organizational philosophy statements remain wall furnishings—ideas that are espoused but never enacted (Argyris, 1976) and, therefore, are nothing more than highly visible examples of the hypocrisy of would-be organizational leaders.

Tactical Policies and Programs

A critical step in making real the leader's vision is for the organization to support words with actions, to "put its money where the [leader's] mouth is." Policies and programs represent critical action elements for carrying out the vision. Policies must be developed and programs initiated; this means that middle and lower levels of management must be involved and that financial as well as human resources must be committed.

An example is Keithley Instruments, a small manufacturer of precision scientific instruments located in northern Ohio near Cleveland. It is a closely held, family-owned firm that, in recent years, has been guided by a vision on the part of its president and top executives (Frohman and Sashkin, 1985). With the help of the vice-president for human resources, a skilled organization development practitioner, the top group worked together to develop an organizational philosophy. The statement began by defining three organizational objectives: high productivity, high product quality, and excellent employee relations. These themes were then spelled out in a brief (less than 150 words) "statement of beliefs" about employees. This statement centered on clear identification of values. General values about employees were defined: "They are trusted." Values relating to the coordination function were detailed: "They [employees] are encouraged to work together and develop teams." Values supporting goal attainment were specified: "They are supplied the tools, conditions, and training and share in setting expectations for performance." Developing this philosophy was hard, but implementing it was harder.

Had the development of a philosophy been the only concrete action, the vision would have ended at that point. At Keithley, however, the values and beliefs contained in the new organizational philosophy became the basis for new policies and programs. One major policy centered on improving product quality through teamwork, with worker teams having increased self-management. The programs implied by this policy not only were expensive, but they were strongly resisted by senior managers. Only after the plant manager was removed was it possible to redesign a traditional assembly line work process in favor of autonomous product teams. The cost was in the millions of dollars.

Ultimately, this major action program proved highly successful. Over the next four years, productivity increased by about 80 percent, while the number of production employees increased by just 28 percent. Output per employee has approximately doubled over the four-year period. At the same time, production costs were reduced by about 50 percent and product quality, as measured by warranty repair rates, improved by about 15 percent.

But how did the employees feel about the program and its consequences? Macy and others (1986) report that while productivity and performance typically improve as a result of sociotechnical changes of the sort described here, workers often exhibit decreased satisfaction. And concern for people was a central theme of the organizational philosophy at Keithley. An answer can be seen, generally considered in part, by a reduction in absenteeism of almost 80 percent over four years. Absenteeism is one indicator of worker satisfaction. Thus, it is clear that at Keithley people wanted to be on the job to a much greater extent than had been true before the program was initiated. This result is consistent with evidence offered by Johns (1987), which suggests that absenteeism is significantly affected by the organization's culture.

Despite the success at Keithley, the changes produced by the programs and policies reflecting the new organizational philosophy took considerable time to pay off in performance and productivity. Though purely speculative, it is notable that the function of adapting and the theme of change were absent from the philosophy statement. Perhaps it seemed self-evident that the policies and programs would produce positive change, yet one cannot help but wonder whether explicitly incorporating such values in a company philosophy might have made the process easier and, perhaps, less lengthy.

Personal Behavior of the Visionary Leader

An organizational philosophy to support the vision is necessary and critical but not enough to make a vision real. A third and often deciding factor concerns the personal actions of the leader. Leaders must communicate their visions in ways that reach out to organization members, gripping them and making them want to get involved in carrying out the vision.

Leaders who are especially effective in getting across their visions are often said to be "charismatic." Bennis and Nanus (1985) observe that "charisma is the result of effective leadership, not the other way around" (p. 224). Charisma is a consequence of effective behavior expressed by leaders to communicate their visions.

Drawing on the work of Bennis (1984) and Bennis and Nanus (1985), one can identify five types of behavior used by effective leaders (Sashkin, 1984a; Sashkin and Fulmer, 1985):

Focusing Attention. The first type of behavior concerns getting others' attention focused clearly on specific key issues. In this way, leaders help others understand and become committed to the leader's visions. This may involve odd, unusual, and creative actions on the part of the leader, all designed to capture and concentrate attention on an important aspect of the leader's vision. For instance, in Chrysler's television commercials, Lee Iacocca physically demonstrated his closeness to employees, emphasized the quality of the product, and referred repeatedly to the "*New* Chrysler Corporation." His aim was to concentrate viewers' attention on the three critical themes: people, goals, and change. Taking a more dramatic, perhaps even odd approach, Frank Perdue grabs television viewers' attention by holding up a chunk of chicken in each hand, one his own and the other a competitor's. Observing that a yellower color indicates health and quality of the chicken (the competitor's a sickly white), he says, "I wonder where the yellow went!"

Communicating Personally. The second set of leader behaviors centers on effective interpersonal communication of the vision. This means listening for understanding ("active listening" [Rogers, 1952]), rephrasing what the other person says to show understanding and to help clarify the message while at the same time identifying and making explicit the feelings expressed (whether implicit or overt). Personal communication skills also include giving feedback effectively (for example, being descriptive rather than evaluative, being specific rather than general), questioning and probing skillfully, and summarizing appropriately. Effective leaders understand that their visions are more likely to be heard, understood, and accepted if they hear and understand the other person. Effective personal communication skills are easy to describe but rare in practice, despite being part of the curriculum of most business schools. These skills are common to all types of effective leaders, from the CEO of a small company to the leader of a nation. In a television interview, Henry Kissinger was asked if Mao Tse-tung actually had two-way conversations when holding the sort of rare private meetings that Kissinger had experienced. Or, he was asked, did Mao simply lecture and more or less ignore the views of the other party? Kissinger responded that Mao insisted on hearing out the other person in detail and made sure he understood before presenting his own views. According to Kissinger, when in a one-to-one situation, Mao never spoke as though he was delivering a position statement; he would first show that he had listened and understood what the other person had said and then explain his own views concisely and clearly. Effective communication on the part of visionary leaders is not just a matter of good media presence, but it is achieved through one-to-one communication skills.

Demonstrating Trustworthiness. The third type of behavior involves consistency and trustworthiness. Bennis (1984) found that outstanding CEOs are very consistent in their actions. They do not "flip-flop" on positions but stand firm, having once taken a position. Thus, it is easy to be sure where they stand. Though one might not always agree with leaders, they are trusted because they say what they mean and mean what they say.

Consider again the example of Jack Welch, CEO of General Electric Corporation. As noted earlier, a key aspect of Welch's vision and of the philosophy he has created for GE is the need for technological innovation and risk taking. To encourage such internal entrepreneurship, Welch insists that no one should be punished for taking a worthwhile risk, even if the risk does not "pan out." If such a failure situation led to sanctions against the risk taker, Welch's credibility would be lost and his vision could fail. Thus, Welch looks for risks that did not work out and has been known to make what would under other circumstances be seen as management awards. For example, it became clear that a long-term effort to produce a very long-lasting, energy-efficient light bulb had failed; after an investment of several million dollars, the project was technically successful, but the product cost far more than customers were willing to spend. Welch closed out the project with a major ceremony and full-scale party. Senior employees involved in the project were given tangible awards, such as VCRs, and some were even promoted—including the person in charge of the project. An executive vice-president observed that this was all part of an effort to get organization members "to understand that you could take a run at something with the management's blessing, give it your best shot, and, if the market wasn't there or we couldn't crack the technology, the individual didn't end up losing" (Potts, 1984, p. G10). But in addition to firmly establishing the reality of a key element of the culture Welch was trying to build, this symbolic rewarding of a failure also reinforced Welch's credibility and trustworthiness, strengthening his position as a visionary leader and increasing the likelihood of attaining that vision.

Displaying Respect. Shows of respect toward ones self, as well as toward others, comprise the fourth set of behaviors exhibited by effective visionary leaders. Rogers (1959) sees positive regard as a critical aspect of both human development and psychotherapeutic treatment. Through "unconditional positive regard" from significant others, one develops positive *self*-regard. This is critical, because without self-respect one cannot really care about others.

Visionary leaders are self-assured, certain of their own abilities. They express this not through arrogance or postures of superiority but in simple self-confidence. Bennis (1984) gives a good example: Dr. Franklin Murphy, former chancellor of the University of California, Los Angeles, and now chairman of the Times-Mirror Company, has been offered several cabinet-level appointments in recent years. He has repeatedly declined what many—and most who feel pressured to prove their personal worth—would find difficult or impossible to refuse. His reason? "I just don't think I'd be good at that sort of thing," Bennis quotes him as saying. This sense of self-respect, of confidence in themselves and their abilities, is apparent also in how visionary leaders treat others.

Organization members feel good around effective visionary leaders. Such leaders boost the sense of self-worth of those around them by expressing unconditional positive regard: paying attention, showing trust, sharing ideas, and making clear how important and valued organization members are. Visionary leaders not only tell organization members they are important but, consistent with Holdstock and Rogers (1977), they also communicate this message through behavioral acts, such as supporting certain policies and programs or providing symbolic and material rewards.

Taking Risks. The fifth type of behavior used by effective visionary leaders involves creating and taking calculated risks and making clear and strong commitments to risks once they are decided on. Bennis (1984) has called this "the Wallenda Factor," after the great tightrope walker, Karl Wallenda. Wallenda failed and fell to his death, Bennis suggests, because he invested all his thought and energy in ways of avoiding failure rather than focusing on succeeding at the risk he was taking. Effective visionary leaders have no energy to spare for covering their rear ends; all of their efforts go toward achieving their goals. This does not mean taking foolish or thoughtless risks; any important risk is carefully evaluated and entered into only after a thoughtful calculation of the chances of success. But, once taken, the focus is on making the risk work, not on avoiding, minimizing, or recovering from failure.

Visionary leaders build opportunities for others into their risks, chances for others to buy in, to take the risk with the leader and share in both the effort and the reward. Visionary leaders motivate by ''pulling'' people along with them, as Bennis (1984) puts it, rather than by trying to push people in the direction desired by the leader.

On a smaller scale, visionary organizational leaders often involve employees in ownership of the organization through stock awards, purchase plans, or formal employee stock ownership plans. Rosen, Klein, and Young (1986) observe that employee ownership is strongly associated with corporate performance; they have found that publicly held companies that are at least 10 percent employee-owned outperform from 62 to 75 percent of comparable competitor firms. They go on to say that visionary leaders ''who are committed to employee ownership see it as a critical part of the company's corporate culture and identity.'' They recognize employee ownership as an important part of their ''managerial philosophy and they translate this . . . into action in concrete ways,'' such as stock-voting rights or opportunities for participation in decisions. With regard to employee ownership programs, Rosen, Klein, and Young found that the strength of management's philosophical commitment made a difference. Employees were more satisfied with their jobs and more committed to the organization. The stronger the managerial philosophy toward employee ownership and involvement, the less likely employees were to say they planned to leave the organization. Again, this illustrates how visionary leaders can create risks with opportunities for others to join in.

Interactions Among Types of Behavior. I have described the five types of behavior as though they are quite separate and distinct, but this is a conceptual convenience; one must recognize that visionary leaders often display specific behaviors that reflect several of the behavior types at the same time. For example, having part of one's pay committed to stock purchases entails certain risks, but Rosen, Klein, and Young note that another important aspect of employee stock ownership plans is that "employees are treated like owners—with respect, trust, and consideration."

Other Behavior. It would be foolish to suggest that the types of behaviors defined and described above represent all of the important personal behaviors of visionary leaders. There are doubtless other specific behaviors and behavior categories that are used by visionary leaders to get across their visions. However, the behaviors initially identified by Bennis (1984) and discussed above are among the more important of such personal expressions used by visionary leaders, as shown by evidence now being accumulated.

Consequences of Personal Behaviors. I have developed a questionnaire based on the five sets of personal leader behaviors just described (Sashkin, 1984a). Subsequent studies using revised versions of the Leader Behavior Questionnaire (LBQ) have shown that the scales are internally reliable, with alphas no less than .78 (Valley, 1986). The LBQ contains a scale to measure each of the five types of personal leader behavior and a sixth scale to assess the degree to which the leader is seen as charismatic by others.

Leaders' self-reports of frequency of behavior were summed across the first five scales and correlated with subordinates' reports of leaders' charismatic affect (scale six), obtained independently (Sashkin and Fulmer, 1985). The correlation is .26 ($p < .05$). When subordinates' reports of leaders' behaviors are correlated with subordinates' reports of charismatic feelings toward the leaders, the correlation increases substantially, with $r = .59$ ($p < .01$). Thus, there is some evidence that the more leaders engage in these behaviors, the more strongly they are seen as charismatic by their subordinates. It remains to be seen, of course, whether engaging in these behaviors leads to the implementation of leaders' visions.

In summary, this section has dealt with how visionary leaders go about making their visions real through three types of action. The first action takes place at the organizational level, involving top managers in designing an organizational philosophy that clearly expresses the leader's vision and is understood by members of the organization. The second action, although initiated at the top, really involves middle managers in designing and implementing specific programs that promote policies derived from the organizational philosophy. The third action of visionary leaders to implement their visions consists of the personal behaviors they use to communicate their visions in specific, explicit detail and to engage individual organization members in concrete actions that will help make the leaders' visions real.

Training Visionary Leaders

Having sketched a theory of visionary leadership, a logical question is whether such leaders can be trained or developed. At this stage, one can only speculate with regard to training in each of the three aspects of visionary ledership: personal characteristics and cognitive skills, understanding the nature of vision, and putting the vision into action.

Personality and Cognitive Skills

I have argued that a prerequisite for effective visionary leadership is a strong need for power, along with the desire to use power in positive, prosocial ways. Thus, we must ask whether it is possible to "train" individuals to have (1) increased levels of need for power and (2) the desire to direct power in ways that benefit the organization and its members as well as the leader. McClelland and Winter (1969) have reported on the success of a program to train entrepreneurs to have a greater need for achievement (which then led to substantial new economic development in their communities). It appears that, at least in theory, it should be possible to train leaders to have a greater need for power.

There are at least two practical methods for producing such leaders. First, there is no doubt that such individuals can be identified and therefore can be selected as potential leaders. Methods for identifying such persons are readily available (McClelland, 1975; Winter, 1987). Second, House (in discussion, May 1987) has suggested that while we may not be able to train leaders to need power more or to want to use it prosocially, we can very likely train leaders to change their power-related behaviors. Thus, it may be possible to train leaders to act more like leaders who have high power needs and to engage in specific prosocial uses of power. The nature of such training can be specified by examining the work of McClelland, his colleagues, and others (such as Howell). Finally, McClelland's earlier work on training in the need for achievement suggests that it may be possible to directly increase need for power through training. Such an approach might be combined with the behavior-specific training suggested by House to show leaders how to channel the power need in productive, prosocial directions. Overall, then, a training approach to alter power-related behavior may be possible.

But what of the four cognitive skills for the process of visioning? Can these be trained? Jaques (1986) raises grave doubts, arguing that one's ultimate time span of vision and level of cognitive development are fixed at birth (genetically) and cannot be modified. Some may be capable of no more than first-level management, others of middle management—but no higher—and still others of top-level or organizational leadership. Jaques (1986) suggests that visionary leadership, at the twenty-year and longer time span, is quite rare. He implies that this is not such a bad state, since the need for such leaders is limited. Although it is possible (according to Jaques) to determine an individual's potential (Stamp, 1978), it is *not* possible to tell when that potential might be actualized, because cognitive development can occur throughout one's life span. It is not, in Jaques's view, possible to predict when a person will reach his or her potential, and some individuals may not live long enough to reach the peak of their innate potential. Jaques also believes that training has no effect on the development of a person's innate potential, neither advancing nor retarding the time when a person can function at a higher cognitive level. If Jaques is correct in his view, there appear to be certain severe limits on training for visionary leadership.

Even assuming that one's level of cognitive functioning is fixed and cannot be modified, I would suggest that Jaques's pessimism regarding the potential contribution of training is ill founded. That is, few human abilities, whether cognitive (for instance, mathematical ability) or physical (such as skill at tennis), fail to benefit from training and practice. While an individual may not have the potential to become a renowned mathematician, few people indeed would fail to benefit from the development of what mathematical talent they possess. Whatever one's current level of cognitive development, it should be possible to improve one's performance at that level through training. Of course, this is an empirical question. While some efforts have been made to develop activities to raise awareness and provide guided practice in visioning (Sashkin, 1986b), it remains to be seen whether this or any form of training has an effect. Despite a lack of knowledge as to the best ways to train cognitive skills in visioning, such efforts may be critical if the trends identified by Hayes and Abernathy (1980) concerning the short-term perspective of senior executives are to be reversed.

Training About the Nature of Vision

Training about the nature of vision is less problematic than is training centered on the personal characteristics of the leader. The former includes developing an understanding about the content themes critical to effective visions and how these themes are connected to the key functions that are driven by the organization's culture. Trainees also need to learn how to assess the four functions represented in Parsons's action framework (Figure 1) and how to identify and measure the values underlying each function—that is, the values that provide continuity and support for the organization's culture.

The training just described implies an element of conceptual and didactic learning along with the need for certain skills in gathering information, analyzing data, and making assessments. I suggest that sophisticated and effective training methods are at our disposal for accomplishing these aims. For example, the basic concepts—vision content themes, organization functions, and culture—could be adequately addressed in a two- or three-day seminar. Of course, understanding how the concepts apply to one's own organization is more challenging. Training leaders to apply the concepts might involve an approach centered on action research (Frohman, Sashkin, and Kavanagh, 1976). That is, trainees could be involved in actually conducting assessments of their own organizations' functions and culture as a precursor to the development of an organizational philosophy and to an action strategy for implementing that philosophy (Sashkin, 1985b). Training *about* the nature of vision is a relatively straightforward matter compared with creating or implementing a vision.

Skill Training for Implementing Visions

Previously it was suggested that visionary leaders engage in three types of action intended to put their visions into practice. At the strategic level of action, they work with top managers to develop an organizational philosophy that incorporates and expresses the leader's vision. At the tactical level, visionary leaders help develop policies that put the philosophy into action and empower mid-level managers to create programs for implementing those policies. Finally, at the level of personal behavior, five types of behaviors that visionary leaders use were identified. Training approaches in each of these three areas are briefly described below.

Strategic Action Training. Creating an organizational philosophy that incorporates and clearly expresses the key elements of a vision is a difficult process calling for strong team-building skills. Leaders who are less sure of themselves in small-group work can be aided by a strong process consultant either from the outside or from within. In Keithley Instruments, the vice-president for human resources, an experienced internal organization development (OD) consultant, had the skills to help the CEO work effectively with the top management team. However, if teamwork is to be an important theme within the leader's vision, it would seem desirable for the leader to demonstrate effective team leadership skills to be consistent with what is being espoused. Fortunately, most OD practitioners, as well as many general management consultants, can provide organizational leaders with the most effective hands-on guidance for developing team-building skills (Sashkin and Burke, 1987). Beyond team-development skills, Sashkin (1985b) has provided a step-by-step guide for leaders and top management groups to assist in the "how-to" stage of developing an organizational philosophy.

Tactical Action Training. The real skills involved at this level of leadership action are the skills by which leaders empower others to take active, self-directing roles in creating specific "pieces" of the leader's vision. But it appears that many executives find it quite difficult to empower others. They may think that the process involves giving up power when, in fact, it increases everyone's degree of influence (Likert, 1967; Tannenbaum, 1968; Tannenbaum and others, 1974).

While there are structured training activities specifically designed to deal with the dynamics of power and influence in organizations (for example, Oshry, 1975), two more generally useful types of training and consultation are available. One approach is to seek the help of a consultant skilled in analyzing and intervening in ongoing organizational processes (for example, see Schein, 1969, 1987). Alternatively, leaders can obtain training or consultation assistance in the area of participative management (also called "employee involvement"; for example, see Lawler [1986]). Some have suggested that participative management is a critical aspect of the sort of organizational culture common to many leaders' visions (Sashkin, 1984b, 1985a), because it is based on strong values highly consistent with effective organizational functioning (adapting effectively to change, attaining goals, and working together effectively).

Personal Behavior Training. Finally we come to the specific interpersonal skills that visionary leaders use to communicate their visions and to get others involved in and committed to carrying out those visions. I suggest that it is quite likely that these types of behavior can be learned. The technology of training and the use of modeling and guided practice provide a strong basis for suggesting that most people can learn to enact some or many specific behaviors in each of the five categories defined and discussed earlier.

Effective communication, for example, can be taught through the development of "active listening" (empathic understanding) skills, questioning skills, and feedback skills. Skill in focusing others' attention can be developed through creativity training (Prince, 1970), using such programs and methods as Gordon's (1961) "synectics" or DeBono's (1971) "lateral thinking." This skill area can also benefit from training in making formal presentations. Leaders can learn the behaviors associated with being seen as consistent and trustworthy by engaging in programs that teach one self-observation skills centering on behavioral process feedback (see Barnett, 1985). Skills involved in actions expressing regard and respect for self and others are incorporated in many interpersonal skill development programs offered through colleges and training institutes (such as National Training Laboratories or the American Management Association). Even such a "quick read" as *The One Minute Manager* (Blanchard and Johnson, 1982) explains how to express personal regard toward others, both when rewarding ("praising") and punishing ("reprimanding"). Finally, creativity training can also help one learn how to create inviting risks, while skill training in decision making (such as that offered through Kepner-Tregoe) can help ensure that the risks are reasonable. But to involve others in sensible risks, risks they can "own" and to which they can fully commit themselves, the leader must also have team leadership skills. Thus, we come full circle in this catalogue of skills with a key skill that is relevant at the strategic, tactical, and personal behavior levels—the skill of working effectively with groups and building them into teams.

Conclusion

I have proposed that visionary leaders have as their aim the transformation of organizational cultures. Such leaders, I have argued, are characterized by a strong desire to obtain and use power and influence as a means of empowering organization members to carry out the leaders' long-range strategic visions. The organization is thus transformed into a stable, high-performing system (Vaill, 1978), while the organization's members, as Bass (1985) has suggested, may be transformed into more capable, involved, and committed members of the system. To achieve such aims, leaders must first possess the characteristics described. Next, they must be able to design and disseminate organizational philosophies that capture their strategic visions. They must help create and support policies and programs that are designed to implement their visions by empowering organization members. Finally, they must be able to enact certain behaviors in interaction with organization members in order to engage those individuals in turning the leaders' visions into organizational realities.

The theory presented here is as much integrative as it is innovative, based on the work of McClelland (1975), Jaques (1986), Parsons (1960), and Bennis (1984). Yet, both in detail and as a whole, the present theory breaks ground and puts forth new concepts. It is concerned with charisma (Weber, [1924] 1947) only as a measurable effect of observable behavior, not as a mysterious force that permeates and directs the relationship between leaders and followers.

Visionary leadership theory is intentionally optimistic. It asserts that within the limits of certain personal capacities (which may themselves eventually prove to be modifiable), leaders can be more visionary and more transformational, if they so choose. This observation contrasts with Schein's (1985) pessimistic outlook in this regard. Visionary leadership theory, as outlined here, can be of great practical use because it does specify tools and their use. Moreover, the present theory identifies the qualifications that users of these tools must possess and, at least in outline, describes the challenging task of constructing an organizational culture.

References

Argyris, C. *Increasing Leadership Effectiveness.* New York: Wiley, 1976.

Bandura, A. *Social Learning Theory.* Englewood Cliffs, N.J.: Prentice-Hall, 1977.

Barnett, B. G. "Peer-Assisted Leadership: Using Research to Improve Practice." *The Urban Review,* 1985, *17,* 47–64.

Bass, B. M. *Leadership and Performance Beyond Expectations.* New York: Free Press, 1985.

Bennis, W. G. "The Four Competencies of Leadership." *Training & Development Journal,* 1984, *38* (8), 14–19.

Bennis, W. G., and Nanus, B. *Leaders.* New York: Harper & Row, 1985.

Blanchard, K. H., and Johnson, S. *The One Minute Manager.* New York: Morrow, 1982.

Burke, W. W. "Leadership as Empowering Others." In S. Srivastva and Associates, *Executive Power: How Executives Influence People and Organizations.* San Francisco: Jossey-Bass, 1986.

Burns, J. M. *Leadership.* New York: Harper & Row, 1978.

Carlzon, J. *Moments of Truth.* Cambridge, Mass.: Ballinger, 1987.

DeBono, E. *Lateral Thinking for Management: A Handbook of Creativity.* New York: AMACOM, 1971.

Frohman, M. A., and Sashkin, M. "Achieving Organizational Excellence." Paper presented at the annual meeting of the Academy of Management, Organization Development Division, San Diego, Calif., Aug. 1985.

Frohman, M. A., Sashkin, M., and Kavanagh, M. J. "Action-Research as Applied to Organization Development." *Organization and Administrative Sciences,* 1976, *7,* 129–161.

Gordon, W. *Synectics: The Development of Creative Capacity.* New York: Harper & Row, 1961.

Hayes, R. H., and Abernathy, W. J. "Managing Our Way to Economic Decline." *Harvard Business Review,* 1980, *58* (5), 67–77.

Hickman, C. R., and Silva, M. A. *Creating Excellence.* New York: New American Library, 1984.

Holdstock, T. L., and Rogers, C. R. "Person-Centered Theory." In R. J. Corsini (ed.), *Current Personality Theories.* Itasca, Ill.: Peacock, 1977.

House, R. J. "A 1976 Theory of Charismatic Leadership." In

J. G. Hunt and L. L. Larson (eds.), *Leadership: The Cutting Edge.* Carbondale: Southern Illinois University Press, 1977.

House, R. J., and Baetz, M. L. "Leadership: Some Empirical Generalizations and New Research Directions." In L. L. Cummings and B. M. Staw (eds.), *Research in Organizational Behavior.* Greenwich, Conn.: JAI Press, 1979.

Howell, J. M. "The Socialized and Personalized Faces of Charismatic Leadership." Paper presented at the International Symposium on Charismatic Leadership in Management, McGill University, Montreal, May 1987.

Hoy, W. L., and Ferguson, J. "A Theoretical Framework and Exploration of Organizational Effectiveness of Schools." *Educational Administration Quarterly,* 1985, *21* (2), 117–134.

Jaques, E. "Taking Time Seriously in Evaluating Jobs." *Harvard Business Review,* 1979, *57* (5), 124–132.

Jaques, E. *The Form of Time.* London: Heinemann, 1982.

Jaques, E. "The Development of Intellectual Capability: A Discussion of Stratified Systems Theory." *Journal of Applied Behavioral Science,* 1986, *22,* 361–383.

Johns, G. "The Great Escape." *Psychology Today,* 1987, *21* (10), 30–33.

Katz, D., and Kahn, R. L. *The Social Psychology of Organizations.* (2nd ed.) New York: Wiley, 1978.

Kelman, H. C. "Compliance, Identification, and Internalization: Three Processes of Attitude Change." *Journal of Conflict Resolution,* 1958, *2,* 51–60.

Lawler, E. E., III. *High-Involvement Management: Participative Strategies for Improving Organizational Performance.* San Francisco: Jossey-Bass, 1986.

Likert, R. *The Human Organization.* New York: McGraw-Hill, 1967.

Lindblom, C. E. "The Science of 'Muddling Through.'" *Public Administration Review,* 1959, *19,* 79–88.

McClelland, D. C. (ed.). *Studies in Motivation.* East Norwalk, Conn.: Appleton-Century-Crofts, 1955.

McClelland, D. C. "Methods of Measuring Human Motivation." In J. W. Atkinson (ed.), *Motives in Fantasy, Action, and Society.* New York: D. Van Nostrand, 1958.

McClelland, D. C. *Power: The Inner Experience.* New York: Irvington, 1975.

McClelland, D. C., and Boyatzis, R. E. "Leadership Motive Pattern and Long-Term Success in Management." *Journal of Applied Psychology,* 1982, *67,* 737–743.

McClelland, D. C., and Burnham, D. "Power Is the Great Motivator." *Harvard Business Review,* 1976, *54* (2), 100–111.

McClelland, D. C., and Winter, D. G. *Motivating Economic Achievement.* New York: Free Press, 1969.

Macy, B. A., and others. "Meta-Analysis of United States Empirical Organizational Change and Work Innovation Field Experiments." Paper presented at the annual meeting of the Academy of Management, Chicago, Aug. 1986.

Mintzberg, H. *The Nature of Managerial Work.* New York: Harper & Row, 1973.

Mintzberg, H., and Westley, F. "Strategic Vision: Iacocca and Levesque." Paper presented at the International Symposium on Charismatic Leadership in Management, McGill University, Montreal, May 1987.

Oshry, B. "Power and the Power Lab." In W. W. Burke (ed.), *New Technologies in Organization Development.* San Diego, Calif.: University Associates, 1975.

Ouchi, W. *Theory Z.* Reading, Mass.: Addison-Wesley, 1981.

Parsons, T. *Structure of Social Action.* New York: Free Press, 1937.

Parsons, T. *The Social System.* New York: Free Press, 1951.

Parsons, T. *Structure and Process in Modern Societies.* New York: Free Press, 1960.

Parsons, T., Bales, R. F., and Shils, E. A. *Working Papers in the Theory of Action.* New York: Free Press, 1953.

Perrow, C. *Organizational Analysis.* Belmont, Calif.: Wadsworth, 1970.

Peters, T. J. *What If Tom Watson Wasn't Your Founder: The Twenty-Five Most Asked Questions.* Special Study No. 82. New York: American Management Association, 1984.

Peters, T. J., and Waterman, R. H., Jr. *In Search of Excellence.* New York: Harper & Row, 1982.

Potts, M. "GE: Changing a Corporate Culture." Part 1. *Washington Post,* Sept. 23, 1984, pp. G1, G10–G11.

Prince, G. M. *The Practice of Creativity*. New York: Harper & Row, 1970.

Pye, L. W. "Mao Tse-tung's Leadership Style." *Political Science Quarterly*, 1976, *91*, 219–235.

Rogers, C. R. "Barriers and Gateways to Communication." *Harvard Business Review*, 1952, *30* (4), 46–49.

Rogers, C. R. "A Theory of Therapy, Personality, and Interpersonal Relations, as Developed in the Client-Centered Framework." In S. Koch (ed.), *Psychology: A Study of a Science*. Vol. 3: *Formulations of the Person and the Social Context*. New York: McGraw-Hill, 1959.

Rosen, C., Klein, K. J., and Young, K. M. *Employee Ownership in America*. Boston: Lexington, 1986.

Sashkin, M. *The Leader Behavior Questionnaire*. Bryn Mawr, Pa.: Organization Design and Development, 1984a.

Sashkin, M. "Participative Management Is an Ethical Imperative." *Organizational Dynamics*, 1984b, *12* (4), 5–22.

Sashkin, M. "Creating a Corporate Excellence Culture: Identifying Levers and How to Use Them." *Emprender* (Spanish; Mendoza, Argentina), 1985a, *21* (145), 36–39.

Sashkin, M. "Creating Organizational Excellence: Developing a Top Management Mind Set and Implementing a Strategy." Paper presented at the annual meeting of the Academy of Management, Organization Development Division, San Diego, Calif., Aug. 1985b.

Sashkin, M. *How to Become a Visionary Leader*. Bryn Mawr, Pa.: Organization Design and Development, 1986a.

Sashkin, M. "True Vision in Leadership." *Training & Development Journal*, 1986b, *40* (5), 58–61.

Sashkin, M. "Why Public Bureaucracies Cannot Be Excellent." Unpublished manuscript, Office of Educational Research and Improvement, U.S. Department of Education, 1986c.

Sashkin, M. "Explaining Excellence in Leadership in Light of Parsonian Theory." Paper presented at the annual meeting of the American Educational Research Association, Washington, D.C., April 1987.

Sashkin, M., and Burke, W. W. "Organization Development in the 1980s." *Journal of Management*, 1987, *13*, 393–417.

Sashkin, M., and Fulmer, R. M. "A New Framework for

Leadership: Vision, Charisma, and Culture Creation." Paper presented at the Biennial International Leadership Symposium, Texas Tech University, Lubbock, July 1985.

Sashkin, M., and Fulmer, R. M. "Toward an Organizational Leadership Theory." In J. G. Hunt, B. R. Baliga, H. P. Dachler, and C. A. Schriesheim (eds.), *Emerging Leadership Vistas*. Boston: Lexington, 1987.

Schein, E. H. *Process Consultation*. Reading, Mass.: Addison-Wesley, 1969.

Schein, E. H. *Organizational Culture and Leadership: A Dynamic View*. San Francisco: Jossey-Bass, 1985.

Schein, E. H. *Process Consultation*. Vol. 2. Reading, Mass.: Addison-Wesley, 1987.

Schiffer, I. *Charisma: A Psychoanalytic Look at Mass Society*. Toronto: University of Toronto Press: 1973.

Stamp, G. "Assessment of Individual Capacity." In E. Jaques, R. O. Gibson, and D. J. Isaac (eds.), *Levels of Abstraction in Logic and Human Action*. London: Heinemann, 1978.

Tannenbaum, A. S. (ed.). *Control in Organizations*. New York: McGraw-Hill, 1968.

Tannenbaum, A. S., and others. *Hierarchy in Organizations: An International Comparison*. San Francisco: Jossey-Bass, 1974.

Thompson, J. D. *Organizations in Action*. New York: McGraw-Hill, 1967.

Tichy, N. M., and Devanna, M. A. *The Transformational Leader*. New York: Wiley, 1986.

Trice, H. M., and Beyer, J. M. "Charisma and Its Routinization in Two Social Movement Organizations." *Research in Organizational Behavior*, 1986, *8*, 113–164.

Vaill, P. B. "Toward a Behavioral Description of High-Performing Systems." In M. W. McCall, Jr., and M. M. Lombardo (eds.), *Leadership: Where Else Can We Go?* Durham, N.C.: Duke University Press, 1978.

Valley, C. A. "The Relationship Between the Leader Behaviors of Pastors and Church Growth." Unpublished doctoral dissertation, Department of Educational Leadership, Western Michigan University, 1986.

von Bertalanffy, L. "The Theory of Open Systems in Physics and Biology." *Science*, 1950, *111*, 23–28.

Weber, M. *The Theory of Social and Economic Organization.* (A. M. Henderson and T. Parsons, trans.; T. Parsons, ed.) New York: Free Press, 1947. (Originally published 1924.)

Winter, D. G. "Leader Appeal, Leader Performance, and the Motive Profiles of Leaders and Followers." *Journal of Personality and Social Psychology,* 1987, *52,* 196–202.

Yukl, G. A. *Leadership in Organizations.* Englewood Cliffs, N.J.: Prentice-Hall, 1981.

Zaleznik, A., and Kets de Vries, M.F.R. *Power and the Corporate Mind.* Boston: Houghton Mifflin, 1975.

6

Profiles of Strategic Vision: Levesque and Iacocca

Frances R. Westley
Henry Mintzberg

At the heart of charismatic leadership is strategic vision—a subject that has been long admired but seldom investigated. Through biographical and autobiographical materials on two acclaimed charismatic leaders, we probe into the nature and context of strategic vision, the strategic styles of the protagonists, the origins of these styles and their contexts of justification, and the processes by which the visions developed.

What is the source of strategic vision? Where and how does it develop? How does it experience demise? How can we characterize the "strategic styles" of leaders with respect to such vision? These important questions have hardly been addressed in the literature of management, even though there has been growing interest of late in the concept of vision.

The New Merriam-Webster Pocket Dictionary (1964) defines vision in a variety of ways: as "(1) something seen otherwise than by ordinary sight (as in a dream or trance), (2) a vivid picture created by the imagination, (3) the act or power of imagination, and (4) unusual foresight in foreseeing what is going to happen." Strategic vision might seem to be most clearly linked to the fourth definition. Certainly in the traditional literature of strategic management, "vision" is prized by all types of organizations, public and private, because it corresponds to an ability to forecast. Recently, vision has also been linked to the transformation of organizations and has been seen as key to "leading" as opposed to managing people (Tichy and Devanna, 1986; Bennis and Nanus, 1985). Hence, vision is valued for its motivating qualities as well.

We view strategic vision as conceptually distinct from, but empirically embedded in, the larger concept of strategic style, a view that differs from that currently prevalent in the leadership literature. Bass (1987) has defined "envisioning" as "creating an image of a desired future organizational state" (pp. 51–52), an ability central to all effective leaders. It is seen as the basis of "empowering others" (Sashkin, 1987; Srivastva, 1983; Mendell and Gerjuoy, 1984) when it is coupled with the ability to communicate (Bennis and Nanus, 1985; Tichy and Devanna, 1986; Gluck, 1984). In general, these three elements—the definition of images of future states, the articulation of these images, and the empowerment of followers through this communication—are seen as three distinct steps in a sequence (Conger and Kanungo, 1987; Bennis and Nanus, 1985; Tichy and Devanna, 1986, perhaps a reflection of Selznick, 1957). While it is useful analytically to distinguish these three, our research suggests that sequencing them in chronological steps does not correspond to reality. In one of our cases, vision seemed not so much a sequential process as an interactive one. What "images," if any, were constructed seem to have had as much to do with the past as with the future. In the other case, vision did seem to correspond to a "design for the future," and its articulation resulted in as much resistance as empowerment.

Much of the literature on leadership and vision also suggests a great deal of control by the leader, who selects, communicates, and thereby orchestrates events (see, for example, Bennis and Nanus, 1985; Meindl, Erlich, and Dukerich, 1985; Gupta, 1984). Again, our research suggests something quite different: Strategic visions are dictated by the contexts in which they arise (Lieberson and O'Connor, 1972). In one case, attention was focused on a leader who embodied an already heartfelt vision, as opposed to creating a new one. In the other case, the vision was to some extent evident, the leader "choosing" classic strategies for the context. It may be that only with a *fit* between inner and outer context, between personality and problem, between the leader and the moment, can the charismatic, empowering response be triggered and the leader thereby be viewed as a "visionary."

Our notion is that strategic visions are complex, novel images that may be more or less conscious, articulate, and realistic. They contain the standard elements of strategy—products, markets, organizational designs, and so on—but contain much more. And they are embedded in contexts: the external strategic contexts of issues and organization, the internal personal context of the life experiences and expectations of the leaders themselves. Visions are contained and expanded in time, tied to the process of evolution itself. Lastly, they are formed by— and, in turn, form—a complex structure of justifications by which the visionary explains and makes meaningful his or her vision (to self and others). It is impossible to detach and view strategic vision apart from these rich contexts and interactions. Taken as a whole, vision and context add up to what we call strategic style—a distinctive configuration of thought, action, interaction, and justification that characterizes an individual leader over time.

Justification is an important component of this configuration and merits an extra word here. In this component, we include both conscious (including self-conscious) and unconscious justifications. The latter include patterns in the data that the leader uses to paint his or her image of the context of the vision, as well as patterns in the nature of the language itself. We can relate here to a number of approaches for interpreting texts, including Boulding's (1965) theory of image analysis, Levi-Strauss's (1955) theory of the structural analysis of myth, and Bernstein's (1975) theory about the significance of linguistic codes. The common element of all these techniques is that they attempt to tap the "deep structures" of justification—that is, the relationships between specific actions and decisions and the meaning these have for the leader—what Pondy (1978) has called the "grammar of leadership." Attempts to uncover these deep structures are important in exploring an unobservable phenomenon such as vision. It is essential if our definition of leadership style is to refer to more than an inventory of characteristics and take into account "the whole manner in which the leader approaches his task, including his attitudes and values" (Pondy, p. 89).

The ultimate aim of this research program is to develop a typology of strategic styles. But we begin here with a different intention—to investigate and pin down our basic concepts, to develop a sense of strategic vision and strategic style. In this chapter, we compare and contrast the visions of two contemporary leaders: Lee Iacocca, to whom is attributed the dramatic turnaround at the Chrysler Corporation, and Rene Levesque, who led the Parti Quebecois to power in Quebec and almost led that province out of the Canadian confederation. In these two men, we have a fascinating comparison of very different strategic styles, one essentially inductive in nature and the other deductive; yet both are men who faced their respective moments of truth—whose whole lives had been dedicated to reaching the points at which they found themselves taking the reins of ultimate power.

Method

In our research, we look for excellent biographies or autobiographies—rich and detailed, especially in terms of the events in question and the thoughts of the protagonists. As coauthors, we read them and write up our respective stories, each of us independently seeking to draw on any concepts available to explain what we find, and then (and only then) read each other's materials, carry our concepts across each other's work, and seek to draw more general conceptual conclusions.

There are, of course, other ways to proceed. While no one can get inside the mind of a strategist, there are different ways to tap strategic thinking. One could interview the leaders, study organizational documents, track down everything written on the individual. Biographies and autobiographies do pose their problems. The act of writing a biography or autobiography requires an ordering and an interpretation of past events, which can introduce distortion. The written word is inherently linear, rational, and historical. Books must have beginnings and ends, events must unfold in a logical progression. This bears only a limited comparison to experience, which is much more haphazard and circular. Moreover, the person recounting his or her own story is required to translate "backstage" experience to "front-stage" presentation of self (Goffman, 1959). The wish, of course, is to present the self in the best possible light. Added to this is the publisher's imperative that the autobiography be a "good story" in order to sell.

To our mind, outweighing these problems are certain unique advantages of these source documents. What biographies and autobiographies offer is the "gestalt" of an intense observer. They are also efficient, providing the comprehensive story—especially in the case of biographies written by professionals. The writer may have spent a career digging out just this kind of data and may have worked intimately within the context for years. (Levesque's biographer, for example, covered Quebec politics for Canadian newspapers and magazines during many of the critical years of this story.) The use of such source documents not only provides us with better data than we might be able to amass ourselves, but it also allows us to consider a larger number of leaders, enabling us to focus attention where we believe our comparative advantage lies—in seeking to draw the conceptual messages behind these stories. As for autobiographers, they offer an especially unique piece of truth—the authors select their own justifications for events and from the patterns among these we learn something of their inner images and the basic assumptions that underlie their visions. Autobiographies may construct these after the fact, but to the extent that certain types of justifications are repeatedly employed, we can uncover important elements of the leader's strategic style.

We open the chapter with each of our two stories. No effort was made to render them equivalent in form, tone, or content. We believe eclecticism is useful at this point: It enriches the chapter conceptually and provides a broader basis for making comparisons. Based on the characteristics of the two men, as well as the source documents (in one case primarily a biography, in the other an autobiography), the Levesque story focuses on process and evolution, the Iacocca one on the structures of justification. After presenting each story, we will explore at some length the strategic and personal contexts of each vision to develop a comparison of the two strategic styles.

Rene Levesque: The Rise and Fall of a Strategic Vision

> "Do you have a plan to release the turtles?"
> "A plan? A dream perhaps, but that's not a plan."
> [from the film *Turtle Diary*]

Rene Levesque created the Parti Quebecois, eventually led it to victory in creating the government of Quebec, directed that government in a referendum that sought a mandate to negotiate "sovereignty-association" with the rest of Canada, and then saw his vision of an independent Quebec collapse in the subsequent defeat of that referendum. That Levesque was a strategist there can be little doubt. But there can be a great deal of doubt that the vision he pursued was exclusively his own. In a sense, Levesque pursued or, more exactly, operationalized and articulated a vision that had long existed in Quebec—and still does, for that matter.

It has been argued elsewhere (Mintzberg, 1987) that five definitions of strategy appear to be in common use (even if only one can generally be found in dictionaries): as a *plan* (a set of clear guidelines of intentions into the future), a *pattern* (consistency in realized actions out of the past), a *position* (the location of an organization in an environment, in business typically in terms of products produced and market served), a *perspective* (the broad sense of how an organization goes about doing things in relation to its "culture"), and a *ploy* (essentially a short-term means to outwit a competitor).

When discussing strategy as vision, the tendency is to view it as perspective based on plan—in other words, as a broad, all-encompassing image, however implicit and personalized, that will deliberately carry an organization into the future. In this case, we will see how the need to operationalize such an image ever more precisely reduced broad perspective to specific position and eventually to narrow ploy. In the film *Turtle Diary,* lines from which are quoted to introduce this description, a dream was realized through a plan. In the case of Rene Levesque's vision, we argue that the plan destroyed the dream.

In this chapter, we consider the story of Rene Levesque's vision of Quebec's independence, from its origins in history through his experiences in politics to his eventual resignation from public life, based primarily on one excellent source document, Graham Fraser's book *PQ: Rene Levesque and the Parti Quebecois in Power* (1984). This is backed up by another source document, Rene Levesque's own autobiography, *Memoirs* (1986, translated by Phillip Stratford), which, interestingly enough, turned out to be far less useful. We trace the case through six phases in a life cycle: origins (roots of the perception), crystallization (definition of the perception), elaboration (ideological pursuit of the perception), institutionalization (practical pursuit of position), crescendo (reduction to ploy), and disintegration (final destruction of the vision).

Phase One: Origins—Roots of the Perception. Rene Levesque did not invent Quebec nationalism by any stretch of the imagination, nor did he conceive the idea of Quebec sovereignty. But it was under his leadership—especially his *strategic* leadership—that the idea began to take tangible shape and was put before the voters of Quebec as an alternate political system.

The origins of the idea go well back in Quebec history: "The first nationalist to articulate clearly the idea that Quebec should break away from Confederation was an American-born ultramontane journalist named Jules-Paul Tardivel, who published his own paper, *La Verite,* beginning in 1881. . . . [By 1885, Tardivel] decide[d] on separation as the long-term necessity for French Canada." More recently, the notorious Quebec asbestos strike of 1949 pitted an "insensitive" English Montreal management against a French Canadian work force in rural Quebec, and "became a rallying point for a generation of Quebec intellectuals" (Fraser, 1984, p. 21; all subsequent references in this section to Fraser's book will give page number only).

Levesque's own movement toward independence was a

gradual one. His father's unfortunate business partnership with an English Canadian named Kelly supposedly "embittered Rene Levesque for life" (p. 15). Fraser describes the asbestos strike as "a turning point in Levesque's development as a nationalist" (p. 21), but he nonetheless did not embrace an independentist position until long after. The 1960s saw him as a minister in the new reform government of the Quebec wing of the Liberal Party (Canada's dominant political party) at the start of Quebec's "Quiet Revolution," after a career as a highly popular journalist. Referring to crowds chanting "Maitres chez nous!" (masters in our own house) during a 1962 election campaign, Levesque comments in his autobiography that "the chant acquired a powerful thrust, but one that was slightly disturbing, for in the uproar I sensed aspirations for a future that, for my part, I was not yet able to imagine with any precision" (Levesque, 1986, pp. 179–180).

As a Liberal minister, his political posture was "on the far left," to use his own words (p. 31), but his stand on Quebec, while clearly nationalistic, also remained ambivalent. He told one journalist in 1963 "that political action in Quebec should start from two fundamental facts: firstly, that French Canada was a true nation, and secondly that it was not politically sovereign. 'It's not a matter of examining for the time being whether we should be or not: we're not,' he said. 'Thus, an authentic nation but a nation that does not possess its sovereignty. It is from these two poles, or in terms of these two realities, that we must work'" (p. 31). But he had also told another journalist a few months earlier that he "wouldn't cry for long" if Quebec separated from the rest of Canada, and several months later he told a student group that only "associate state" status would be acceptable for Quebec, which would have to be negotiated peacefully with the rest of Canada, but that "if they refused this status to Quebec, we should separate." Some months after that, in December 1964, he perhaps best summed up his position with the comment "I am not a separatist—but I could become one" (p. 32).

Phase Two: Crystallization—Definition of the Perception. The pressures on Levesque began to increase, but he remained on the knife's edge, officially a cabinet minister in the Liberal government but feeling increasingly uncomfortable with the federalist position. Soon the pressures would reach a head and force him (as well as others) off that knife's edge. On the one hand, the Rassemblement pour l'Independance Nationale (RIN) had formed to express the separatist position, with a vengeance. That left Levesque in between, an "opportunist," as a student in one meeting shouted to him as others booed him (p. 36). On the other hand, he was feeling increasingly isolated among the Liberals, whose personal philosophies tended to be quite different from his own. His position on independence began to firm. At a Liberal retreat in 1967, he made a call for dramatically more powers for Quebec, his first statement of "sovereignty-association" (p. 40), this just two months after French President Charles de Gaulle's famous "Vive le Quebec libre!" pronouncement on the steps of the Montreal City Hall.

Then "things suddenly began to move very quickly" (p. 41). A thirty-five-page statement that called for "the essential components of independence" along with economic association with the rest of Canada took a group of his associates, including Robert Bourassa (later Liberal premier of Quebec), by surprise (p. 41). Finally, at a Liberal Party convention in October 1967, after a last-ditch effort to swing the party behind his nationalist stand (which met with overwhelming resistance, indeed animosity), Rene Levesque "made a short statement and walked out of the ballroom of the Chateau Frontenac, and out of the Quebec Liberal Party." As the *Toronto Star* had noted earlier regarding the speech that was to define his position at the convention: "Partisans of Quebec independence waited seven years for Rene Levesque. He arrived last night" (p. 43).

Thus, we have a gradual shift in mind set—not one that moved very far, but in the nature of politics far enough to tilt off one plane and onto another. Rene Levesque had shifted his position slightly or, perhaps more accurately, had articulated his true feelings more clearly; but the most influential among his Liberal colleagues had not done so—perhaps had even shifted slightly the other way in reaction to the extremist views in currency then—and that was enough to produce a major schism between them. So Levesque was launched on his new venture: Now he could begin to articulate his vision, literally in earnest.

But it must be borne clearly in mind what that vision was at that point: no more than a concept, really a single idea— Quebec independence in the form of sovereignty-association. In Levesque's words, "it was the complete mastery of every last area of collective decision making, along with economic association with the rest of Canada. This means that Quebec must become sovereign as soon as possible" (p. 41). Andrews has emphasized in *The Concept of Corporate Strategy* (1987) that strategies should be kept simple. Rene Levesque concurred to a degree that almost seemed to border on naivete:

> The more I thought about this project, the more it seemed logical and easy to articulate. Its main lines were beautifully simple and there was paradoxical added advantage that was far from revolutionary. In fact, it was almost banal, for here and there throughout the world it had served to draw together people who, while determined to be masters in their own house, had found it worthwhile to enter into associations of various kinds with others. So association it was to be, a concept that had figured for a long time in our vocabulary and a word that would marry well with sovereignty, sovereignty-association making a euphonious pair. . . . [Independence, on the other hand, had acquired] an absolute, rigid character from demonstration to demonstration as if independence were an end in itself, that the name was not much more, alas, than an invitation to the riot squad! Like the rose, however, wouldn't it smell as sweet by any other name [Levesque, 1986, p. 214]?

This broadest of perspectives would form the basis for Rene Levesque's later articulations. The strategic management literature tends to portray strategies as complete and definitive; in reality, most strategies seem to be more like umbrellas— broad guidelines under which the specifics are worked out in an emergent fashion (Mintzberg and Waters, 1985). This perspective was Rene Levesque's umbrella, at this point not much more than a single concept.

Phase Three: Elaboration—Ideological Pursuit of the Perspective. Vision was not enough, however, especially just as a concept. There was a need to elaborate the concept, to explain what it meant, both in and of itself and in its consequences. And there was a need to build an organization to bring the concept to fruition, a process that strategic management people like to call "implementation." Articulation and organization are the necessary vehicles to collectivize a vision, to draw others into it formally in order to mobilize the social energy needed to realize it. There is, unfortunately for Levesque, another concept in the literature of administration called "institutionalization"— the displacement of goals by the very fact of having to pursue them formally. Even if Levesque's vision had been fully articulated at the outset, the dangers of institutionalization would have been present. With so much articulation still to come, these dangers were magnified. In effect, while Levesque was implementing, he still had to be formulating, albeit under cover of the umbrella. Moreover, implementation was proceeding too fast, capturing formulation and in a way displacing the initial vision.

In our view, elaboration proceeded in two stages. The first was of an ideological nature, relatively unimpeded by the pressures of pragmatism. But the success of that stage—it helped get the Parti Quebecois elected to power in 1976—led to a second stage of elaboration dictated by the exigencies of holding political office, which required a more pragmatic form of elaboration. And that had to be accomplished between two major sets of political forces, which became an ever narrowing band on which to stand.

Levesque founded the Mouvement Souveraineté-Association (MSA) in late 1967 and a few months later published his book *An Option for Quebec* (1968), which spelled out the ideas in the speech he had given to the Liberals. Everything remained on a relatively general level, except for some ideological specifics which were of little importance at that point: "By the time of

the [April policy] convention, the MSA had a provisional executive, and a set of policy proposals, ranging from the essentials
of sovereignty-association to the creation of new ministries of
planning, compulsory civic service for young people, a modest
army, and the suggestion that all lawyers should be employed
by the state'' (p. 46).

But the pressures that were to plague Levesque soon arose
nonetheless, notably those from the left of his party pushing to
move farther and more radically than he was prepared to. A
floor fight broke out at this convention, setting a pattern for
those to come, this time on harsh proposals to contain or elimi-
nate certain uses of the English language in Quebec. Levesque
urged moderation, stressing the positive aspects of encouraging
a French-speaking society rather than the negative ones of discouraging an English-speaking one, and won the fight—also a
pattern that was to repeat itself many times over the years.
(Among the radical proposals brought up at this convention were
proposals to tax companies wishing to use English on signs and
to cut off social security for immigrants not enrolling their children in French schools; as a government years later, the party
was simply to outlaw both behaviors! Another proposal was to
phase out state support for English-language schools; this came
up again at the 1971 convention and was again defeated, after
Levesque threatened to resign if it passed.) ''The convention
established a pattern of giving him most of what he wanted,
but not everything'' (p. 58).

Thus, from the very beginning, Levesque was forced to
walk a tight line between the more radical elements to his left
and his own sense of moderation, defined by the pressures from
the right. ''The dilemma which Levesque had wrestled with since
he conceived the party in 1968 was how to balance the ardor
of the party militants with the demands of electoral pragmatism''
(p. 303). He had a vision, but its evolution over time was to
be mightily influenced by the field of forces that was growing
up around him. How to sustain strategic vision in such a force
field became Rene Levesque's greatest problem.

We should note here that it was *his* problem. As Fraser
points out, Rene Levesque was hardly one for teamwork in any

event; at this stage, the negotiations took place largely inside his own brain. Levesque noted in his memoirs: "Maybe I should say straight off that I believe I could never be a party man, no more Pequiste [member of the Parti Quebecois] than Liberal. For me any political party is basically just a necessary evil" (Levesque, 1986, p. 261). Earlier, he had said, "it's not always easy, this teamwork"! (p. 47).

What were the elements of Levesque's strategic vision at this point? The core element, of course, was his notion of sovereignty-association, as we noted only vaguely articulated, but situated clearly between the existing Canadian confederation and outright independence. As Levesque notes in his memoirs: "I tried out the various formulas then current: special status, or particular status, opting out (the right to withdraw, with financial compensation, from various federal programs), and finally a new or renewed federalism, within which we would constitute an associate state, free from dependence as a minority. With regard to all these concepts one idea stood out: equal rights for the two collectivities" (Levesque, 1986, p. 201). Levesque in fact attributes the idea to Daniel Johnson (Union Nationale [conservative] premier of Quebec in the late 1960s); but, having adopted it, Levesque claimed it "suited me perfectly." The RIN option of "straight ahead and right now," otherwise characterized as "clean hard independence," Levesque "didn't agree with" (Levesque, 1986, p. 201).

The relative moderation reflected in this stand permeated the rest of the vision: Levesque was generally tolerant of other people's rights, as was clearest in his own particular preferences on the issue of English-language rights (though hardly tolerant of his perceived adversaries; some of his comments in his memoirs about the Quebec anglophones ["unilingual sneer of a dominant majority," p. 288] or about the Quebec francophones who served politically at the federal level [for example, "the Good Lord in Ottawa," p. 264], especially Pierre Elliott Trudeau, were little short of infantile).

Another element, again consistent with those above, was his search for middle-class support, of "normal people" (p. 48) as opposed to the radicals of the movement. And then there was the belief in grass-roots involvement in decision making, at least in principle—for, as we have seen, Levesque was intent on getting his way. But it is true that getting his way generally meant convincing others of the correctness of his way, even if that involved threats of resignation.

Overall, then, the vision was broad, again little more than an umbrella under which specifics could be debated. But it somehow held the whole disparate conglomeration of beliefs called the MSA together.

In 1968, the movement became the Parti Quebecois, which encompassed almost all the independentist forces of the province. In subsequently contesting elections, it had to temper its more extremist elements and gradually specify its stands, particularly after it became a serious political force. In the 1973 election campaign, the promise of a referendum on Quebec independence was added to its electoral platform; at the 1974 party convention, this was taken to mean that a referendum would be held to ratify Quebec's constitution after independence was declared by a victorious Parti Quebecois. "Now, just as he had watered down the party policy in 1973, Levesque changed this to mean that a [Parti Quebecois] government would not proceed towards achieving independence until it had got the authorization of a referendum" (p. 65). The other side of the Party's platform consisted of a series of social democratic commitments— "nitty-gritty, bread-and-butter promises," such as free drugs for the elderly and agricultural zoning (p. 65).

All of this had an impact, because in 1976, perhaps more to their shock than anyone else's, the Parti Quebecois was elected to form the government of Quebec.

Phase Four: Institutionalization—Practical Pursuit of Position. Election was a mixed blessing. It brought what the Parti Quebecois needed to realize its vision: power. On that famous night in 1976, "Everything seemed possible . . . even probable . . . and, why not, assured!" (Levesque, 1986, p. 275). But it also brought even greater forces to temper the vision. On the very morning after the election, in conducting some business with the president of Hydro-Quebec, an institution that had a great deal to lose from political instability, Levesque's old friend told him to "cool it" (p. 72). Levesque did and he didn't. He stressed the party's profound respect for democracy and sought to "reassure, calm, and conciliate" (p. 73). Also, shifting within his strategic umbrella, he hinted that the referendum would precede negotiations with Ottawa, a direct contradiction of the party's program, as well as his own position in an article a few months earlier that called for immediate negotiations followed by a referendum if those failed. However, in a speech to the Economic Club of New York, Levesque made comments on politial sovereignty as the party's "prime objective" that shocked his audience and convinced him never again to read a speech text handed to him by someone else.

Public relations was in a sense the first and perhaps the most important aspect of the process of institutionalization that was now setting in quickly. As the party in power, the Parti Quebecois had to manage what it said very carefully. Having to implement the ideological vision in the pragmatic world of power politics meant an ever tightening system of constraints. Governments *do* things by *saying* things, and so the management of the word became a prime aspect of policy—especially for this government, with the delicate issue it was trying to promote.

The second aspect of institutionalization was the need now to implement through others. As an opposition party with an ideal, the Parti Quebecois could operate largely on the word of one man; as the party in power, there was a plethora of governmental issues to deal with—some unrelated, others only peripherally related to the central element in the vision, and many far beyond the capacity of one man. So Levesque had to learn to delegate, or more exactly to leave a lot of decision making to the discretion of others. And that made it increasingly difficult to keep a rein on the vision. The vision now had to be operationalized through others, which necessarily meant crudely, with a good deal of slippage. Naming his cabinet was Levesque's first encounter with this. True to form, Levesque named a cabinet primarily of "moderates: ideological pragmatists, politically liberal, favoring a strong interventionist state" (p. 82). But Levesque also had a "juggling act . . . to perform . . . to balance the forces for change against those for stability'' (p. 74). This meant that the pressures he had experienced in the party were now reflected in his own cabinet, though hardly to the same degree, since he could exercise much greater control over a group of people that he had the power to appoint and dismiss and that he met on a regular, face-to-face basis.

The third force for institutionalization was the nature of the legislative process itself. Legislation certainly clarifies vision, but it also disjoints it, reducing it to a series of independent, rather precisely defined statutes. Each was debated and fought over in cabinet, with Levesque, for example, giving in on the legislation concerning access to English schools. In favoring his grass-roots norms, Levesque necessarily ceded tight control over strategic vision, at least in terms of how it was being operationalized. As the practical realities of political power manifested themselves, integrated vision gave way to incremental policy making, much in the way that Cyert and March (1963) describe "sequential attention to goals"—the reconciliation of conflicting forces by attending to each in turn, without regard to the contradictions. Strategy, which until then had been perception, was now becoming position, or, more exactly, sets of positions as expressed in the different pieces of legislation.

The field of forces was also becoming ever clearer. At the apex was still Rene Levesque, a moderating influence in a volatile context. The position he had placed himself in after he left the Liberal Party was hardly moderate, but in the context of the nationalistic forces of the Parti Quebecois, Rene Levesque was a moderate. Of course, the end sought by his moderate stand seemed radical, but even this was not clear (as we shall see later). Then there were the ever present pressures from the left, which were constantly gnawing away at his moderation. These were manifested especially at party conventions, where they continually tried to redefine Levesque's more moderate stands. One convention, for example, called for abortion on demand, a position that Levesque considered politically insane. Thus, while the cabinet was struggling with the realities of political office, the party remained in the state of political idealism. Not having to make the practical commitments, the party radicals could keep the ideological heat on Levesque. As Fraser puts it: ''there is a fundamental tension between pragmatism and principle, the responsibilities of office and the ideology of the membership'' (p. 119).

The pressures from the right came in part from Quebec members of the federal parliament, including former colleagues of Levesque—Pierre Trudeau, Jean Marchand, and others who had fallen on the other side of the knife's edge. But perhaps more important (and what gave Trudeau and his colleagues their real power) was the fact that these pressures came from the population at large as well, the majority of which was moderate and hardly sympathetic to rupture in their established routines. In this respect, Levesque well reflected their beliefs, at least compared with the more radical elements of the Parti Quebecois.

Thus the party came to adopt a '' 'good govenment' strategy'' (p. 169), putting its ''political perspective for the future on the back burner'' (p. 181). Unfortunately, that did not always prove easy to do. Part of being good government meant providing new services, and those were often costly. ''In the minds of the new men in power, men who were planners and intellectuals with roots in the public sector, good government was inevitably more government'' (p. 168). Worst of all were the concessions to the trade unions, whose support the government felt it needed. Jacques Parizeau, ostensibly the brilliant and responsible finance minister, found himself drawn deeper and deeper into deficit spending, which eventually would come to haunt not only him but the entire cabinet. Parizeau's intended financial strategy of restraint reversed itself in emergent fashion. ''Each minister argued that his pet project was crucial to the success of the referendum. Parizeau had held the purse strings tight the first year, but relented. . . . The result was a continuous growth in Quebec's deficit'' (p. 168).

When the time came to face it, no pressures or choices experienced by the Parti Quebecois were greater than those associated with the referendum. Caught within the party between those who believed in outright independence and those who preferred a more careful and moderate stand on the issue as well as the means to get to it, the government had to tread a very fine line, at times so fine that there seemed no room to maneuver. As a result of this "hesitant waltz" the government was dancing, there was sometimes the feeling that the object of the whole exercise was being lost. To quote one party activist, the good government strategy had "been shown to be false and debilitating."

However, Levesque had not lost sight of his own strategic vision. So far, he was managing to tread that fine line: "Levesque's personal goal remained the complex, ambiguous idea he had developed in 1967: political sovereignty and economic association with the rest of Canada. Much of the party and the program was independentiste; however, bit by bit, convention by convention, Levesque had brought the party back, nearer to his original conception" (p. 170).

But in order to realize this, Levesque had to accept what can be called a "process strategy"—one of how to proceed, not what to achieve (Mintzberg and Waters, 1985), that came to be called "étapism": proceeding gradually, step-by-step, a way of "sugaring . . . the pill of independence" (p. 171). Rene Levesque did not oversee this strategy; his minister Claude Morin did. In 1974, Morin had said: "The achievement of independence cannot be instantaneous, or swift, still less abrupt" (p. 195). By 1976, Morin, who had the full support—and, more importantly, the sympathy—of Levesque, had gained full control of the referendum strategy, "despite periodic grumblings that the étapes would stretch on to infinity" (p. 195).

> First, in 1974, there was the introduction of the idea of a referendum—but only if negotiations to achieve independence reached an impasse. This became, during the 1976 campaign (as it had, in the last days of the 1973 campaign), a commitment to seek a mandate in a referendum first, and then begin negotiations. This was endorsed at the 1977 convention. Then, on October 10, 1978, Rene Levesque rose in the National Assembly to announce a crucial new wrinkle in the ideology of sovereignty-association.

"We have no intention of first obtaining sovereignty and then negotiating an association," he
said. "We do not want to end, but rather to radically transform, our union with the rest of Canada,
so that, in the future, our relations will be based
on full and complete equality."

As Claude Morin put it a few days later,
"Sovereignty-association is a single word." This
became known instantly as the "hyphen strategy";
it was a significant step backwards from all previous
positions the party had taken. Economic association
had become a precondition for independence; thus,
Quebec sovereignty would depend, not on the will
of Quebec voters, but on the success of negotiations
with the rest of Canada [p. 171].

But étapsim may have extracted an enormous price—
the conversion of the vision into steps for implementation that
may have blurred that vision. When Robert Burns, "a symbol
of the left-wing energy of the party" (p. 180), quit politics in
1979, an earlier interview was published "in which he had predicted that the government would lose the referendum and the
next election" (p. 180).

Phase Five: Crescendo—Reduction to Ploy. The referendum brought all the pressures to a head. And it exacerbated
the growing threat to the strategic vision of having to operationalize that vision in an ever narrowing field of influencing
forces. Election to power had narrowed perspective to position;
the referendum was to narrow position to ploy.

In a sense, working out the details of the referendum
brought Levesque back to the stage of ideological pursuit of his
vision, for unlike the other Parti Quebecois legislation—such
as enacting a language law—this did not pertain to anything
immediately operational. Étapism had dictated that the government was merely to seek a "mandate" to negotiate sovereignty-
association. And so the debates raged around the wording of
the question. Sovereignty-association had become "a bargaining

position rather than an objective in itself'' (p. 201)—in other words, a ploy.

On the one hand, the debate was lofty, concerned with the deepest ideals of the party. On the other hand, it was trivial, reduced to arguments over dashes and commas in the referendum question in order to entice the greatest number of votes. "We were obsessed by the wording," one member of cabinet was to recall later. A policy statement on the issue—"practically everybody" had "a hand in its preparation" (p. 196)—was later challenged as "devious and unclear" (p. 198). Given the referendum question,* when the campaign did begin, everything centered on that one "x"—oui or non. As Fraser puts it in reference to the different groups of Quebec's political elite, "The referendum was their battleground. But in many ways, it only highlighted their interwoven past" (p. 210). As ploy, the question probably worked—to the extent that it could. In other words, assuming the intention was to maximize votes, the étapist wording of the question probably did get the maximum number of votes the Parti Quebecois could hope for. Over the years, polls had indicated that there was always a hard-core separatist group of perhaps 20 percent of the population at best; another group sympathetic to Quebec autonomy, if not outright independence, made up perhaps another 20 percent. And that was the percentage that finally supported the question—just a shade over 40 percent.

The Parti Quebecois really did get its act together for the referendum. The whole exercise was extremely well orchestrated. The federalist forces, in contrast, were slow to get started and organized. Unfortunately for the Parti Quebecois, however, by a quirk in Ottawa the federal Liberals, led largely by a strong

---

*"The government of Quebec has made public its proposal to negotiate a new agreement with the rest of Canada, based on the equality of nations; this agreement would enable Quebec to acquire the exclusive power to make its laws, levy its taxes and establish relations abroad—in other words, sovereignty—and at the same time to maintain with Canada an economic association including a common currency; no change in political status resulting from these negotiations will be effected without approval by the people through another referendum; on these terms do you give the Government of Quebec the mandate to negotiate the proposed agreement between Quebec and Canada?"

core of French Canadians under Pierre Trudeau, had displaced the largely English Canadian Conservative government of Joe Clark. Thus the "non" forces did not have an influential set of spokesmen from Quebec. Even more unfortunate was another quirk, a disparaging comment made by a feminist member of the Parti Quebecois cabinet (in which she tried to put down the wife of the leader of the "non" forces as a tradition-bound homemaker) that angered large numbers of French Canadian women, whose traditional conservatism had made them very suspicious of the whole exercise. That one comment suddenly activated them, for the most part for the first time publicly (fifteen thousand of them filled the Forum in Montreal one evening in what seemed to be a largely spontaneous reaction). And that may have swung the tide at a critical point in the campaign, causing deep questioning among other undecided or only marginally favorable voters.

Whether the strategy was right or wrong, whether ploy did in fact work better than vision, to which the more radical party members would have preferred to have remained true, the Parti Quebecois never got the popular support it needed to realize its dream.

Phase Six: Disintegration—Final Destruction of the Vision. Although the loss of the referendum had a debilitating effect on Rene Levesque and the Parti Quebecois, the party was, in fact, easily reelected to office less than a year later due to a combination of factors. Not the least of these was the negative image of the new leader of the provincial Liberal party, but also there was the perception of the Parti Quebecois as having provided honest, effective, and innovative government. In April of 1981, Quebec did not want sovereignty, but it did want the rest of what this party had stood for. But after 1981, that perception eroded quickly.

Debates continued, some about the relevance of including proposals on independence in the party's election platform. (By the mid 1980s, even sovereignty-association was for all practical purposes deleted from the party's election platform.) Other debates continued about a variety of issues associated with governing Quebec. But the air had gone out of the Parti Quebecois balloon. "The referendum defeat seemed to have broken [the cabinet's] spirit" (p. 257). Moreover, the one belief that held this disparate group of people together under the label of the Parti Quebecois was now gone, and the forces of entropy set in, eventually driving the more left-wing elements out of the party. "The Humpty-Dumpty alliance—the odd coalition of idealists and pragmatists, nationalists and social democrats that had united behind Rene Levesque in 1968—was broken and could not be repaired" (p. 368).

Most curious was the treatment of the independence issue. It was not just that the expediency of including it in the election platform was debated as a practical matter. It was almost as if the vision itself, having failed to gain enough popular support, never really did exist. For example, some months after the referendum, while Levesque was negotiating in good faith with the Trudeau government and the other provincial premiers on achieving a new arrangement for Quebec within the federal system, a rumor (later proved false) circulated in the Executive Council offices in Quebec City that Levesque had reached a deal. Fraser describes the response: "The reaction was pure visceral elation: cheers, hugs, shouts of joy. One senior civil servant who had once been a Parti Quebecois official watched with a wry sense of discovery: even there, even at the heart of the government's planning secretariat, the deep-rooted, fundamental desire was not for rupture and liberation from Canada—but for reconciliation" (p. 298).

After the last time Levesque brought the Parti Quebecois convention over to his position, this time to ensure that sovereignty-association would not be a part of the election campaign, he told the convention: "We have, in effect, for all intents and purposes, gone back to our roots. . . . That is to say that we are still, as we have been since the beginning, sovereignists, but with the realism that the special situation that history and geography has made in Quebec demands. It is not for nothing that from the beginning, seventeen years ago, we evoked not only associate states, but even, do you remember, a sort of new Canadian community" (p. 370). Fraser concludes: "Now, Levesque had clearly rejected rupture in favour of conciliation, active striving for independence in favour of a passive belief in it'' (p. 370).

In effect, the results of the referendum campaign had forced Levesque up over the knife's edge and down the other side. Peeling off the sovereignty-association position, a deeper, more stable vision seemed to be revealed. But that was a vision that needed neither a special party nor special political power; in a sense, it was a vision that had been shared by Quebec's leaders throughout its history.

The Parti Quebecois exhibited a classic case of what organizational sociologists call ''goal succession''—the displacement of the primary goal of an organization because it either can no longer be achieved or has already been achieved (Sills, 1957). Protecting Quebec within the confederation, promoting its rights and spheres of autonomy, became the new goal, one remarkably similar to that of Levesque's predecessors, including the Liberal premier under whom he had served and the previous Union Nationale one he had so resisted. Even the social democratic posture changed, partly in response to the party's overspending in earlier years and partly in response to the demise of the party's more left-wing elements after the referendum. The cabinet's fights with Quebec labor unions became notorious, ironically reminiscent of pre-1960s days of union bashing.

The Parti Quebecois eventually became a party ''comme les autres'' (like the others). The referendum ''transformed the Parti Quebecois from a national movement into a provincial party'' (p. 240). It no longer had any real integrating vision, any central element beyond wanting to maintain power. As one minister later announced: ''A party exists in order to get elected'' (p. 360). Even with respect to independence, Levesque was later to argue, in Fraser's words, that ''sovereignty would remain an ideal,'' and he ''called on party members to keep the faith. But it seemed clear that he no longer believed that Quebec independence was on the public agenda for the foreseeable future. Sovereignty was, he said, an insurance policy'' (p. 364).

Eventually the pressures got to Rene Levesque—the humiliations in his negotiations with Trudeau on the Canadian constitution, the battles with the unions, the disagreements within his own party followed by the resignations of key members of his cabinet. By late 1985, ''he was clearly exhausted, dispirited, and unable to articulate his new vision for the Parti Quebecois'' (p. 366). As one former Parti Quebecois minister had earlier remarked, ''There are so many good ordinary people in the party who adore Levesque. They have a blind faith that he can lead them through the fog, that he has a vision, a grand design. . . . Levesque is leading them nowhere'' (p. 313). On June 20, 1985, Rene Levesque—who, in the opinion of Graham Fraser, ''had a stronger commitment to Quebec itself than to the ideal of independence'' (p. 372)—announced his resignation from the post of Premier of Quebec. On September 29, he was replaced as Parti Quebecois leader and Premier by Pierre Marc Johnson, who had earlier ''told the cabinet that if the next election were to be fought on sovereignty, he would not be a candidate'' (p. 361).

Lee Iacocca: The Weaving of a Strategic Vision

What brought the kindred spider to that height,
Then steered the white moth thither in the night?
What but design of darkness to appall?—
If design govern in a thing so small.

[from "Design," by Robert Frost]

This is the story of technical imagination—a genius for making things work without apparent design. In the poem ''Design,'' Robert Frost describes taking a walk one morning and coming across a white heal-all—a flower that is normally blue. Adding to this anomaly was a white spider hanging from the flower and holding a trapped white moth. Frost ponders about such serendipity, such unlikely juxtaposition of elements, which functions to appall ''design of darkness . . . if design govern in a thing so small.'' Iacocca's story shows a similar genius at work, the genius of serendipity, of the juxtaposition of elements, of a deep understanding of process. Our discussion of this story is based on Iacocca's autobiography (written with W. Novak, 1984; all subsequent references in this section will give page number only). Our focus is on Iacocca himself, his personal background, and his descriptions of the actions he took as president of Ford and later of Chrysler. In particular, we will look at the structure of Iacocca's justifications for his actions in two instances: the Mustang case and the turnaround at Chrysler.

Lee Iacocca is the youngest child of first-generation Italian immigrants. He and his sister Delma grew up in Allentown, Pennsylvania, in what he describes as a family "so close it sometimes felt as if we were one person with four parts" (p. 3). Iacocca paints his family as close, affectionate, resourceful, deeply religious, and committed to fulfilling the American dream.

Young Lee attended elementary and high school in Allentown, where he learned about bigotry and that "life wasn't always fair." He was a good student, graduating near the top of his class. In ninth grade, he was elected school president—owing, he admits, to the genius of a school friend, who was his campaign manager. He only retained the presidency for one semester because he "lost touch with his constituency." From this experience, he determined that "the ability to communicate was everything" (p. 18).

Iacocca entered Lehigh University and graduated with honors in industrial engineering, although in retrospect he felt that many of his most "valuable" courses were in psychology—"the fundamentals of human behavior." It was these courses, Iacocca claims, that taught him to "read" people quickly and easily.

After Lehigh, Iacocca went to Princeton, where he finished his master's program in two semesters. In August 1946, he began work as a student engineer at Ford Motor Company in Dearborn, Michigan. It had been his lifelong ambition—colored, Iacocca claims, by his father's intense love of cars—to work at Ford. However, soon tiring of engineering work, Iacocca decided to switch to marketing. He found a low-level desk job in Chester, Pennsylvania, in fleet sales.

From this point, Iacocca's rise was meteoric. In 1949, he was a zone manager; by 1953, he was an assistant sales manager in Philadelphia. In 1956, he became district manager in Washington; in 1959, he became national truck and marketing manager; and by 1960, he was named vice-president and general manager of Ford division. In 1970, he became president of Ford Motor Company. Along the way, he was helped by a number of mentors, from each of whom he claims to have learned certain discrete lessons. During his time as president, Iacocca was responsible for a number of successful cars—most notably the Mustang in 1963-1964 and the Mark III in 1968. Between 1970 and 1974, he also led Ford into the era of "downsized" cars with the Ford Fiesta and the ill-fated Pinto.

In 1978, Iacocca was abruptly fired from Ford—by his own account because of Henry Ford's paranoia and jealousy. In that same year, he accepted the presidency of the Chrysler Corporation. It was as president of the Chrysler Corporation that Iacocca rose to national prominence. He joined Chrysler as the organization was teetering on the brink of bankruptcy. Through a tour de force of organizational retrenchment and public relations, Iacocca spearheaded a dramatic organizational turnaround between 1979 and 1982.

This discussion focuses on two key strategic initiatives in Iacocca's career—one of product and one of organization. We will examine the events and justifications centering around the introduction of the Mustang and those centering around the Chrysler turnaround. Then we will draw comparisons between these two cases in order to create a profile of Lee Iacocca's strategic style.

The Mustang Case. A particular product strategy makes an interesting study of strategic vision, because in some ways the "vision" is made manifest in the product itself. The Mustang was launched on April 17, 1964, and within a year Ford had sold 418,000 cars, surpassing the Falcon's highest yearly sales by 1,000 cars. In the next twenty years, the original Mustang was to be remembered as a classic, with Iacocca claiming the credit as the "father of the Mustang."

Work on the car began in 1960. Soon after Iacocca became president of Ford, he brought together a team "to work on his own projects." From that point on, the development of the project was in the hands of this team. With few exceptions (outlined below), Iacocca uses the term *we* when he describes actions and decisions. He claims that the context of these early team discussions was his perception that the market was changing, becoming more youthful. "We only sell what people are willing to buy," he argued.

The group collected data, which continued to fuel this perspective. They focused on the Corvair, General Motors's hottest-selling sports car, the customers' expressed nostalgia for the Thunderbird, and market research that pointed to the rise of the baby boomers. The image was brought into somewhat sharper focus by the team's analysis of market data. In particular, Iacocca directed the team's attention and the market research toward Ford's Falcon customers, who were buying a lot of features for an inexpensive car, and the increasing importance of women who bought second family cars. The conclusion: market conditions called for a small, light, and inexpensive car that could hold four people and that had great styling and strong performance.

Iacocca claims personal responsibility for some of the "nostalgia" that he feels characterized the car's design. In his love for cars, he reports, he would pore over old pictures in *Auto Universum*. One of his favorite cars was the (Lincoln) Continental Mark, with its "long hood and short deck," which Iacocca classified as everyone's dream car. He also claims to have originated the decision to use existing Falcon components in order to save money, providing a platform (and engine) on which to construct the new body of the new Ford dream car. Iacocca states that by mid 1962 "we still didn't have a design. . . . Our styling people produced no less than eighteen different clay models in the hopes that one of them would be the car we were after. Several of them were exciting, but none of them seemed exactly right" (p. 67). In short, the team's discussion and Iacocca's nostalgia seemed to have generated a list of criteria expressive, at least for Iacocca, of a certain gestalt. That, however, did not correspond to a design.

In July 1962, Iacocca decided to stage a competition. Three "top stylists" were requested to enter into "an unprecedented open competition by designing at least one model of the small sports car we were determined to build" (p. 67). It is not clear what other criteria were given to the designers, but one of them, Dave Ash, seemed to capture what Iacocca wanted. Whether the model corresponded to a vision Iacocca had or whether he "discovered" in the model the crystallization of unformed ideas is difficult to determine. His justification for his choice was highly emotional. "As soon as I saw it, one thing hit me instantly: although it was sitting there on the studio floor, this brown clay model looked like it was moving" (p. 67).

The choice of a name was the next hurdle. Here Iacocca got help from an advertising agency, which generated thousands of animal names. Mustang was selected (he does not indicate by whom or how) because it "had all the excitement of wide open spaces and was American as all hell" (p. 70). Finally, in the choice of price and marketing techniques, Iacocca draws heavily on anecdotes of personal responses to justify and explain his choices. He tells of customers who saw the Mustang, heard the price, and said, "It doesn't look like an ordinary car—and at that price what you get is an ordinary car" (p. 71). He tells of dealers who reported "that the crush of customers was so thick he couldn't get his Mustang off the wash rack" (p. 72) and of customers who wrote "to express their gratitude and their enthusiasm" (p. 75).

It is very difficult to separate Iacocca's personal vision from the vision of his team. Iacocca selected with great care a team of creative people. Ostensibly their goal was to work on his projects, but it would seem that, even by his own admission, his vision was extremely unfocused—really no more than a germ of an idea at the outset. Certain data helped clarify this idea and focus it on a "youth market waiting to be tapped."

The data Iacocca selected to flesh out this picture were of three kinds. One kind described demographic processes, such as the growing economic power of the young, and aspects of the competition, such as the kind of cars General Motors was producing. Using Boulding's (1965) theory on the six aspects of mental image (spatial, historical, relational, affectionate, personal, and value), these may be termed *relational* data, as they suggested certain causal relations between products, markets, and competitors. Secondly, Iacocca selected *personal* data. Throughout his justifications of his choices, Iacocca recounts anecdotal evidence of a highly personal nature, elevating particular customers and dealers to oracular levels by quoting from their letters or speeches at length. Last were *historical* data: Iacocca searched through images of old cars to piece together a new dream car. This is a pattern we see repeated throughout his biography. For example, when the Mark III was introduced to newspaper publishers, Iacocca drew heavily on historical continuity: "Rather than placing the car on the turntable, which was the normal way of introducing a new model, we put the *publishers* on a turntable. As their viewpoint shifted, they saw a series of historic Lincolns and Marks. Finally, the curtains opened and there was the new Mark III" (p. 84).

In the case of the Mustang, we see clearly the way in which strategic images, embedded in justifications, may evolve through teamwork, as opposed to being implemented by subordinates. Iacocca seems, at least in terms of the Mustang, to exemplify not Selznick's (1957) institutional leader with a clear vision but Wrapp's (1967) manager who doesn't make policy decisions, "borrowing bits and pieces" of the plans of others and giving an open-ended sense of direction while avoiding policy straitjackets. This becomes even clearer in our second case.

The Chrysler Turnaround. Iacocca's reactions to Chrysler may be summed up in the following vivid first impression: "The office of the president . . . was being used as a thoroughfare to get from one office to another. I watched in amazement as executives with coffee cups in their hands kept opening the door and walking right through the president's office. Right away I knew the place was in a state of anarchy. Chrysler needed a dose of order and discipline—and quick" (p. 152). The themes of dry rot, lack of teamwork, and poor information ("I couldn't find out anything") (p. 154) color Iacocca's account of his first days. His response, similar to that of his first days as president of Ford, was to build a team.

Throughout his biography, Iacocca makes a point of

underlining his commitment to teamwork. He feels that "inter-actions between the different functions in a company are ab-solutely critical" (p. 153) and that at Chrysler "there was no team, only a collection of independent players" (p. 157). One of his first actions upon moving to Chrysler was to begin to build his team—in fact, he had prepared for this before he left Ford. "When I came to Chrysler I brought along my notebooks from Ford, where I had tracked the careers of several hundred Ford executives" (p. 167).

Iacocca used these notebooks to look up top Ford talent and attempt to woo them to Chrysler. An entire chapter of his autobiography is devoted to describing in detail the personalities and qualifications of the people he wooed. (For example, of Gerald Greenwald in finance he says: "Jerry has the talent and know-how of the entrepreneur"; of Hal Sperlich: "Hal's a vi-sionary, but a very pragmatic one"; and so on.) As described by Iacocca, the first reactions of these men upon coming aboard at Chrysler seemed eerily like his own. The chief complaints were "no information, no clear job responsibilities, need for discipline, a lack of order." Again, Iacocca selectively recounts their reactions, and it is noteworthy that what he remembers are those orientations that link up with his own. One presumes he selected the players he did because they shared his "vision," which at this point seemed merely an unfocused need to clean up a mess in ways that were traditional in a smoothly running American automobile firm.

Having formed the team, it seems unlikely that the turn-around in all its complex elements was an enactment of Iacoc-ca's vision; rather, it more likely grew or coalesced through the actions and interactions of these team members. Even with the logical sequence necessarily imposed by book writing, it is dif-ficult for Iacocca to separate his identification of the problem from his building of the team. Mention of team members pre-cedes the chapter on team building, for example, making it unclear which came first: diagnosis of a problem resulting in a team or the forming of a team resulting in a diagnosis. In any event, he undertook a series of decisive actions (for exam-ple, developing the K-car, selling certain operations, firing

15,000 employees) that culminated in going to the United States government for a loan.

Almost all of these activities are similar to those taken by many companies in a retrenchment mode—what the strategic management literature refers to as an "operating" rather than a "strategic" turnaround (see, for example, Hofer, 1980). Except for the development of the K-cars, these actions do not represent vision in the proactive, anticipatory sense of the word; they were largely reactive. "Everybody talks about 'strategy,' but all we knew was survival. Survival was simple. Close the plants that are hurting us the most. Fire the people who aren't absolutely necessary or who don't know what's going on" (p. 186).

However, as we noted earlier, vision is more than the sum of discrete strategic initiatives. It involves the context of justification, too—the way in which these initiatives are embedded in a structure of explanation, definition, and language. In this context, we find Iacocca repeatedly resorting to metaphor and analogy, not unlike many decision makers (Neustadt and May, 1986).

Analogy, as a rhetorical device, bridges unlike contexts and works to mobilize energy and emotion. Iacocca may or may not have "believed" in his own analogies, but they seemed to work powerfully for those around him. His choice of metaphor/analogy was vivid and created a rich justification for discrete strategic initiatives.

First and foremost, Iacocca likens the crisis at Chrysler to that of America in two twentieth-century crises—world war and economic depression. For example, the necessity of closing the plants is described in terms of triage: "I felt like any army surgeon. The toughest assignment in the world is for the doctor who's at the front during a battle. . . . it's a question of priorities. . . . They would pick the ones who had the best chance of survival" (p. 186). This metaphor suggests that the plant closings were painful for all concerned, that they were undertaken in the interests of healing, and that Iacocca was in charge of healing a wounded organization at war with an enemy.

This theme of war is reiterated in Iacocca's discussion of

the mass firings. In 1979 and 1980, Chrysler laid off 15,000 blue- and white-collar workers. Included in this number were most of the staff. "When the bullets start to fly," notes Iacocca, "the staff is always the first out the door" (p. 190). This metaphor reaches bathetic heights in his justification of renewed firings: "But our struggle also had its dark side. To cut expenses, we had to fire a lot of people. It's like a war—we won, but my son didn't come back" (p. 230). By this time, all of Chrysler's employees have become Iacocca's children—innocents cut down by enemy fire. The image of a country at war concealed the culpability of Chrysler in its own bankruptcy, as well as the divergence of interests of its managers and workers, while it underlined the need for loyalty and joint action.

The intelligent use of metaphor reached an apex in Iacocca's attempt to convince the government to guarantee an enormous loan. In response to the negative media coverage and to political figures who felt that the government should not bail out Chrysler, Iacocca created a comparison between Chrysler as a company and America as a whole. "We were a microcosm of what was going wrong in America" (p. 201), he says at one point. Later, to counteract the popular view that such a "big monolithic company" didn't need help, he says: "We explained that we're really an amalgam of little guys. We're an assembly company. We have eleven thousand suppliers and four thousand dealers. Almost all of these people are small businessmen— not fat cats. We need a helping hand—not a hand out" (p. 212).

This is an ingenious image: pushing the boundaries of the company outward to include suppliers and dealers—the whole of America's heartland. It is a metaphoric sleight of hand, but it creates a vision "as American as apple pie," to use Iacocca's own terminology. Moreover, Iacocca drew on history to justify his pitch to the United States Senate. The Chrysler case was not unique, he argued: "Loan guarantees, I soon learned, were as American as apple pie. Among those who had received them were electric companies, farmers, railroads, chemical companies, shipbuilders, small businessmen of every description, college students, and airlines. In fact, a total of $409 billion in loans and loan guarantees were outstanding when we made our one billion dollar request. . . . Setting a precedent? On the contrary. We were only following the crowd'' (p. 199).

A final example of Iacocca's use of analogy was his dramatic move (which he sees as central to winning concessions from the union) of cutting his salary to one dollar per year. Here again, Iacocca invokes the war metaphor: ''I didn't take one dollar a year to be a martyr. I took it because I had to go into the pits.'' He was the general fighting alongside his men. Later he intensifies and further personalizes his action by drawing an analogy to the family: ''I call this equality of sacrifice. . . . It wasn't the loans that saved us, although we needed them badly. It was the hundreds of millions of dollars given up by everybody involved. It was like a family getting together and saying 'We've got a loan from our rich uncle and now we're going to prove that we can pay him back''' (p. 230).

In a sense, by his gesture, Iacocca identified himself personally with the Chrysler cause and with the workers of Chrysler. There is some reason to believe that Iacocca actually felt such an identification, and by acting it out he powerfully communicated an element of his strategic vision. Throughout his book, Iacocca draws analogies between his family and America in general. He begins and ends the book by drawing a comparison between Christopher Columbus and his father. He closely identifies his family's fortunes (during the depression, for example) with the fortunes of America. He also draws a parallel between Chrysler and America. And, in a final connective leap, he equates his role at Chrysler with his parents' role in caring for their children during hard times: ''When the chips were down, my mother found nothing wrong with working in the silk mills so I could have lunch money for school. She did what she had to do. When I got to Chrysler, I found a royal mess, but I did what I had to do'' (p. 340).

This chain of connections is what Levi-Strauss (1955), in his theory of mythology, calls ''structural equivalents''— unlike things that become related through a chain of smaller equations, as in algebraic formula equations. In this case: Iacocca's family = America; Chrysler = America; therefore Chrysler = Iacocca's family. Chrysler is not ''like'' Iacocca's family

except to the extent that both are "like" America. Once the
equation is established, however, it provides a powerful justification for particular ploys.

Returning to the notion of strategic vision, it is obvious
that, in Chrysler's case, the visionary elements are contained
in the context of justification, in particular in the analogies in
which the turnaround strategies were embedded. The essence
of the vision was mythical and clearly ideological; it had to do
with Iacocca framing or imaging the Chrysler bail-out, as well
as his own role in it, in terms that would turn his potential opponents (unions, workers, bankers, senators) into a community
motivated to support his particular tactics. That image was that
Chrysler *was* America: Chrysler was a loyal, hard-working American family, of which Iacocca was the father, struggling to survive in the face of war and famine. In building this vision, Iacocca
used structures similar to those used in developing the Mustang—
bringing together previously unrelated people, ideas, and images. As in the case of the Mustang, the justifications used were
characterized by relational, historical, and personal data.

This consistency across the two cases suggests a particular
strategic style at work, which we will discuss in greater detail
later. Unlike the case of the Mustang, however, in the Chrysler
case the justifications themselves contained the creative, expan-
sive, and intuitive aspects we associate with vision. Vision in
the Chrysler case had little to do with desired future states for
the organization: rather it had to do with justifications for its
continued existence.

Having completed our stories of Levesque and Iacocca,
there remain two loose ends to tie together. We have emphasized
the context of justification in the Iacocca story and the strategy
process as the interaction of various views of strategy in the story
of Levesque. At this point, we wish to review Levesque's context of justification, as well as Iacocca's strategic process.

Levesque's Structure of Justification

In contrast to Iacocca's use of personal, historical, and
relational imagery to justify his actions, Levesque's orientations

were overwhelmingly slanted toward justification through values. His value orientations can be clearly separated into two somewhat contradictory ideologies.

The first is an ideology of oppression. Within the parameters of this ideology, the English are viewed as the single-minded oppressors, the French as the victims. Levesque evokes this image in times of trial and disappointment, yet as a justification it restricts as much as empowers him. It represents a cliché—an image decidedly dropped for some individual anglophones—and seems to operate as what Bernstein (1975) would call "restricted code," functioning to signal an allegiance and to reduce anxiety but not to progress in resolving problems or dilemmas. It is ritualistic but not constructive.

The second ideology is profoundly democratic and represents his strength as a problem solver. His democratic image is a complex justification—what Bernstein would call an "elaborate" code—which allows for discussion and resolution of problems. As a democrat, he deliberately resisted the extreme separatist position, at times going against his own most deeply felt emotions to defend the majority of French Canadians.

From the point of view of the issue (Quebec sovereignty) and the political reality (a deeply divided population), Levesque's vacillation between restricted and elaborate codes of ideology made him a natural leader. He belonged but was a loner, resented anglophones but defended their rights, loved the "people" but was impatient with their refusal to become masters in their own house. However, in view of his own personality and career, one gets the feeling that Levesque *served* his ideology rather than acting as its master. This is perhaps always true of the dreamer, the believer. His vision is clear but it is also rigid. Energy is spent in defense of the vision; avenues of progress are rejected as compromises.

Justification through values often involves individuals in the process of equating their values with their self-identity; they view their own value orientations as definitional of who they are. This rendered Levesque susceptible to manipulation. He recounts a story of when Pierre Trudeau, as prime minister of Canada, managed to manipulate him into supporting the idea of a national referendum by saying "you . . . the great democrat . . . don't tell me you're afraid to fight?" (Levesque, 1986, p. 331). Levesque could not resist the appeal to his values, despite the fact that he understood Trudeau's motives and that the referendum was not in his best interests.

Thus, unlike Iacocca, who could use justifications to serve his ends, Levesque at times became the servant of his justifications. Like a turtle's shell, his values acted both to protect and to inhibit him.

Iacocca's Strategy Process

As can be seen in Figure 1, we have shown the process of the evolution of Levesque's vision as deductive and destructive—from *perspective* to *position* to *ploy*. Ironically, though destructive, this sequence represents a convergence on specific *plans*. As in *Turtle Diary*, the dream came first; the plan had to be developed.

Figure 1. Levesque's Deductive Strategy Process.

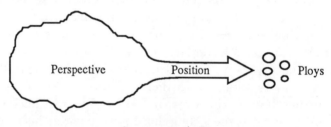

Convergence on Plan

Iacocca's inductive process is shown in Figure 2. In essence he began with strategy as *process*, not content: the construction of a team that itself would develop the strategy. From that process, the team developed a series of *positions*—tangible elements about specific automobiles, loan guarantees, and so on. Some of these positions also required *ploys*, most evident in the lobbying and negotiations that took place while Chrysler was trying to secure the government loan guarantees. Then Chrysler's

plans were developed as the tangible manifestations of these positions and ploys—the means to operationalize or implement
them. (For a discussion of this view of planning as program-
ming, see Mintzberg and Waters, 1982.) The *perspectives* that
eventually emerged in the Iacocca story—the ultimate manifestations of strategic vision—represented the combination and convergence of these various positions and ploys as plans. In other
words, strategy grew out of the patterns that formed among the
elements.

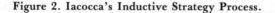

Figure 2. Iacocca's Inductive Strategy Process.

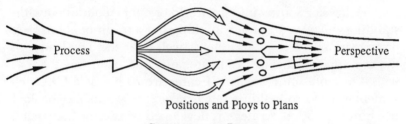

Positions and Ploys to Plans

Convergence on Pattern

Strategic Context

Having developed the role of strategic process and the
context of justification in the visions of both Levesque and Iacocca, it remains to explore the strategic and personal contexts
of these visions. We begin with the strategic context: institutional, issue, product, and market. Beyond the few but basic
similarities—notably two highly charismatic men negotiating
their organizations through highly threatening environments—
there are a number of evident (as well as some more subtle) differences between their contexts.

The Institutional Context. Lee Iacocca had the advantage
of the clear goals that come with the business enterprise—to ensure its viability through profitable operations. For Levesque,
of course, the system itself contained no such clear goals, although his own vision for it obviously did. Iacocca's context,

however, was hardly purely free enterprise, at least at the outset
at Chrysler: Its crisis propelled it into the public arena, where
its leader had to negotiate its survival through government intervention. In fact, these actions constitute a form of turnaround
not mentioned in the strategic management literature—"political
turnaround." Of course, Levesque would likely have defined
the problem in Quebec as one of turnaround, too, but that would
have been his own perception (and one not shared by 60 percent of the Quebec population). Thus, in one case turnaround
was an exogenous condition, defined by the events; in the other,
it was a way to define a problem, endogenous and ultimately
strategic.

Chrysler's foray into the world of public politics notwithstanding, Iacocca never led anything but a traditional business
organization. There, hierarchy is well defined: The leader at
the top appoints his or her lieutenants and dismisses them at
will. To quote him: "Where I come from, if I as a CEO tell
someone to do something and I never get an answer back, I
fire him" (p. 300). Strategy is developed within the hierarchy,
and everyone defers to that strategy. Of course, when the organization is threatened and others have a major stake in its survival, they worry about those strategies. But as nonexperts, few
deem themselves capable of questioning them. And once the
threat passes, few outsiders really care at all. Even the ostensi-
ble owners, the shareholders, generally keep quiet—unless, of
course, individuals have a significant stake in the enterprise
(Berle and Means, 1968; Mace, 1971).

The contrast here with Levesque and the Parti Quebecois
is marked. Everyone seemed to care passionately about everything the Parti Quebecois government did. In some ways, Levesque had the greatest trouble with certain of his closest allies,
over whom he could not exercise formal power, and even with
some of his own cabinet ministers, whom he did appoint. Thus,
while Iacocca's external context may have been somewhat political, Levesque had to struggle in a context both internal and
external that was constantly and intensely political. That is why,
while "the enemy without" may have served the vision of Iacocca, it helped to destroy that of Levesque.

Moreover, Levesque continually had to make strategy in a fishbowl; Iacocca was spared that after the firm became viable and to some extent while he was making it so. In business, you appoint a leader and then hope for the best. You don't second guess that leader: at worst you replace him or her and put your faith in another leader. In addition to the differences in their intrinsic personalities, the difference in the extent of their public visibility helps explain why Iacocca could make such effective use of teamwork while Levesque could not and, moreover, why Iacocca could continually pull the pieces together to integrate a strategic vision while Levesque saw his initial strategic vision reduced to ploy before it *dis*integrated.

The Issue Context. The main issue in question was, of course, very different too. Levesque wanted to act proactively to remake a society; his strategic intentions, if realized, would have profoundly affected not just a cabinet or a party, not even just a civil service or political system, but every one of six million Quebecers, not to mention more than twice that number of other Canadians.

The issue facing Iacocca was to save several hundred thousand jobs—in effect, to maintain an economic status quo. No one expected much else to change; indeed, even Iacocca's two big American competitors could not have expected to be much influenced by the issue. (Domestic "competition" in the American automobile business had long been such that few entertained the idea that Chrysler could threaten Ford or General Motors; no one dreamed that Iacocca could ever be *that* successful.)

So while everyone in Canada hung on Rene Levesque's every word, the Iacocca experience at Chrysler really became home entertainment of the very best sort. Horatio Alger came to life in a characteristically late twentieth-century reincarnation. We all followed the serial with glee; it was the best soap opera around, and its star performer relished the part. Meanwhile, north of the border, investments were being transferred frantically, troops were occupying Montreal, families were torn apart over "oui" and "non." The Canadians were in it for real, while the Iacocca show entertained the Americans. The effect on strategic vision, as we have shown and will show in the following sections, was profound.

The Product Context. Besides the issue itself, what the issue dealt with was fundamentally different. As we noted for Iacocca, "'vision' is manifest in the product itself." While it may be true that every strategy is an abstract invention, a concept that can be seen only in the mind's eye, the Chrysler strategic position was manifested in cars that took visual shape. The strategic vision almost literally came to life in visual design, as reflected in the Iacocca comment about a clay model of a car that looked "like it was moving." In contrast, the only thing that moved for Levesque was hope—which moved both up and down. In effect, the Parti Quebecois strategy remained an abstraction that never took any tangible shape at all. Moreover, the Chrysler cars that defined strategic position themselves took shape on assembly lines—that most tangible of production processes. The Parti Quebecois strategies took shape through people debating words in closed offices or open conventions.

The Market Context. Iacocca went after markets "waiting to be tapped." So did Levesque, in a sense. But while Iacocca could segment his markets—create differentiated products, each of which could capture its own niche—Levesque never had any choice but to go for that one comprehensive market. And to win he needed the largest market share, which, against a single competitor, meant more than 50 percent. That never proves easy, especially when your product means so much disruption in the lives of your potential customers.

A niche is not so much a way to compete directly as it is a way to avoid head-on competition. No segmentation, no niche, means outright competition. So while Iacocca could play straight and creatively in his own niches, Levesque faced a game of zero sum: For every single move he made, he could expect a countermove from his opponents. And when you represent disruptive change while your competitor sits comfortably with the status quo, strategy making becomes difficult indeed. No wonder perspective was reduced to ploy.

Levesque faced a further problem. Iacocca was able to go with markets as they were: He had less need to create demand per se than to find potential demand and satisfy it. Levesque was certainly catering to pent-up demand, but he knew that it constituted less than the 50 percent he needed. So he had to convince people to perceive demand. He was the one who had the difficult selling job! His problem was that the market resisted. While in America there was a natural propensity to save Chrysler—doing so, after all, would preserve the comfortable status quo—in Canada the natural tendency was to reject sovereignty-association: Confederation was the comfortable status quo. So Iacocca was able to go with the natural flow, and he won, while Levesque could not, and he lost.

To conclude, both men began with intrinsic charisma in their respective contexts; both were earthy, in touch, intuitive men disrespectful of unnecessary constraint. Yet the behavior of the two diverged dramatically due, in good part, to strategic context.

Personal Context

Despite the similarities just noted, in many ways these two men are a study in contrasts. They shared a destiny—to be the right man for the job—which most charismatic leaders seem to share, but as their jobs varied so, too, did their characters. Levesque's defining characteristic would seem to have been a deep-seated and often admirable ambivalence—a man divided, ideally suited to represent a people divided. The cover photo from his autobiography (Figure 3) epitomizes this. In addition, his approach was fundamentally *deductive:* He began with an ideal and attempted to construct or find its mirror image in reality. In contrast, Iacocca radiated an unconflicted self-confidence, evident in the photo from the cover of his autobiography (Figure 4). In a sense, these characteristics tell the whole story. Iacocca's ability to align himself with the forces in his environment, using their energy to his ends, was significant. His approach was fundamentally *inductive*—his vision or ideal growing from and in response to the stream of his operational decisions and day-to-day encounters. We shall explore these contrasts along two dimensions: first, these two leaders' relationships with their fathers and, second, their relationships with their careers.

Relationships with Their Fathers. In both autobiographies, the father figured prominently as a life influence. Iacocca's father was something of a hero, and certainly a role model. Nicola Iacocca loved cars, and he loved America. Iacocca attributes to his father his instinct for marketing, as well as most of his values. He saw his father as the backbone of the family, able to keep everyone's spirits high, a continual optimist. Iacocca constantly refers to his experiences with his father in reference to later life events: "Many years later, when I was trying to save Chrysler from bankruptcy, I missed my father's comforting words. I'd say, 'Hey Pop, where's the sun, where's the sun!' He never let any one of us surrender to despair. . . . I kept my sanity in those days by recalling his favorite saying: 'It looks bad right now, but remember, this too shall pass'" (Iacocca and Novak, 1984, p. 10). Iacocca accumulated innumerable lessons from his father, which he claimed to use as guides throughout his career. Certainly, throughout the book, he refers to them.

Levesque is much more guarded in his mentions of his father. He describes himself as "'a sad child,' by which they meant difficult." He cites as a primary influence on his childhood a neighboring family with four boys, with whom he "hung out." His early childhood was spent outdoors in the beautiful countryside of the Gaspesie and in the company of peers, not family. "From one season to the next, we ran free between the forest and the sea" (Levesque, 1986, p. 51). Levesque's father is introduced first as providing a house bursting with the books Levesque loved and as a man "resigned" to a life less fulfilling than he had hoped. "My father was a young lawyer, who, when the Spanish influenza came within a whisper of carrying him off, had to resign himself to a rural practice" (p. 53).

Levesque and his father shared a love of books and a penchant for crossword puzzles. Dominique Levesque told his son stories of the English-owned companies and their oppression of workers and of how he himself had suffered at the hands of his

Irish partner. He had dreamed of a political life but ended up in a country practice. In recounting the story of his father's early death, Rene Levesque writes: "He had been a good man, perhaps more upstanding and discreetly dedicated to the service of others than anyone I have ever met. He was a cultivated man but never flaunted it; he had lost none of his idealism, only his illusions, and he was so honest that he died in perfect poverty" (p. 76).

Hence, Levesque, Sr., is seen as something of a victim of circumstance and oppression. As we shall see, Levesque shared that outlook or at least strongly empathized with the victim or underdog stance and frequently fell into defining the world in the black-and-white terms of oppressor and oppressed. This formula for interpreting reality may be related to his relationship with his father. Yet, at his father's death, Levesque felt a distance, in contrast to the closeness Iacocca experienced with his father.

Levesque emerged from childhood with a desire to fight for those who were victimized and oppressed, a preference for dreams and ideals, and a refusal to compromise values—all of which were traits he shared with his father. He does not refer to his father, however, to justify or explain his adult behavior; rather, Levesque, Sr., is a remote, shadowy figure in the autobiography. This may be due to Levesque's sense of privacy. The intense positive experiences of his childhood were times he spent with his peers, which may have contributed to the deeply democratic ideals he exhibited. Iacocca focuses much more squarely and self-consciously on his family as the primary group of his childhood and on his father as his first mentor. He defines his father as a source of strength, pragmatism, and optimism—qualities he internalized. He continued to draw on his father as role model and inspiration in his adult life. He chose filial roles in relation to superiors and paternal roles in relation to subordinates, seemingly replicating this satisfactory relationship.

Relationships with Their Careers. A second point of comparison between these two men, which reveals their distinctive personalities, is their attitude toward their careers. Similar to his attitude toward his relationship with his father, Levesque's attitude toward his career had a deeply ambivalent quality. He loved school but resented how it restricted his freedom. He was bored and irritated by law school and dropped out despite his mother's hope that he would follow in his father's footsteps and take the law office she continued to rent for him. He drifted into the war as a correspondent, the choice dictated more by instinct than by reason: "No wish to fight to kill, but a ravenous hunger for war experience, to see it close up, to learn what it was about" (Levesque, 1986, p. 84).

A similar impulse took him into politics. He was put up to run in a district where he "wasn't exactly a stranger. But at the corner store, they weren't exactly killing the fatted calf either." As Minister of Public Works, he threw himself into nationalizing Hydro-Quebec, but he felt somewhat an outsider—"a black sheep"—with his colleagues. By 1965, despite his successes, the endless struggle was getting to him, and he spoke of "packing it in." In addition to his sense that the French Canadians were a marginal people due to English domination, he perceived himself as something of an outsider. In his own words, "I believe I could never be a party man, no more Pequiste than Liberal." Levesque, a man forced to live in a team context, was not a team player.

But Levesque was an outsider with roots, with connections. It is not coincidence that his ideal was sovereignty-*association*—a partnership of equals, each of whom was master in his own house. And while Levesque was forced into prominence as the leader of the Parti Quebecois, he did not find ultimate satisfaction in that role. His most enthusiastic commentary is reserved for his role in nationalizing Hydro-Quebec, when he was a Liberal cabinet minister. In a sense, Levesque's Hydro-Quebec was the equivalent of Iacocca's Mustang—a project successfully planned and executed while working within the framework of another man's party/company.

Iacocca portrays himself as being as undivided about his career as he was about his family: "School was a very happy place for me. I was a diligent student. I was also a favorite of many of my teachers" (p. 15). The only deviation from a straight course Iacocca took was to switch from mechanical to industrial engineering. Despite this change, he finished his engineering degree in three years. His dream, when he graduated, was to work at Ford: "Even before I graduated, I wanted to work for Ford. I drove a beat-up 1938 six-horsepower Ford, which is how I got interested in the company. . . . Cars were what I cared about" (p. 28). He started working in August 1946, and, by his own avowal, he loved it as much as he had expected. When he was fired from Ford, he was approached by a number of companies. "Some of these offers were very tempting, but I had trouble taking them seriously. I had always worked in the car business and that's where I wanted to stay. . . . Cars were in my blood" (p. 141).

Iacocca demonstrated a singleness of purpose and an identification with his business that were quite distinct from Levesque's attitudes. If Levesque's desire was to separate himself, Iacocca's was to belong. As we have seen, Iacocca identified with his family, with his company, and with his country. He was a team player par excellence and approached each new challenge by first constructing a team. He defined himself as someone who would and could and did win. While some individuals got in his way—most notably Henry Ford—Iacocca defines these people as "paranoid" (in the case of Ford, p. 99), "living in the last century" (*Wall Street Journal*, p. 211), "ideologues" (senators, p. 213), and criminals (Congressman Richard Kelly, p. 217). In contrast, Levesque characterized the English as extremely powerful "potentates," "mini-magnates," "feudal baroners," a "monolithic bloc," and a "formidable opponent." Of one anglophone minister in the Liberal cabinet, Levesque wrote: "Speaking French as well if not better than us, this superbly attired gentleman represented with exquisite courtesy the most upper-crust circles of the dominant minority" (Levesque, 1986, p. 175). These definitions of those who opposed them fit with Levesque's mild pessimism and Iacocca's unbounded optimism.

In sum, then, the personalities of these men were profoundly different. Levesque was a private man, an idealist, a bit of a dreamer, a victim of circumstance like his father, an outsider yet a participant who was able through the profound tension of his own ambivalence to forge a vision of sovereignty-association and to hold together the ambivalent elements of his party. Iacocca, in contrast, was a self-defined winner, an extrovert, an actor with a fundamental self-confidence and optimism and a gift for clothing his actions in patriotic allusions, which he may or may not have felt. Both men, through the force of their personalities, were creators of change: the one by a stubborn refusal to renounce democratic ideals and a vision, the other through his ability to align himself with the winning forces, to use energy from the outside for his own purposes, to choose people who enacted a vision and to "market" that vision in the appropriate ideological clothing. In this sense, their personalities matched the strategic contexts in which they found themselves and help explain the charismatic force of each. Levesque's notion of sovereignty-association expresses his self-image, as well as his political vision. Iacocca's tactics in reshaping Chrysler express his own approach to life, as well as his approach to organizations.

Conclusion: Two Strategic Styles

As we pull together the various elements of strategic style we have introduced, we end up with two quite distinct configurations. We call one the "tightrope walker," the other the "bricoleur." Their elements are summarized in Table 1.

The Tightrope Walker. We label Rene Levesque's strategic style the "tightrope walker." He had lofty ideals and high-wire dreams but had to manifest them in a balancing act between a conservative populace on one side and a missionary party on the other; this was reflected in his own personal ambivalence. Levesque's path on that tightrope, however, seemed to be clear (at least until the referendum was lost), from the unacceptable status quo of Canadian federalism to some form of sovereignty for Quebec, along a straight line that amounted to a deductive process: "Levesque was no bargainer, no negotiator. He and his government developed a position with careful, Cartesian logic, based on a set of principles from which the argument flowed. The result was a closed logical circle, a final offer with no bargaining room, no fall-back position" (Fraser, 1984, p. 284). Moreover, to mix our metaphors, Levesque really was the turtle, standing on that tightrope encumbered with a heavy ideological shell. This made his passage from dream to reality a perilous one, and ultimately ill fated. No plan really did develop that realized the dream, and so he fell all that much harder.

The Bricoleur. The term "bricoleur" refers to a common figure in France: a man who frequents junkyards and there picks up stray bits and pieces which he then puts together to make new objects. We have selected this image, drawn from Levi-Strauss (1955), for Lee Iacocca because neither in the case of the Mustang nor in that of Chrysler did he really present the world with anything startlingly new or original. In the one case, he produced a product that represented a recombination of "classic" Ford parts from old models tailored to fit on existing car platforms and over existing engines. In the other, he executed a turnaround in almost textbook fashion, clothing it in evocative images composed of personal, historical, and patriotic analogies. In both cases, he recognized certain set financial and political parameters and played within them—in one case pursuing a fairly conservative approach, in the other a conservative cost-cutting strategy. Iacocca's unique style does not reside in any of the individual elements as much as in his ability to combine elements inductively—whether people, facts, or images—and then infuse the combinations with intense personal affect.

Iacocca seemed able to build his strategic vision, as Wrapp (1967) and Quinn (1980) have described, piece by piece by building a team and taking advantage of opportunities, and yet he was also able to create a powerful ideology to move his organization in the broader sense that Selznick (1957) so eloquently portrayed in *Leadership in Administration.* The act of piecing together people, parts, and processes resulted in the Mustang; the act of piecing together images resulted in a powerful survival

Table 1. Two Strategic Styles.

Iacocca: The Bricoleur	
Process	Discovers vision in the process of piecing together people, ideas, events
Structure of justification	Accent on the personal, the historical, relationships between things; ideology is servant
Strategic context	Private sector; clear goals; well-defined hierarchy; turnaround situation; tangible product; segmented markets
Personal context	An optimist; identifies with family and father; single-minded in career; self-defined winner; master of metaphor
Levesque: The Tightrope Walker	
Process	Vision begins as perspective, gradually eroded through compromise, political pressure
Structure of justification	Emphasis on the ideology as master, value dimensions
Strategic context	Public sector; missionary political party; volatile issue; abstract product; one central market
Personal context	Pessimist; loner; divided against self; true to ideals; limited by ideology

myth for Chrysler—perhaps the key to its turnaround. Such "bricolage" represents serendipity as an art form—the final outcome representing a process of discovery as much as implementation.

To mix our metaphors once again, as shown in Figure 5, Iacocca really was the inductive spider, weaving his web, perhaps by instinct, perhaps by design, combining the elements he caught into sustaining strategies. Spiders generally don't fall, or at least they don't get hurt when they occasionally do. They merely land and move on to weave another web. Levesque, as shown, in contrast, was the deductive turtle, walking the tightrope high above the world, from the pragmatic "non" of the Quebec population to the idealized "oui" of the Parti Quebecois.

Figure 3. Rene Levesque.
(Photo by Bernard Bohn.
Used by permission)

Figure 4. Lee Iacocca.
(Photo by Anthony LOEW, Inc.
Used by permission)

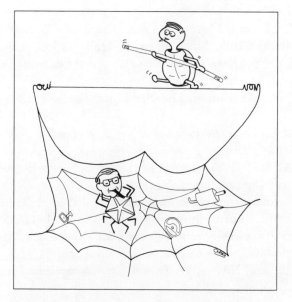

Figure 5. The Tightrope Walker and the Bricoleur.

References

Andrews, K. R. *The Concept of Corporate Strategy*. Homewood, Ill.: Irwin, 1987.

Bass, B. M. "Charismatic and Inspirational Leadership: What's the Difference?" Proceedings of the International Symposium on Charismatic Leadership in Management, McGill University, Montreal, May 1987.

Bennis, W., and Nanus, B. *Leaders: The Strategies for Taking Charge*. New York: Harper & Row, 1985.

Berle, A. A., and Means, G. C. *The Modern Corporation and Private Property*. San Diego, Calif.: Harcourt Brace Jovanovich, 1968.

Bernstein, B. B. *Class, Codes and Control: Theoretical Studies Towards a Sociology of Language*. New York: Schocken Books, 1975.

Boulding, K. E. *The Image: Knowledge in Life and Society*. Ann Arbor: University of Michigan Press, 1965.

Conger, J. A., and Kanungo, R. N. "Towards a Behavioral Theory of Charismatic Leadership in Organizational Settings." Proceedings of the International Symposium on Charismatic Leadership in Management, McGill University, Montreal, May 1987.

Cyert, R. M., and March, J. G. *A Behavioral Theory of the Firm*. Englewood Cliffs, N.J.: Prentice-Hall, 1963.

Fraser, G. *PQ: Rene Levesque and the Parti Quebecois in Power*. Toronto: Macmillan, 1984.

Gluck, F. W. "Vision and Leadership." *Interfaces*, 1984, *14* (1), 10–18.

Goffman, E. *The Presentation of Self in Everyday Life*. New York: Doubleday, 1959.

Gupta, A. K. "Contingency Linkages Between Strategy and General Manager Characteristics: A Conceptual Examination." *Academy of Management Review*, 1984, *9*, 399–412.

Hofer, C. W. "Turnaround Strategies." In W. F. Glueck (ed.), *Business Policy and Strategic Management*. New York: McGraw-Hill, 1980.

Iacocca, L., and Novak, W. *Iacocca: An Autobiography*. New York: Bantam Books, 1984.

Levesque, R. *An Option for Quebec*. Toronto: McClelland and Stewart, 1968.

Levesque, R. *Memoirs*. (P. Stratford, trans.) Toronto: McClelland and Stewart, 1986.

Levi-Strauss, C. "The Structural Study of Myth." *Journal of American Folklore*, 1955, *68*, 428–444.

Lieberson, S., and O'Connor, J. F. "Leadership and Organizational Performance: A Study of Large Corporations." *American Sociological Review*, 1972, *37*, 117–130.

Mace, M. L. *Directors: Myth and Reality*. Boston: Harvard Business School, Division of Research, 1971.

Meindl, J. R., Ehrlich, S. B., and Dukerich, J. M. "The Romance of Leadership." *Administrative Science Quarterly*, 1985, *30*, 78–102.

Mendell, J. S., and Gerjuoy, H. G. "Anticipatory Management or Visionary Leadership: A Debate." *Managerial Planning*, 1984, *33* (3), 28–31, 63.

Mintzberg, H. "Five P's for Strategy." *California Management Review*, 1987, *30* (1), 11–24.

Mintzberg, H., and Waters, J. A. "Tracking Strategy in an Entrepreneurial Firm." *Academy of Management Journal*, 1982, *25*, 465–499.

Mintzberg, H., and Waters, J. A. "Of Strategies, Deliberate and Emergent." *Strategic Management Journal*, 1985, *6*, 257–272.

Neustadt, R. E., and May, E. R. *Thinking in Time: The Uses of History for Decision-Makers*. New York: Free Press, 1986.

Pondy, L. R. "Leadership Is a Language Game." In M. W. McCall and M. W. Lombardo (eds.), *Leadership: Where Else Can We Go?*. Durham, N.C.: Duke University Press, 1978.

Quinn, J. B. *Strategies for Change: Logical Incrementalism*. Homewood, Ill.: Irwin, 1980.

Sashkin, M. "A Theory of Organizational Leadership: Vision, Culture and Charisma." Proceedings of the International Symposium on Charismatic Leadership in Management, McGill University, Montreal, May 1987.

Selznick, P. *Leadership in Administration: A Sociological Interpretation*. New York: Harper & Row, 1957.

Sills, D. L. *The Volunteers: Means and Ends in a National Organization.* New York: Free Press, 1957.

Srivastva, S., and Associates. *The Executive Mind: New Insights on Managerial Thought and Actions.* San Francisco: Jossey-Bass, 1983.

Tichy, N. M., and Devanna, M. A. *The Transformational Leader.* New York: Wiley, 1986.

Wrapp, H. E. "Good Managers Don't Make Policy Decisions." *Harvard Business Review,* 1967, *45* (5), 91–99.

7

Two Faces of Charisma: Socialized and Personalized Leadership in Organizations

Jane M. Howell

As several chapter authors have discussed, charismatic and transformational leadership have recently emerged as important concepts among organizational leadership scholars. Political scientist James MacGregor Burns (1978) initiated the distinction between exchange-oriented transactional leaders, who reward followers for reaching established objectives, and transformational leaders, who inspire followers to transcend their immediate self-interests for superordinate goals. In their best-selling book, *In Search of Excellence,* Peters and Waterman (1982) observe that at some point in the histories of successfully managed companies transformational leaders have arisen and instilled purpose, shaped values, and engendered excitement. In his recent book, *Leadership and Performance Beyond Expectations,* Bass (1985) argues that transformational leadership is necessary to promote follower performance beyond ordinary limits. Finally, House and Singh (1987), in reviewing the burgeoning research on the behavior and effects of charismatic and transformational leaders, conclude that such leaders profoundly influence follower effort, performance, and affective responses toward them.

Despite the increased attention being focused on transformational and charismatic leadership in both the academic literature and the popular press, to date no scholarly consensus has emerged on the precise application of the concept of charisma.

The term *charismatic* has been applied to very diverse leaders emerging in political arenas (Adolf Hitler, Benito Mussolini, Fidel Castro, Franklin Delano Roosevelt), in religious spheres (Jesus Christ, Jim Jones), in social movement organizations (Mahatma Gandhi, Martin Luther King, Jr., Malcolm X), and in business organizations (Lee Iacocca, Mary Kay Ash, John DeLorean). However, such a widespread application of the term obscures the term's meaning.

If the concept of charisma is to serve a useful purpose in scientific inquiry, then it cannot embrace leadership styles as disparate as those cited above. By distilling the elements that differentiate the range of leaders captured within this broad concept, the explanatory power of charisma will be increased. Therefore, a theory that distinguishes among different forms of charisma is proposed in this chapter. The theory looks not only at the possibilities of charismatic leadership, but, importantly, also at its limitations. For while the reader of this volume may be developing a sense of charisma's profound impact, it must be seen both in its positive and negative light.

Following several authors of this book (Bass, Chapter Two; Conger and Kanungo, Chapter Three; House, Woycke, and Fodor, Chapter Four), I define charisma in terms of particular leadership abilities. These include the leader's ability to: articulate a captivating vision or mission in ideological terms; create and maintain a positive image in the minds of followers; show a high degree of confidence in him- or herself and his or her beliefs; set a personal example for followers to emulate; behave in a manner that reinforces the vision or mission; communicate high expectations to followers and confidence in their ability to meet such expectations; show individualized consideration toward followers and provide them with intellectual stimulation; and demonstrate a high degree of linguistic ability and nonverbal expressiveness. These abilities of a leader represent a "generic" conceptualization of charisma. However, it is the intent of this chapter to tease out the distinctive components of charisma that delineate different charismatic forms.

It should be underscored that, in accordance with Weber's example ([1924] 1947), charisma is used in a value-neutral manner. As Willner (1984, p. 12) points out, charismatic leadership is "inherently neither moral nor immoral, neither virtuous nor wicked . . . such questions arise only when we wish to evaluate whether a particular charismatic leader has used the relationship in the service of good or evil."

An Overview of the Theory

McClelland (1985), in his work on power motives, suggested two types of power: socialized and personalized. Based on such a distinction, the theory of charismatic leadership proposed in this chapter distinguishes two types of charisma: one based on the use of socialized power and the other based on the use of personalized power. The theory further suggests that these two types of charisma are exercised through different social influence processes (Kelman, 1958) and behaviors and that they result in different effects on followers and on the perpetuation of the leader's mission. Table 1 summarizes the components of the theory and their interrelationships.

Table 1. Components of Socialized and Personalized Leadership.

Antecedent		
Power motive	Personalized	Socialized
Process		
Social influence	Identification	Internalization
Behavior	Articulate goals based on leader's private motives; recognize followers' needs for benefit of leader's goals	Articulate goals based on followers' needs; recognize followers' needs to develop them in their own right
Consequences		
Effects on followers	Willing obedience; submission; habituated followership	Empowerment; autonomous followership
Perpetuation of mission	Dependent on leader; unstable	Independent of leader; stable

While this chapter distinguishes between two types of charisma—socialized and personalized—these leadership types are not mutually exclusive. It is conceivable that socialized leaders might revert to personalized leadership or personalized leaders might become socialized, depending on follower responses, situational contingencies, or a leader's personal development. In addition, a leader might simultaneously display behavior that reflects some aspects of both socialized and personalized tendencies. Although such transitional or mixed forms of charisma might be noticed in a leader's behavior, the extreme or pure types of charismatic leadership—socialized and personalized—are analyzed here for the purpose of differentiating the two faces of charisma. To achieve this purpose, the chapter is organized into six sections.

I begin by reviewing the work of McClelland and his colleagues on the power motive and deriving hypotheses concerning the two types of charismatic leadership based on a differential exercise of power. In the second section, I review Kelman's (1958) theory on social influence processes and deduce from it hypotheses concerning a differential use of social influence processes by socialized and personalized leaders. In the third section, I describe the behaviors of the two charismatic types. In the fourth section, the effects of socialized and personalized leaders on followers and on the perpetuation of the mission are outlined, citing examples from the literature to illustrate the varying effects. In the fifth section, I discuss the implications for theory on organizational and individual effectiveness. Directions for further theoretical development and research are proposed in the final section.

The Power Motive

Several scholars have postulated that charismatic leaders possess high needs for power or influence. Etzioni (1961, p. 203), for example, contends that charisma is the "ability of an actor to exercise diffuse and intensive influence over the normative orientations of other actors." In his theory of charismatic leadership within organizations, House (1977) argues that charismatic leaders have extremely high levels of dominance and need for influence over others. In order to further our understanding of the different forms of charisma, it is instructive to examine the literature on power motivation.

McClelland and his colleagues have extensively studied the motivational aspect of power—the desire to have a strong impact on others (McClelland, 1970, 1975, 1985; McClelland and Boyatzis, 1982; McClelland and Burnham, 1976). They contend that individuals with a high need for power can be expected to take an activist role with respect to their work environment and thus more frequently attempt to influence the outcomes of important decisions.

In an examination of an individual's need for power (measured by content analysis of stories written in response to the Thematic Apperception Test [TAT]), McClelland, Davis, Kalin, and Warner (1972) found that the expression of power varied qualitatively, depending on activity inhibition. Activity inhibition is defined as the degree of restraint one feels toward the use of power. It determines whether power is expressed in socialized and controlled ways or in self-aggrandizement and impulsive aggressiveness (McClelland, 1985, p. 302).

More specifically, the socialized face of power (high need for power and high activity inhibition) is in theory characterized by efforts to assist organizational members in formulating higher-order, transcendent goals and by instilling in them a sense of power to pursue such goals. The power drive is "socialized" in the service of others. In contrast, the personalized face of power (high need for power and low activity inhibition) is characterized by the exertion of personal dominance or by seeking to "win out" over adversaries. Life is seen as a zero-sum game; power is used for personal gain or impact.

Research supporting the distinction between high and low activity inhibition is presented by McClelland. In a 1975 study, he found that individuals with greater needs for power than for affiliation but with a highly inhibited sense of power exhibited behavior characterized by respect for institutional authority, discipline, self-control, caring for others, demonstration of public concern, and a strong sense of justice. Correlations between the need for power and the presence of these behaviors with individuals high in activity inhibition ranged from .23 to .48. In contrast, for individuals low in activity inhibition, correlations were either insignificant or negative, ranging from .07 to − .35.

A longitudinal test comparing what McClelland describes as the "leadership motive pattern" (moderate to high need for power, low need for affiliation, and high activity inhibition) with long-term management success at AT&T further supports the differential effects of activity inhibition (McClelland and Boyatzis, 1982). The results revealed that managers in nontechnical jobs who possessed the leadership motive pattern upon entry into management (in comparison with nontechnical managers who did not possess this pattern) had significantly higher levels of advancement after eight and sixteen years of experience. No correlation was found between the leadership motive pattern and the level of promotion attained for technical managers.

Other studies have provided consistent support for the positive association between this leadership motive pattern and management success. For instance, McClelland and Burnham (1976) found that the subordinates of managers characterized by this pattern had higher morale and hence better sales performance than did subordinates of managers with other motive patterns. In another study, Winter (1979) reported that the leadership motive pattern was associated with success for nontechnical leadership positions in the United States Navy. There was no association between the leadership motive pattern and success for high-ranking technical officers.

In summary, the theoretical formulations and supportive research evidence presented by McClelland (1985) and McClelland and Boyatzis (1982) suggest that individual expression of the power motive varies qualitatively depending on the degree of activity inhibition. Accordingly, charismatic leaders, given their high need for power, might be differentiated by a high or low degree of activity inhibition in their expression of power. This leads to the following hypotheses:

Hypothesis 1. Charismatic leaders high in activity inhibition (socialized leaders) will express and sat-

isfy their need for power through socially constructive and egalitarian behaviors.

Hypothesis 2. Charismatic leaders low in activity
inhibition (personalized leaders) will express and
satisfy their need for power through personally
dominant and authoritarian behaviors.

Exercise of Social Influence

Given the different power motives of personalized and
socialized leaders, it may be postulated that such leaders utilize
different social influence processes. In his theory of attitude formation and change, Kelman (1958) describes three conceptually
distinct processes of social influence: compliance or exchange,
identification or affiliation, and internalization or value congruence.

Compliance occurs when individuals adopt attitudes and
behaviors in order to gain specific rewards or avoid certain
punishments. This induced behavior is instrumental in producing a satisfying social effect. Under this process, the power of
the influencing agent is based on control of rewards and punishments.

Identification occurs when an individual accepts outside
influence in order to establish or maintain a satisfying relationship with the influencing agent. Opinions adopted through identification thus are dependent on an external source and on social
support. As such, they are not integrated with the individual's
value system. The satisfaction derived from identification is due
to the act of conforming, not the specific content of the induced
behavior. According to Kelman (1958), in the identification process, the power of the influencer is based on attractiveness: The
individual possesses qualities that make a continued relationship with him or her desirable.

Internalization occurs when an individual accepts the influence of another's ideas and actions because they are congruent
with his or her own value system. The adopted behavior becomes part of a personal system as opposed to a social role

expectation; it is independent of an external source. The satisfaction derived from internalization is due to the content of the new behavior: It is intrinsically rewarding or appropriate for the context, and therefore it is instrumental. In this case, the power of the influencing agent is based on credibility—that is, expertise or trustworthiness.

Parallels between the three social influence processes proposed by Kelman and writings on transactional, charismatic, and transformational leadership can be drawn. The social influence process of compliance appears to be associated with transactional leadership. In his incisive analysis of transactional leadership, Burns (1978) suggests that the relationship between transactional leaders and their followers is entrenched in a bargaining process. Both parties to the exchange pursue their respective purposes and maintain the relationship as long as the individual needs of leader and follower can be met through a reciprocal exchange of rewards for services provided. However, as Burns (1978, p. 20) observes, while a leadership act has occurred, it is not one that "binds leader and follower together in a mutual and continuing pursuit of a higher purpose."

The process of identification appears relevant to charismatic leadership. According to Dow (1969, p. 315): "It [charisma] involves a distinct social relationship between leader and follower in which the leader presents a revolutionary idea, a transcendent image or ideal which goes beyond the immediate, the proximate, or the reasonable; while the follower accepts this course of action not because of its rational likelihood of success . . . but because of an affective belief in the extraordinary qualities of the leader. Thus the leader appeals to . . . the revolutionary image and his own exemplary qualities with which the follower may identify." Dow further states (1969, p. 308): "It is this irrational bond, or identification between leader and led, that provides the follower with an opportunity for transcendence and requires the leader, in turn, to maintain the revolutionary quality of the movement."

In accordance with Dow, other leadership scholars have argued that charisma involves strong follower identification with the leader (see Bass, Chapter Two; Downton, 1973; House,

1977; Willner, 1984). For example, in his 1976 theory of charismatic leadership, House (1977, p. 191) argues that the charismatic leader is "an object of identification by which the followers emulate the leader's values, goals, and behavior." Downton (1973), in his incisive analysis of charismatic and inspirational leadership, contends that followers form a strong commitment to the person of the charismatic leader as revealed in their unquestioning obedience to the leader's desires, in their capacity to criticize the leader, and in their tendency to impute special powers to the leader.

The process of internalization is closely linked to the notion of transformational leadership. Burns (1978, p. 4) posits that the transformational leader "looks for potential motives in followers, seeks to satisfy higher needs, and engages the full person of the follower." Such leaders appeal to higher-order values that encompass followers' more fundamental and enduring needs (Burns, 1978, p. 42). Accordingly, followers' goals and aspirations transcend their immediate self-interests and are focused on the collective purpose.

A similar analysis of the social influence process employed by inspirational (socialized) leaders is presented by Downton (1973). He contends that followers' willingness to accept the leader's initiatives stems from their belief that the leader shares their social philosophy. In essence, the leader represents the collective world view of his or her followers.

Regarding charismatic leadership, power motive patterns and social influence processes may be linked together as follows. For socialized leaders, the primary focus of the power motive is the communication of higher-order values: understanding of others, tolerance, and serving the common good. I would hypothesize that the primary source of social influence employed by socialized leaders is internalization, which emphasizes the value congruence of behavior. It should be noted, however, that socialized leaders probably employ identification as a secondary mode of social influence in order to gain followers' respect and trust in themselves and in the mission they espouse.

For personalized leaders, the focus of the power motive is to exert dominance or influence over others. It is therefore postulated that the primary source of social influence utilized by personalized leaders is identification, which emphasizes the social relationship with followers. This leads to the following hypotheses:

Hypothesis 3. Socialized leaders will exert their influence primarily through the process of internalization, which emphasizes value congruence.

Hypothesis 4. Personalized leaders will exert their influence primarily through the process of identification, which emphasizes affiliation between leader and led.

Behaviors of Socialized and Personalized Leaders

Socialized and personalized leaders appear to exhibit a common core of behaviors associated with charisma, including the ability to set high expectations for followers and express confidence in their ability to meet these expectations; create and maintain a positive image in the minds of followers, peers, and superiors; provide personal examples for followers to emulate; behave in a manner that reinforces the vision; show a high degree of confidence in themselves and their beliefs; and exhibit linguistic skill and nonverbal expressiveness (Bass, 1985; Conger and Kanungo, Chapter Three; House, 1977; House, Woycke, and Fodor, Chapter Four). These charismatic behaviors create favorable perceptions on the part of followers and foster their receptivity toward the charismatic image.

However, given the employment of different power motives and social influence processes by socialized and personalized leaders, different leader behaviors may be delineated. Socialized leaders, who make followers feel stronger and more in control of their own destinies, appear to exhibit qualitatively different behaviors than do personalized leaders, who foster followers' unquestioning trust and loyal obedience. It is argued that three behaviors differentiate socialized from personalized leaders: the articulation of a captivating vision and a set of values and beliefs to which leaders want followers to subscribe; the leader's recognition of the individual needs of followers; and the intellectual stimulation of followers.

Expression of Goals and Values. Socialized leaders express goals that are follower driven—that is, they appeal to subordinates' fundamental and enduring needs. More specifically, socialized leaders articulate general and comprehensive values that reflect the felt needs, wants, and aspirations of both leaders and followers (Burns, 1978). Goals are mutual and shared. Hence, leaders and followers are bound together in the pursuit of a common purpose.

In contrast to socialized leaders, personalized leaders articulate goals that come from within themselves—that is, they are leader driven. In particular, a leader's private motives are displaced onto followers and rationalized in terms of follower interest (Burns, 1978). These personal motives may or may not coincide with follower needs; it is the leader's intention that predominates (Burns, 1978).

Since personalized leaders express their own views, not followers' views, it is likely that more radical missions that break with tradition may be espoused. Leaders are not constrained by followers' needs, aspirations, and desires; they are driven by a highly personalized vision. Accordingly, the expression of "explosively novel" innovations and solutions (Shils, 1965, p. 199) is more probable.

Recognition of Follower Needs. Another distinctive behavior of socialized leaders is individualized consideration: the leader's developmental and individualistic orientation toward followers (Bass, 1985). According to Bass, the leader, by recognizing the needs, aspirations, and values of followers, provides examples and assigns tasks to followers on an individual basis to help them significantly alter their abilities and motivation. Therefore, through individualized consideration, socialized leaders engage followers and help them develop in their own right (Avolio and Bass, 1987).

Personalized leaders recognize followers' wants and needs only to the degree necessary to achieve their goals. Burns (1978) argues that such leaders search for the lowest common denominator of motives among and within followers and exploit those motives for their own rather than followers' benefit. Thus, personalized leaders objectify their followers, viewing them as objects to be manipulated. Adolf Hitler provides an illustration of this depersonalization of followers. According to biographer Richard Hughes (1962, p. 266), Hitler saw the universe as containing no persons other than himself—only things. Personalized leaders appeal to follower wants and needs not for developmental purposes but to advance their own purposes.

Intellectual Stimulation. According to Burns (1978) and Bass (1985), a distinctive behavior of transforming leaders is intellectual inspiration and stimulation of followers. In Burns's (1978, p. 163) view, transformational leaders in the political arena have "a capacity to conceive values or purpose in such a way that ends and means are linked analytically and creatively and that the implications of certain values for political action and governmental organization are clarified." Therefore, a fundamental component of transformative power is the expression of analytical and normative ideas in order to change social milieus (Burns, 1978).

Bass (1985), in his discussion of transformational leadership, has extended Burns's conceptualization by explicitly recognizing the impact of the leader's intellectual creativity on followers' thinking. According to Bass, intellectual stimulation encompasses the leader's ability to suggest creative, novel ideas that result in a discrete leap in the followers' conceptualization, comprehension, and discernment of the nature of problems and their solutions. Avolio and Bass (1987) contend that the transformational leader attempts to instill in followers the ability to question not only established views but, eventually, those espoused by the leader. Through intellectual stimulation, the socialized charismatic leader coaches followers to think on their own and to develop new ventures that will further the group's goals.

Based on the above contentions, the following hypotheses are advanced with respect to the behaviors of socialized and personalized leaders:

Hypothesis 5. The behaviors of socialized leaders include articulating goals that originate from followers' fundamental wants, recognizing followers' needs in order to help them develop in their own right, and stimulating followers intellectually.

Hypothesis 6. The behaviors of personalized leaders include articulating goals that originate from leaders' private motives or intentions and recognizing followers' needs only to the degree necessary to achieve leaders' goals.

The Effects of Personalized and Socialized Charismatic Leaders

The different power motives, social influence processes, and behaviors discussed above have interesting implications with respect to their effects. Two can be readily identified: (1) in the followers' response to the leader, and (2) in perpetuation of the leader's charisma.

Followers' Response to Leaders. By expressing goals that followers want and by communicating confidence in their followers' abilities to accomplish these goals, socialized leaders strengthen and inspirit their followers to accomplish these goals (McClelland, 1975). Followers appear to become empowered and ultimately converted from followers to leaders. Graham (1982) terms this phenomenon "autonomous followership." She suggests that preserving the capacity of followers to act autonomously is essential to maintaining the possibility of effective leadership in the future.

Writings on transformational leadership effects support this view of follower autonomy. According to Burns (1978, p. 4), the result of transformational leadership is a "relationship of mutual stimulation and elevation that converts followers into leaders and may convert leaders into moral agents." A consistent view of follower effects is offered by Bass (1985). He proposes that transformational leaders cause followers to become more independent, self-directed, self-actualized, and altruistic.

Examples of socialized leadership effects on promoting follower autonomy and empowerment are prevalent in the literature. For instance, in an experiment designed by Winter (1967), business school students viewed a film of John F. Kennedy delivering his inaugural address. After viewing the film, the students wrote short imaginary stories to a series of TAT stimuli. Content analysis of the thoughts of students revealed that they felt strengthened, inspired, and more confident relative to a group of students exposed to a neutral control film. Using a similar methodology, consistent findings have been reported by Stewart and Winter (1976) and Steele (1977).

To cite a further example, in a case study of a charismatic superintendent in a midwestern school district facing a budgetary crisis, Roberts and Bradley (see Chapter Nine) observed that a crucial component of her charismatic power was the superintendent's ability to help people see what their skills were and to encourage them to take risks and apply their talents. According to Roberts, this socialized leader empowered or energized people by providing opportunities for personal initiative, responsibility, and participation in decision making. In this case, the leader encouraged people to use their ideas and see if they worked.

According to McClelland (1975, p. 259), personalized leaders, by force of their overwhelming persuasive powers and authority, evoke feelings of obedience or loyal submission in followers. Followers appear to surrender their power to the leader and become dependent on him or her. Graham (1982) calls this phenomenon "habituated followership": Followers embrace their subordinate status so completely that failure to comply with the leader's requests is unthinkable.

Followers' unquestioning trust and obedience is a common theme in writings on charisma (Downton, 1973; House, 1977; Weber, [1924] 1947). In his discussion of charismatic authority, Weber (pp. 358–359) observed that charisma involves a purely personal relationship between leader and led. Due to their love, passionate devotion, and enthusiasm, followers willingly subscribe to the charismatic leader and his or her mission. In his theory of charismatic leadership, House (1977) proposes similar charismatic effects on followers: willing obedience to the leader, unquestioning acceptance of the leader, loyalty to and affection for the leader, identification with and emulation of the leader, and trust in the correctness of the leader's beliefs.

Illustrations of the effects of personalized leaders in creating follower dependence are observed in the literature. For example, Smith and Simmons (1983) give a detailed account of leader effects on followers in a new facility for emotionally disturbed children. The medical director, labeled by these investigators as charismatic, had a personally powerful presence and captivating dream of an ideal service organization. Interviews with new staff members revealed that a compelling force in their joining the medical facility was the opportunity to work with the director, who had such a clear vision of their organization's future. In delegating program planning to his clinical staff, the director, however, demanded control. When action plans were proposed by the staff, the director often vetoed them because they did not meet his vision. Accordingly, he fostered dependency and compliance among his clinical staff leading to an avoidance of needed confrontations and to an undermining of the staff's capacity and willingness to take initiative. Ultimately, the staff revolted and began working to undermine him.

An in-depth analysis of the strategies employed by the Reverend Jim Jones to foster an extraordinary degree of psychological submission among his followers is presented by Johnson (1979). Jim Jones used several means to strengthen his position of power and thereby create follower dependence: Members were required to sever their ties with the outside (including their families), contribute all their resources to the group, and migrate to an isolated environment in Guyana. Accordingly, followers became highly dependent on their leader for meeting their social, emotional, and material needs. Jim Jones's unwillingness to allow followers to be individualistic precluded their growth toward autonomy. Rather, through his actions, Jim Jones developed an adoring and totally compliant fellowship (Rutan and Rice, 1981).

The preceding theoretical arguments and illustrations lead to the following hypotheses regarding socialized and personalized effects on followers:

Hypothesis 7. Socialized leaders, by strengthening and inspiriting their followers to accomplish higher-order goals, create follower autonomy and empowerment.

Hypothesis 8. Personalized leaders, by evoking feelings of obedience and loyal submission in followers, create follower dependence and conformity.

Perpetuation of Charisma. For each social influence process, Kelman (1958) has described the conditions under which it manifests. He contends that behavior through *identification* occurs when an individual's relationship to the influencing agent is salient. As noted earlier, behavior adopted through identification not only is tied to an external source (that is, the influencing agent), but it also depends on social support. It is further argued that if a satisfying self-defining relationship is not maintained, identification will be discontinued. The effect of identification on an individual's responses is consistent with Weber's ([1924] 1947) notion of charismatic authority. As Weber notes (pp. 358–359), if charismatic leaders fail to benefit their followers, their charismatic authority will likely disappear.

These conceptual arguments have implications for the perpetuation of the personalized leader's charisma. Specifically, continuing identification with the personalized leader depends on the maintenance of a satisfying relationship with the leader. If this condition is not met, the potency of the ideas and actions espoused by personalized leaders and their effects on followers will decline.

According to Kelman (1958), behavior through *internalization* occurs under conditions when values are perceived to be shared and relevant regardless of the salience of the relationship with the influencing agent. As Kelman (1958) observes, if individuals change their perceptions of the conditions for value maximization, the induced response will be extinguished. This suggests that followers' accomplishment of a mission is independent of the leader's presence. Accordingly, the potency of ideas and actions espoused by the socialized leader should be perpetuated given the continuing relevance of the mission for the followers.

From the above conceptual arguments, the following hypotheses are proposed regarding the perpetuation of charisma:

Hypothesis 9. The potency of ideas and actions espoused by the socialized leader should be perpetuated beyond the tenure of the leader given the continued meaningfulness of the values for followers.

Hypothesis 10. The potency of ideas and actions espoused by the personalized leader will only be perpetuated given the maintenance of a satisfying relationship between leader and follower. If this relationship is attenuated, then the potency of the personalized leader will decline.

Implications of Socialized and Personalized Leadership for Organizational and Individual Effectiveness

The theory of socialized and personalized charismatic leadership developed in this chapter has important implications for organizational effectiveness and individual well-being. The functional and dysfunctional consequences of these leaders are briefly outlined below.

Personalized Leadership. From an organizational perspective, personalized leaders may have both desirable and deleterious effects. In times of crisis, for example, personalized leaders might be very beneficial for organizational health. By espousing a radical vision that offers a possible functional solution for overcoming distressful conditions, personalized leaders may serve as a source of organizational renewal and redirection. Moreover, by virtue of their overwhelming presence and dominance, these leaders can harness the energies of followers to single-mindedly devote themselves to the cause and to the leader. Such sustained efforts on the part of followers may speed organizational revitalization.

Beyond the crisis phase, however, the long-term effectiveness of an organization may be jeopardized by personalized leaders. For example, in order to perpetuate their charismatic image, these leaders may create stressful circumstances. They may subvert institutional innovations in order to pursue their own course of action or propound values that are personally based, not organizationally derived. Therefore, in the long run, personalized leaders may represent a very unsettling and disruptive force in the organization, inappropriate for the stability and continuity of the existing structure, systems, and culture.

From an individual perspective, personalized leaders appear to have negative effects on followers' personal growth and career development. By fostering followers' dependence, conformity, and obedience, personalized leaders undermine followers' motivation and ability to challenge existing views, develop independent perspectives, and undertake new ventures. In the short run, followers' capacity for independent thought and action may be impaired. Ultimately, the personalized leaders' effort to win devotion and commitment of followers may turn to the tyranny of thought control and brainwashing.

Socialized Leadership. Adopting an organizational view, socialized leaders appear to have a positive effect on organizational life. By expressing followers' wants, needs, and aspirations, socialized leaders represent a force for evolutionary, not revolutionary, changes that are aligned with organizational interests. In addition to serving as a positive force for change, socialized leaders raise the level of consciousness of human conduct and the ethical aspirations of both leader and led (Burns, 1978). Accordingly, socialized leaders may transform and elevate the values and conduct of the organization.

Socialized leaders also appear to enhance individual effectiveness. By encouraging followers to think on their own, to question established ways of doing things, and to focus on their collective purpose, socialized leaders mobilize their followers' potential for the independent pursuit of activities, creative action, and personal development. Accordingly, these leaders may develop a cadre of possible future leaders, not followers (Burns, 1978). Therefore, the pool of talent necessary for executive succession may be expanded.

Toward the Future: Implications
for Theoretical Development and Research

In this chapter, I have proposed a theory to explain the variances we see in charismatic leaders. However, further theoretical developments are clearly required. As discussed in the introduction, transitions between socialized and personalized leadership are conceivable. In addition, leaders may manifest both socialized and personalized behaviors, utilize a variety of social influence processes, and obtain a range of follower responses. For example, a personalized leader might utilize all three influence processes (compliance, identification, and internalization) with primary emphasis on identification. Given certain circumstances, a different influence process might be employed as a secondary mode.

Further theoretical development is also needed with respect to other predispositions (in addition to need for power) that distinguish socialized and personalized leaders. For example, the level of socioemotional maturity or of generalized self-efficacy may differ for these leadership forms. As well, personality characteristics that predispose followers to support or oppose leaders need to be explored. For instance, are followers with an external locus of control, a low need for dominance, and low tolerance for ambiguity more receptive to a personalized leader than are followers with an internal locus of control, a high need for dominance, and high tolerance for ambiguity?

Situational contingencies that might influence followers' receptiveness to and acceptance of socialized and personalized leaders need to be determined. Perhaps followers may be more willing to embrace a personalized leader during times of crisis. As several leadership scholars have observed (Halpin, 1954; Korten, 1968; Mulder, Ritsema van Eck, and de Jong, 1970; Mulder and Stemerding, 1963; Torrance, 1954; Tucker, 1970; Weber, [1924] 1947; Ziller, 1955), people in need of deliverance from distress more easily respond with great emotional fervor to a leader who offers or strengthens faith in that possibility. A state of acute distress predisposes people to perceive extraordinary qualities and to follow with enthusiastic loyalty a leader offering salvation from distress (Tucker, 1970; Weber, [1924] 1947). Under these circumstances, personalized leaders who exert personal dominance and authority may be more appropriate from the followers' perspective. However, to speculate, as crisis subsides or pressures abate, receptivity to the personalized leader may decline.

It also seems probable that socialized leaders emerge during times of crisis. Franklin Delano Roosevelt, for example, won the American presidency at the nadir of the nation's worst depression. However, in contrast to personalized leadership, there may be more opportunities for socialized leadership in less intense situational contexts. For example, House and Singh (1987) contend that egalitarian (socialized) charismatic leaders may be appropriate for situations requiring creativity, adaptability to changing conditions and uncertain environments, extraordinarily high initiative, and personal assumption of responsibility on the part of followers.

Another area for further exploration is the emotional responses of followers to socialized and personalized leadership. Do both leadership forms equally inspire love and hatred in followers? Or are personalized leaders, given their focus on personal dominance, more likely to polarize followers, commanding allegiance, reverence, and loyalty among supporters and generating hatred, animosity, and fear among opponents? A related issue to be addressed is the basis for follower commitment to the leader. For instance, followers' willingness to accept personalized leaders' initiatives, which may be interpreted as a manifestation of devotion to the leader, might be a facade rooted in followers' fear of punishment (Downton, 1973, p. 77).

In addition to theoretical developments, testing of the hypotheses advanced in this chapter is required. Three research methodologies can be proposed for such testing. First, following the methodology used in Chapter Four, the motivational imagery in the speeches of charismatic leaders could be content analyzed for low and high activity inhibition. Second, field studies might be conducted to test the proposed theory. Using Bass's Multifactor Leadership Questionnaire, profiles of charismatic (personalized) and transformational (socialized) leaders could be obtained.

To determine the differential use of social influence processes by these leaders, followers' identification and internalization could be measured using O'Reilly and Chatman's (1986) instrument. Third, laboratory experiments could be designed in which confederate leaders would be trained to display either personalized or socialized behaviors. Their effects on their followers' task performance, task identification, and satisfaction and the followers' relationship with the leader could then be measured. The convergence of findings from these multiple methodologies would strengthen the validity of the theory's propositions.

Conclusion

A significant gap in our current thinking about charisma is the lack of delineation between different forms of charisma. To date, a wide range of leadership has been captured by the generic label "charisma." However, in order to aid scientific inquiry, it is critical for organizational scholars to distill the elements that differentiate leaders as disparate as Mahatma Gandhi, Adolf Hitler, Franklin Delano Roosevelt, Jim Jones, and Martin Luther King, Jr. To that end, this chapter has attempted to distinguish between socialized and personalized leaders with respect to their power motives, social influence processes, behaviors, and effects on followers and on the perpetuation of charisma. By differentiating these two forms of charismatic expression, the possibilities and limitations for organizational and individual effectiveness are highlighted. It is hoped that by identifying socialized and personalized leaders in advance we can eventually enhance the effectiveness of such leaders and minimize their dysfunctional outcomes in organizations.

References

Avolio, B. J., and Bass, B. M. "Charisma and Beyond." In J. G. Hunt (ed.), *Emerging Leadership Vistas.* Elmsford, N.Y.: Pergamon Press, 1987.

Bass, B. M. *Leadership and Performance Beyond Expectations.* New York: Free Press, 1985.

Bennis, W., and Nanus, B. *Leaders: The Strategies for Taking Charge.* New York: Harper & Row, 1985.

Burns, J. M. *Leadership.* New York: Harper & Row, 1978.

Clark, B. R. *The Distinctive College: Antioch, Reed and Swarthmore.* Hawthorne, N.Y.: Aldine, 1970.

Dow, T. E. "The Theory of Charisma." *Sociological Quarterly,* 1969, *10,* 306–318.

Downton, J. V. *Rebel Leadership: Commitment and Charisma in the Revolutionary Process.* New York: Free Press, 1973.

Etzioni, A. *A Comparative Analysis of Complex Organizations.* New York: Free Press, 1961.

Graham, J. W. "Leadership: A Critical Analysis." Paper presented at annual meeting of the Academy of Management, New York, Aug. 1982.

Halpin, A. W. "The Leadership Behavior and Combat Performance of Airplane Commanders." *Journal of Abnormal and Social Psychology,* 1954, *49,* 19–22.

House, R. J. "A 1976 Theory of Charismatic Leadership." In J. G. Hunt and L. L. Larson (eds.), *Leadership: The Cutting Edge.* Carbondale: Southern Illinois University Press, 1977.

House, R. J., and Singh, J. V. "Organizational Behavior: Some New Directions for I/O Psychology." *Annual Review of Psychology,* 1987, *38,* 669–718.

Howell, J. M. "Charismatic Leadership: Effects of Leadership Style and Group Productivity on Individual Adjustment and Performance." Unpublished doctoral dissertation, Faculty of Commerce and Business Administration, University of British Columbia, Vancouver, 1986.

Howell, J. M., and Frost, P. J. "A Laboratory Study of Charismatic Leadership." *Organizational Behavior and Human Decision Processes,* forthcoming.

Hughes, R. *The Fox in the Attic.* New York: Harper & Row, 1962.

Johnson, D. P. "Dilemmas of Charismatic Leadership: The Case of the People's Temple." *Sociological Analysis,* 1979, *40,* 315–323.

Kelman, H. C. "Compliance, Identification, and Internalization: Three Processes of Attitude Change." *Journal of Conflict Resolution,* 1958, *2,* 51–60.

Korten, D. C. "Situational Determinants of Leadership Structure." In D. Cartwright and A. Zander (eds.), *Group Dynamics: Research and Theory*. New York: Harper & Row, 1968.

McClelland, D. C. "The Two Faces of Power." *Journal of International Affairs*, 1970, *24*, 29–47.

McClelland, D. C. *Power: The Inner Experience*. New York: Irvington, 1975.

McClelland, D. C. *Human Motivation*. Glenview, Ill.: Scott, Foresman, 1985.

McClelland, D. C., and Boyatzis, R. E. "Leadership Motive Pattern and Long-Term Success in Management." *Journal of Applied Psychology*, 1982, *67*, 737–743.

McClelland, D. C., and Burnham, D. H. "Power Is the Great Motivator." *Harvard Business Review*, 1976, *54* (2), 100–111.

McClelland, D. C., Davis, W. N., Kalin, R., and Warner, R. *The Drinking Man*. New York: Free Press, 1972.

Mulder, M., Ritsema van Eck, J. R., and de Jong, R. D. "An Organization in Crisis and Non-Crisis Situations." *Human Relations*, 1970, *24*, 19–41.

Mulder, M., and Stemerding, A. "Threat, Attraction to Group and Need for Strong Leadership: A Laboratory Experiment in a Natural Setting." *Human Relations*, 1963, *16*, 317–334.

O'Reilly, C., and Chatman, J. "Organizational Commitment and Psychological Attachment: The Effects of Compliance, Identification, and Internalization on Prosocial Behavior." *Journal of Applied Psychology*, 1986, *71*, 492–499.

Peters, T. J., and Waterman, R. H., Jr. *In Search of Excellence*. New York: Harper & Row, 1982.

Roberts, N. C. "Transforming Leadership: Sources, Process, Consequences." Paper presented at annual meeting of the Academy of Management, Boston, Aug. 1984.

Rutan, J. S., and Rice, C. A. "The Charismatic Leader: Asset or Liability?" *Psychotherapy: Theory, Research, and Practice*, 1981, *18*, 487–492.

Shils, E. A. "Charisma, Order, and Status." *American Sociological Review*, 1965, *30*, 199–213.

Smith, K. K., and Simmons, V. M. "A Rumpelstiltskin Organization: Metaphors on Metaphors in Field Research." *Administrative Science Quarterly*, 1983, *28*, 377–392.

Steele, R. S. "Power Motivation, Activation, and Inspirational Speeches." *Journal of Personality,* 1977, *45,* 53–64.

Stewart, A. J., and Winter, D. G. "Arousal of the Power Motive in Women." *Journal of Consulting and Clinical Psychology,* 1976, *44,* 495–496.

Tichy, N. M., and Devanna, M. A. *The Transformational Leader.* New York: Wiley, 1986.

Torrance, E. P. "The Behavior of Small Groups Under Stress Conditions of Survival." *American Sociological Review,* 1954, *19,* 751–755.

Trice, H. M., and Beyer, J. M. "Charisma and Its Routinization in Two Social Movement Organizations." *Research in Organizational Behavior,* 1986, *8,* 113–164.

Tucker, R. C. "The Theory of Charismatic Leadership." In D. A. Rustow (ed.), *Philosophers and Kings: Studies in Leadership.* New York: Braziller, 1970.

Weber, M. *The Theory of Social and Economic Organization.* (A. M. Henderson and T. Parsons, trans.; T. Parsons, ed.) New York: Free Press, 1947. (Originally published 1924.)

Willner, A. R. *The Spellbinders: Charismatic Political Leadership.* New Haven, Conn.: Yale University Press, 1984.

Winter, D. G. "Power Motivation in Thought and Action." Unpublished doctoral dissertation, Department of Psychology, Harvard University, 1967.

Winter, D. G. *Navy Leadership and Management Competencies: Convergence Among Tests, Interviews, and Performance Ratings.* Boston: MA, McBer, 1979.

Ziller, R. C. "Leaders' Acceptance of Responsibility for Group Action Under Conditions of Uncertainty and Risk." *American Psychologist,* 1955, *10,* 475–476.

8

Origins of Charisma:
Ties That Bind
the Leader and the Led

Manfred F. R. Kets de Vries

The concept of charisma not only has fascinated sociologists, political scientists, historians, psychologists, and organizational theorists, but it has also captured the imagination of the popular press. It has become a household word. Yet, notwithstanding the existence of a literature on the topic, remarkably little insight has been shed on the psychological origins of charisma. The question of what psychological forces make for the mysterious, almost mystical, bind between leader and led has been largely left unanswered.

Etymologically, charisma means a gift of grace, being favored by the gods. Church historian Rudolf Sohm (1892) used this term for the first time, although in the context of religious transformations. As Conger and Bass have pointed out, it was the sociologist Max Weber ([1924] 1947) who popularized and broadened the concept to describe qualities of a leader "by virtue of which he is set apart from ordinary men and treated as endowed with supernatural, superhuman, or at least specifically exceptional powers or qualities." According to Weber, these powers or qualities are "not accessible to the ordinary person, but are regarded as of divine origin or as exemplary, and on the basis of them the individual concerned is treated as a leader" (pp. 358–359).

237

Unfortunately, in widening the scope of charisma, Weber did not really solve the mystery of the strange bond between leader and led. His analysis of charismatic authority remained largely at a descriptive level. He glossed over the concept and emphasized more traditional and rational or legal authority.

What Weber did say, however, is that charismatic individuals differ in their capacity to inspire personal loyalty apart from the authority derived from an office or status. Charismatic leadership is extraordinary; it is a gift of grace possessed mainly by prophets or religiously inspired reformers. Such leaders are regarded with a sense of awe and mystery and are expected to perform heroic deeds. Thus, charismatic leadership has a salvationistic or messianic quality. Charisma becomes "the quality which is imputed to persons, actions, roles, institutions, symbols, and material objects because of their presumed connection with 'ultimate,' 'fundamental,' 'vital,' order-determining powers" (Shils, 1968, p. 386). Furthermore, charismatic leaders are products of their times. They seem to emerge particularly during periods of uncertainty and unpredictability—in short, at crisis points in history. At the same time, they, in turn, succeed in influencing the events that helped them rise to power. According to Weber, charismatic leaders become prominent in times of psychic, physical, economic, ethical, religious, or political distress. In stable, well-functioning societies, there is less need for the services of such individuals.

To some extent, it might appear that charismatic leadership is a function of the need for order. Yet, paradoxically, in providing "deliverance," truly charismatic leadership tends to be revolutionary in that it may conflict with the established order. But charismatic leaders resolve this dilemma by creating order out of disorder: They provide their followers with new systems of coherence, continuity, and justice. It appears that charismatic leaders are very skilled in channelling grievances and diverging interests into a common goal; they provide a focus for others. And, by behaving in this way, they become creators of meaning. Thus, charismatic leaders "offer salvation in the form of safety, or identity, or rituals, or some combination of these" (Tucker, 1968, p. 740). But this search for renewal has limits, since "the pure charismatic hero bases his prophecy on values that have been central to the past; those values, in order to be radical or revolutionary, must be deviant or at least not central to ongoing established institutions" (Bensman and Givant, 1975, p. 584).

When we study the life histories of truly heroic charismatic leaders, we find that they seem to have gone through a difficult period of gestation before coming to power. During this period—which may be a real or an imaginatively reconstructed portrait of their personal history—the themes of ordeal and adversity, so common in myths, come to the fore. It appears that such leaders may create a "family romance," a kind of fairy tale, which narrates in great detail how after many adversities the real origin of the pure, poor, persecuted prospective leader is finally discovered. As with a mythical hero, the prospective charismatic leader may paint a picture of having been subjected to certain rites of passage—trials, if you will—to prepare him or her for the formidable tasks at hand. Thus, in the behavior and actions of mythical heroes and charismatic leaders we can find many parallels.

Although Weber may have been aware that certain— not necessarily conscious—forces are at work, he did not have the advantage of psychoanalytical insights to help him understand the deeper structures that influence behavior and action (Geertz, 1973, 1983; Kets de Vries and Miller, forthcoming). Furthermore, his view on what charisma really is and when it applies may have been too limited. In fact, what is called charisma can be considered part of a more widely spread phenomenon. Even quite ordinary people who find themselves in a position of leadership cannot escape it. Thus, journalists may have a point in using a rather loose definition of charisma, applying it to any leader with popular appeal. Charismatic elements are present in *all* forms of leadership and derive from a complex psychological interaction process between leaders and followers. To further explain this complex process, a psychoanalytical approach to the origin and limits of charisma is offered in this chapter. I explore and identify some of the psychological forces that affect both leaders and followers and suggest possible conditions under which charisma may or may not manifest. I also examine the potential negative effects that charismatic leadership may have on both the leader and the led.

Taking Advantage of the "Historical Moment"

For leaders to be effective, some kind of congruence is needed between their own and societal concerns. What gives truly effective leaders such conviction and power is their ability to articulate the underlying issues of a society. In trying to resolve their own personal struggles, they manage to project them onto their involvement in and solution of the problems of society at large. What seems to happen is that a leader's vision becomes the concern of all. According to Erikson (1958, 1969), using such dramatic examples as Martin Luther and Mahatma Gandhi, such leaders transform their own personal struggles into universally shared concerns, trying to solve for all what they originally could not solve for themselves; internal, private dialogues are transformed into external public concerns.

This identification of the connection between a public and a private crisis was noted by the political scientist Harold Lasswell in his seminal work, *Psychopathology and Politics* (1960). According to Lasswell, the distinctive mark of the *homo politicus* is the displacement of private motives onto public objects and, at the same time, the rationalization of these motives in terms of the public interest. Intrapsychic conflicts are acted out on the public stage. The effectiveness of this process of externalization, however, depends on "the leader's ability to draw upon and manipulate the body of myth in a given culture and the actions and values associated with these myths to legitimize his claims by associating with himself the sacred symbols of the culture" (Willner and Willner, 1965, p. 77; Willner, 1984).

Thus, collective symbols are made proxy for self-symbols (Lasswell, 1960, p. 186). Part of the leadership phenomenon, therefore, seems to be a myth making process whereby the leader's role in the myth is to make sense by creating continuity between past, present, and future. Charismatics facilitate the transformation of a historical or mythical ideal from a remote abstraction into an immediate psychological reality (Zaleznik and Kets de Vries, 1985). Thus, one aspect of leadership seems to be " 'cultural management,' in part conscious and deliberate, in part probably unconscious and intuitive" (Willner and Willner, 1965, p. 83). Speeches, ceremonies, and rituals are some of the vehicles that make this a successful process. To quote Marshall McLuhan, "the medium becomes the message."

Because of the effects of the mass media on contemporary leadership, the term *pseudocharisma* has been introduced (Bensman and Givant, 1975, p. 602). We can observe today the manipulation of propaganda techniques and the use of opinion polls to create an image of leadership: "The procedures employed are no different from those used in the creation of movie, theatrical, or television plays" (Bensman and Givant, 1975, p. 606). And, when the polls do not oblige and support the leaders' ideas, they can always resort to such rationalization devices as "the silent majority" to give their actions credibility and create support, even if imaginary.

Playing an important role in making people susceptible to manipulation, contributing thereby to the presence of charisma, is the process of projection. A leader is legitimized by the perceptions of his or her followers. Projective processes seem to play a major role in the myth making and symbolic action that form these perceptions. Propelled by the ambiguity and complexity of the events around us, we choose leaders to make order out of chaos. Leaders become the ideal outlets for assuming responsibility for otherwise inexplicable phenomena. Ascribing power to leaders becomes our way of dealing with helplessness. Thus, it seems that even if no one with leadership abilities were available, we would have to create such a person. The mere presence of an individual willing to take on the leadership role facilitates the organization of experience and in doing so helps us acquire a sense of control over our environment—even if this is only illusory (Meindl, Ehrlich, and Dukerich, 1985).

Through these attributional, projective processes, leaders become the recipients ("container") of other people's ideals, wishes, desires, and fantasies (Bion, 1959). They become imbued with mystical, charismatic qualities, whether they possess them or not. And, in accepting this role, they may turn into master illusionists, keeping those fantasies alive and conjuring up images of hope and salvation that may replace reality. Naturally, in this attributional process of projecting themes of one's own inner world onto the leader, role expectations by the followers of appropriate leader behavior—or what can be called the rules of the game—will have a boundary effect as to what is permissible. In one way or another, leaders are expected to recognize these boundaries, making them an essential factor in guiding their behavior.

As I mentioned before, these attributional-projective mechanisms occur particularly in times of distress. Anomie, upheaval, and crisis make for a sense of helplessness and may give rise to forms of collective regression. We should remember, however, that not only do leaders induce regression in others, but they also can fall victim to it themselves.

When followers fall victim to regression, they may revert to primitive patterns of behavior, demonstrating quite clearly how easily archaic psychological processes can emerge and affect action. Freud described what can happen when people get together in groups in this way: "All their individual inhibitions fall away and all the cruel, brutal and destructive instincts, which lie dormant in individuals as relics of a more primitive epoch, are stirred up to find gratification" (Freud, 1921, p. 70).

The Influence of Transference

According to Freud (1921), the appeal of leaders is that at a symbolic, unconscious level they represent the return of the primal father. What seems to happen psychologically is that, in fantasy, the followers replace their own ego ideal—the vehicle by which they measure themselves—with their unconscious version of the leader's ego ideal. When this occurs, the leader facilitates a reconciliation between the two agencies of the mind, the ego—the mental structure that mediates between the person and reality—and the ego ideal. Reconciliation between these two agencies reduces tension and thus can lead to a sense of euphoria. When this happens, all the followers' exaggerated wishes will be projected onto the leader. With their own demands and prohibitions dissipated and transferred to the leader, they feel a sense of community. The leader becomes the conscience of the group. The followers no longer feel harassed by prohibitions; they have no more pangs of conscience. A group ego ideal comes into being that serves all, and with it comes an abdication of personal responsibility. Followers now identify not only with the leader but also with each other in that they share a common outlet of identification. Freud noted: "We know that in the mass of mankind there is a powerful need for an authority who can be admired, before whom one bows down, by whom one is ruled and perhaps even ill-treated . . . that all the characteristics with which we equipped the great man are paternal characteristics. . . . The decisiveness of thought, the strength of will, the energy of action are part of the picture of a father . . . but above all the autonomy and independence of the great man, his divine unconcern, which may grow into ruthlessness. One must admire him, one must trust him, but one cannot avoid being afraid of him too" (1939, pp. 109–110).

Freud compared the bond between leader and followers to the act of falling in love or the state of trance between hypnotist and subject. When this identification process occurs, followers may indulge in an "orgy" of simple and strong emotions and may be swept along by the leader's appeal. Although Freud does not discuss this explicitly, at the heart of this psychological process is a dynamic called transference. Leaders facilitate transference reactions. They are ideal outlets for the crystallization of primitive and unstable identifications.

Transference is a universal phenomenon. It can be described as some kind of "false connection" (Breuer and Freud, 1893–1895), a confusion in time and place. Individuals perceive others and respond to them as they would have reacted to important figures in their past. Attitudes from early family life repeat themselves in the present. It can be said that every long-standing interpersonal relationship is in some ways a new edition of an old alliance. In many ways, individuals transfer what they experienced in relationships of the past onto those of the present (Greenson, 1967; Langs, 1976).

Transference is the basis for all enduring human relationships. But it is also a major source of distortion. Instead of remembering relationships of the past and adapting this knowledge to build better current relationships, individuals often misunderstand the present in terms of their past. They relive the past in current actions, repeating the same mistakes. In an effort to cope with their early conflict-ridden relationships, they may fall back upon older, stereotyped behavior patterns. Unconsciously, they may try to relive bygone relationships in a way that lays them to rest, that resolves their own inadequacy. This revives irrational, archaic structures of personality, causing behavior that is overreactive, underreactive, or bizarre. The careful observer may notice that the person in question responds to others as if they were mother, father, sibling, or some other important figure from the past.

As authority figures, leaders are prime outlets for these types of emotional reactions. Leaders easily revive previously unresolved conflicts with significant figures from the past. In these situations, regressive behavior may occur: Followers may endow their leaders with the same magic powers and omniscience they attributed in childhood to parents or other significant figures. Moreover, transference reactions can be acted out in different ways and may affect both leaders and followers. Conceptually, we can distinguish three types: idealizing, mirror, and persecutory reactions (Kets de Vries and Miller, 1984).

In the type of transference called *idealization,* subordinates may begin to idolize their leaders, to ascribe ideal and thoroughly unrealistic qualities to them. This can be seen as an attempt to revive an earlier phase of life, when parents were looked upon as all-powerful and perfect. In such situations, a strong wish persists to recapture this original state of bliss through union with the person perceived as omnipotent (Kohut, 1971; Kohut and Wolf, 1978). This childhood illusion is not easily given up. Fantasies linger on about the powers of the early caretakers. Although at one level of consciousness they know that it cannot be, some people prefer to pursue this make-believe throughout life. Doing so helps maintain the fantasy that some of the qualities of the admired person will be acquired. Having a relationship with others whom they can admire makes those who behave in this way feel better. Projecting one's own opinions and values onto others and identifying with them becomes a way of affirming one's own existence and can enhance self-esteem.

As authority figures, leaders reactivate lingering dependency needs and often act in such a way as to help create and maintain these illusions. Thus, one facet of the leadership function is the leader as magician—the master illusionist. In a magical way, the leader seems to become a "go-between"—the person able to reinstate for followers the illusion of absolute self-sufficiency and lost perfection. And, when drawn in, followers may seem intoxicated, behaving like sleepwalkers. They may have so much invested in an unreal image of their leader that they are blinded to the leader's faults.

Particularly during periods of upheaval, this search for "paradise lost" comes to the fore. At such times, followers experience increased dependency needs. They may feel lost and torn in different directions, and they may even experience a sense of loss of identity. A leader can reverse this process of identity confusion by providing a focus. By responding to and accommodating their needs for identity, security, and protection, the leader may develop followers who will do anything in the form of appeal, support, or ingratiation. They will please and charm the leader; they will give in to any whim or fancy. This type of behavior, however, puts great pressure on the leader to come through. And, unfortunately, no matter what he or she does, the leader will never be able to satisfy the followers completely.

In the case of mirror transference, we are dealing with the other side of the coin. This involves individuals' love of self-display—their desire to get attention from others. And although this inclination tends to be universal, leaders are more susceptible to it than most people. It is very hard to imagine, unless one has had the experience, what it means to be the object of excessive admiration by followers—even in instances in which some of it may be warranted. The leader's display of narcissism reverberates in the followers; followers recognize themselves in the leader.

Some leaders, in being exposed to a great deal of attention, eventually may find it hard to maintain a firm grasp on reality and thus distinguish fact from fantasy. Too much admiration can have dire consequences for the leader's mind: He or she eventually may believe it all to be true—that he or she really is as perfect, as intelligent, or as powerful as others think is the case—and act accordingly. Moreover, this belief may be intensified by the fact that leaders have something going for them that ordinary mortals don't have: They frequently have the power to turn some of their fantasies into reality. If this happens, we may see the beginning of a self-propelled cycle of grandiosity.

Of course, also bringing such wishes to the fore is the fact that at the base of mirror transference is an archaic memory of grandiose omnipotence—the remembrance of when the individual, as a child, wanted to display his or her evolving capabilities and be admired for them. In order for leaders to experience their "grandiose sense of self," they need others to provide "nourishment" through confirming and admiring responses (Kohut, 1971; Kohut and Wolf, 1978).

Often, however, this strong need to display oneself represents an attempt to counteract a sense of worthlessness and a lack of self-esteem. At a deeper level, such individuals view those with whom they interact as the parents who were never empathetic enough, who never had much patience or were uninterested in their children. These individuals are still searching for mirroring parents; they crave constant attention and admiration. Unfortunately, their own overwhelming needs make them unable to have empathy for others. It is "their turn" now, and they surround themselves with obsequious yes-men who are willing to provide accolades and worship on a regular basis.

Mirror transferences, then, become complementary to idealizing transference reactions—the former being the desire to be applauded, admired, and revered; the latter the propensity to comply with that desire. Thus, idealizing and mirror transference reactions mutually reinforce each other, enhancing the leader's narcissism. Of course, the distinction between mirror and idealizing reactions is only a conceptual one. In practice, these processes occur simultaneously.

If leaders fall victim to these regressive forces, they may

become preoccupied with fantasies of unlimited success and power. They may constantly search for attention and may wish to demonstrate their mastery and brilliance. Encouraged by their subordinates, they may take on overly ambitious projects and engage in unrealistic actions. Because of their desire for grandiosity, they tend to gravitate toward subordinates with high dependency needs, people in search of an all-knowledgeable, all-powerful, and care-giving leader. But the followers may be in for a shock. Preoccupied with grandiosity and having become intolerant of criticism, such leaders can become callous about the needs of their subordinates. They may exploit them and then drop them when their followers no longer serve their purposes.

Given the likely enhancement of narcissistic tendencies in leaders, blaming them for callous behavior may be a realistic complaint. It is another matter altogether, however, for the followers to blame the leader for failing to live up to their own exaggerated expectations. This, unfortunately, is what tends to happen. No leader can really sustain the primitive idealization of the followers; no one can be a perfectly gratifying object. There are always going to be frustrating experiences. The outcome of not meeting the "tacit promise" is predictable. We should not forget that rebellious hatred is the counterpart of idealization. Angry about the frustration of their dependency needs, and perhaps aggravated by callous, exploitative behavior, subordinates eventually may react by vengefully devaluating their leaders. Highly dissatisfied, they may engage in hostile, rebellious acts. Thus, not only is the leader the recipient of praise and admiration, but he or she may be the target of a considerable dose of overt and covert aggression.

The probability that aggressive feelings will emerge is facilitated by early developmental experiences. Even in the early years, a child's parents or caretakers cannot always be completely satisfying. At times, they may not be available, which may cause frustration. This results in childhood anger directed at the caretakers. However, for fear of losing those who are the main source of satisfaction (combined, perhaps, with the belief in the mythical world of the young child that angry feelings can kill), a switch occurs: These feelings are split off and directed toward others. The child reasons that the "good object" didn't do it, so "others" are to blame; they are the ones responsible, causing it to happen (Klein, 1948; Kernberg, 1976, 1985; Mahler, Pine, and Bergman, 1975).

Studies of human development indicate that this primitive way of dealing with the stresses and strains of life is not limited to childhood. Some people easily revive this way of behaving in adulthood. People who are so inclined will divide, in an overly simplified way, all experiences, perceptions, and feelings into unambiguously "good" and "bad" categories. Of course, in doing so they ignore the complexity and ambiguity inherent in all human relationships; instead, they rely on simple, strong, polarized feelings between unbridled hatred, fear, and aggression on the one hand and overidealization on the other. Such people refuse to accept that the same person can have both "good" and "bad" qualities.

When this psychological process occurs, we see how attitudes of idealization can quickly change into devaluation when people feel that their needs are not being met. Followers are fickle; they can easily change their minds. There seems to be no middle road. Thus, subordinates will unload their anger onto their leaders, who, for their part, may not be able to "contain" this anger and therefore counterreact. Hence, given the pressures placed upon them, leaders may feel persecuted. Unable to control their aggressive feelings, they look for victims and retaliate. They themselves will "split" the world into those who are with them and those who are against them. If they take this route, it will make for a delusory world filled with saints, heroes, victims, and scapegoats. No wonder paranoia is considered one of the major "diseases" of leadership.

Projection and projective identification are defense mechanisms that accompany splitting (Ogden, 1982). These defense mechanisms help ward off persecution by "bad" objects. What seems to happen is that unwanted aspects of the self are externalized and attributed to (projected onto) others. People who act in this way never experience a sense of personal responsibility but always blame someone or something else.

In the context of these three interdependent transference reactions, it is interesting to note a not uncommon defense called "identification with the aggressor" (Freud, 1936; Kets de Vries, 1980). This defense mechanism explains why followers continue to be attracted to leaders in spite of their abhorrence, at another level, of the leaders' violent acts. At the core of it all is the followers' illusion—which they cling to as a way of overcoming their own fears—that through identification they can incorporate aspects of the perceived omnipotence of the leader.

The followers' unconscious wish behind this "merger" is that they will become as powerful as the aggressor. Hence, an illusory transformation occurs whereby instead of being the helpless victim the follower convinces him- or herself that he or she is in control. Thus, followers may behave as insensitively toward "outsiders" as their leaders do, having appropriated the latters' particular symbols of power. Meanwhile, their feelings toward their leaders will alternate between love, affection, and fear. Naturally, followers who adopt this defense mechanism share the outlooks of their leaders and support them even if the leaders engage in unrealistic, grandiose schemes or imagine the existence of malicious plots, sabotage, and enemies.

Conclusion

Charisma loses some of its mystery when we understand the influence of transferential processes. Transference, which, according to Jung, is the alpha and omega of clinical treatment (Storr, 1979), is also the key to understanding what otherwise would remain a puzzling phenomenon. We have seen how transferential processes can exert an enormous regressive pull—in the process blurring the boundaries between reality and fantasy. It is this potential for distortion that is the corrupting power of charisma. The limits of charisma are broken when we no longer can distinguish fact from fantasy, when reality testing becomes suspended. If that is the case, we may be swept away by these human dynamics. So we begin to understand some of the potential problems and dangers that charismatic leadership can present—that it has a potentially negative side as well as a positive one.

Paradoxically, although these same regressive forces may give rise to irrational, even pathological behavior—in normal circumstances, a cause of deep concern—in specific situations these may be exactly the kinds of qualities needed for effective leadership. The leader's unique vision, the unrestrained abandonment to achieving a certain aim, distorted as it may be— his or her way of managing aggression may be very functional, as it can break an existing state of inertia. In the process, powerful forces will come to the fore, which, if not closely monitored, may eventually run out of control. And remembering that leaders can wield enormous power and that their actions can have a fateful effect on many, that prospect is frightening. We should never forget that the more positive boundaries of charisma are easily broken. Given the existence of a bipolar self (Kohut, 1971), with its dormant needs of mirroring and idealizing and its potential for excess, charismatic processes require constant vigilance.

It is important for both leaders and followers to be cognizant of the existence of the destructive side effects of charisma, for this realization is the first step toward corrective action. Clinical research has revealed that if individuals are made aware of their transference reactions, these valuable insights into behavior can be stepping stones to productive change. When we notice frequent mood shifts, sudden irritability, feelings of envy, a sense of being watched, an excessive concern about what others think, or the continuous need for an audience, we may be on the track to possible transference distortions.

Charismatic leaders and their followers can minimize transference distortions. This requires not only mature leadership but also mature followership. Unfortunately, rare is the leader who balances action with reflection and distinguishes fact from fantasy. And even rarer is the leader who recognizes the need for boundaries when the formidable forces that make for charisma have been unleashed.

References

Bensman, J., and Givant, M. "Charisma and Modernity: The Use and Abuse of a Concept." *Social Research,* 1975, *42* (4), 570–614.

Bion, W. R. *Experiences in Groups.* London: Tavistock, 1959.

Breuer, J., and Freud, S. "Studies on Hysteria." In J. Strachey (ed. and trans.), *The Standard Edition of the Complete Psychological Works of Sigmund Freud.* Vol. 2. London: Hogarth Press and the Institute of Psychoanalysis, 1893–1895.

Erikson, E. H. *Young Man Luther.* New York: Norton, 1958.

Erikson, E. H. *Gandhi's Truth: On the Origins of Militant Non-violence.* New York: Norton, 1969.

Freud, A. *The Ego and the Mechanisms of Defense.* (Rev. ed.) New York: International Universities Press, 1936.

Freud, S. "The Interpretation of Dreams." In J. Strachey (ed. and trans.), *The Standard Edition of the Complete Psychological Works of Sigmund Freud.* Vol. 5. London: Hogarth Press and the Institute of Psychoanalysis, 1900.

Freud, S. "Group Psychology and the Analysis of the Ego." In J. Strachey (ed. and trans.), *The Standard Edition of the Complete Psychological Works of Sigmund Freud.* Vol. 18. London: Hogarth Press and the Institute of Psychoanalysis, 1921.

Freud, S. "Moses and Monotheism." In J. Strachey (ed. and trans.), *The Standard Edition of the Complete Psychological Works of Sigmund Freud.* Vol. 23. London: Hogarth Press and the Institute of Psychoanalysis, 1939.

Geertz, C. *The Interpretation of Culture.* New York: Basic Books, 1973.

Geertz, C. *Local Knowledge.* New York: Basic Books, 1983.

Greenson, R. R. *The Technique and Practice of Psychoanalysis.* Vol. 1. New York: International Universities Press, 1967.

Kernberg, O. *Object Relations Theory and Clinical Psychoanalysis.* New York: Aronson, 1976.

Kernberg, O. *Internal World and External Reality.* New York: Aronson, 1985.

Kets de Vries, M.F.R. *Organizational Paradoxes: Clinical Approaches to Management.* London: Tavistock, 1980.

Kets de Vries, M.F.R., and Miller, D. *The Neurotic Organization: Diagnosing and Changing Counterproductive Styles of Management.* San Francisco: Jossey-Bass, 1984.

Kets de Vries, M.F.R., and Miller, D. "Interpreting Organizational Text." *Journal of Management Studies,* forthcoming.

Klein, M. *Contributions to Psychoanalysis, 1921–45.* London: Hogarth Press, 1948.

Kohut, H. *The Analysis of the Self.* New York: International Universities Press, 1971.

Kohut, H., and Wolf, E. S. "The Disorders of the Self and Their Treatment: An Outline." *International Journal of Psychoanalysis,* 1978, *59,* 413–426.

Langs, R. *The Therapeutic Interaction.* 2 vols. New York: Aronson, 1976.

Lasswell, H. D. *Psychopathology and Politics.* (Rev. ed.) New York: Viking Penguin, 1960.

Mahler, M. S., Pine, F., and Bergman, A. *The Psychological Birth of the Human Infant.* New York: Basic Books, 1975.

Meindl, J. R., Ehrlich, S. B., and Dukerich, J. M. "The Romance of Leadership." *Administrative Science Quarterly,* 1985, *30,* 78–102.

Ogden, T. H. *Projective Identification and Psychotherapeutic Technique.* New York: Aronson, 1982.

Shils, E. "Charisma." In D. L. Sills (ed.), *International Encyclopedia of the Social Sciences.* Vol. 2. New York: Macmillan and Free Press, 1968.

Sohm, R. *Kirchenrecht.* 2 vols. Leipzig, E. Germany: Duncker & Humblot, 1892.

Storr, A. *The Art of Psychotherapy.* New York: Methuen, 1979.

Tucker, R. "The Theory of Charismatic Leadership." *Daedalus,* 1968, *97,* 731–756.

Weber, M. *The Theory of Social and Economic Organization.* (A. M. Henderson and T. Parsons, trans.; T. Parsons, ed.) New York: Free Press, 1947. (Originally published 1924.)

Willner, A. R. *The Spellbinders: Charismatic Political Leadership.* New Haven, Conn.: Yale University Press, 1984.

Willner, A. R., and Willner, D. "The Rise and Role of Charismatic Leaders." *Annals of the American Academy of Political and Social Science,* 1965, *358,* 77–88.

Zaleznik, A., and Kets de Vries, M.F.R. *Power and the Corporate Mind.* (Rev. ed.) Chicago: Bonus Books, 1985.

9

Limits of Charisma

Nancy C. Roberts
Raymond Trevor Bradley

This chapter describes a longitudinal study of a charismatic leader. The study used a theoretical framework (Bradley, 1987) that distinguishes three levels of charisma: charisma as a social category, charisma as a social relationship, and charisma as a social structure. In our in-depth study of a school district superintendent, we observed the manifestation of charisma at each of these three levels. Interestingly, when the superintendent was later appointed a state commissioner of education, no evidence of charisma was to be found. From a comparative analysis, we discovered that the requisite elements for charisma at all three levels were absent in the second setting. By specifying the necessary and sufficient ingredients at each level, we suggest that there are inherent limits to the transfer of charisma. In the following sections, we describe the context of the study, the theoretical framework used in the study, the design, empirical assessment, and implications of the results for both theory and practice of charismatic leadership.

Note: Funds for the support of this study came from the Research Foundation of the Naval Postgraduate School, Department of Administrative Science, Monterey, California. Earlier research, from 1983 to 1985, was supported by the Minnesota Research Program, which in turn received its funding from the Organizational Effectiveness Research Program, Office of Naval Research (Code 4420E), under contract no. N00014-84-K-0016. We would like to express our thanks to the commissioner and to others who gave so generously of their time and energy to make this research possible.

Context

The governor's appointment of the "midwestern" super-intendent as his commissioner of education came as no surprise to school personnel. Her work as superintendent of a large, midwestern, suburban district had drawn much media atten-tion and legislative interest during her two-year tenure in of-fice. She had gained wide acclaim for her massive grass-roots program to cut $2.4 million from the budget while at the same time successfully avoiding the "bloodletting" of retrenchment. The superintendent's encouragement of innovation also had opened a floodgate of new ideas, many coming from teachers who enthusiastically participated in brainstorming sessions to envision the school system of the future. Ultimately, the super-intendent's "horizons speech" to the state legislature, outlin-ing the challenges to education and the need for restructuring on a statewide basis, won support for her goals and an appoint-ment from the governor, who was committed to change and in-novation in public education.

The superintendent's appointment as commissioner was significant for several reasons. From a political perspective, the governor was willing to invest some of his political capital to change the law concerning the appointment process. His successful action angered traditional education groups, which fought to prevent the "politicization of education" and to maintain the State Board of Education's control over the com-missioner's appointment. This controversy began a two-year battle with "the education establishment" over policy initia-tives and legislative reform, which culminated in name call-ing and a media fight during the legislative session of 1984–1985 (Mazzoni, 1986a).

From an educational perspective, the commissioner was a self-proclaimed change agent who called for a "restructuring of the schools." Her ideas introduced a new vision for public education: decentralized schools with greater teacher-parent con-trol; foundations to manage business ventures, employee health care, and investment and retirement programs; joint business activities with corporations; new relationships with colleges and universities; expanded learning opportunities for students; and statewide testing to assess competency and measure learner outcomes (Mazzoni and Sullivan, 1985; Roberts and King, 1987).

More importantly, from a research perspective, the commissioner's appointment provided a unique opportunity for an indepth, longitudinal assessment of a charismatic leader (Roberts, 1985). Opportunities to observe charismatic leadership over time, other than those afforded by historical data (see Schweitzer, 1984; Willner, 1984), have been rare (Zablocki, 1971, 1980; Trice and Beyer, 1986; Bradley, 1987). What is unique is that during the course of this study the charismatic leader was promoted from her position as a district superintendent to the much more complex job of state commissioner of education. This unanticipated development made it possible to ask an important question: Would she have the same charisma in her new office that she had had in her old one? In other words, can charisma transfer from one setting to another?

While the two positions and their situations were very different—with different constituencies, offices, and contexts—they shared an important element: namely, the person in the leadership position. This presented a strategic research opportunity. With the individual "held constant" in this way, the relative contribution of contextual, structural, and individual factors to the emergence of charisma could (to some extent) be identified. Thus, by observing this person in both positions, as well as the events that unfolded in each setting, it would be possible to make a comparative assessment of an individual's contribution to a charismatic "effect." Furthermore, since this leader purposely set out to duplicate the effect she believed she had initiated as superintendent, the question of whether charisma can be deliberately created (Bass, 1987; Howell, 1987) or re-created (Willner, 1984) could be examined as well. At the very least, the novelty of the research setting promised some determination of the conditions associated with the extent of an individual leader's charismatic effect.

Theoretical Framework

The theoretical framework described in this section is taken from Bradley's earlier work (1987; see the chapter on rethinking charisma in his book for more detail). This framework formed the basis of our study. In our everyday thinking, we see charisma as a variable phenomenon. We recognize that it can occur in a variety of ways, at different levels in society, and with varying degrees of intensity—producing a wide range of possible consequences. Most often, the term is used to capture the inexplicable powers of persuasion that a particular individual is believed to possess. These powers represent a great potential for influence and change; they are in some special way magical or mystical in nature. The person who possesses them is set apart from everyone else.

At other times, we use the term to acknowledge that something more is present—that a powerful, all-encompassing relationship exists between the charismatic individual and his or her followers. So strong is the belief in the leader's charismatic powers that the followers place their destinies in his or her hands. It is as if they have fallen under a magical spell; they become submissive, obedient, enraptured—blind in their absolute loyalty. The charismatic's authority over them seems boundless.

Finally, we occasionally use the term *charisma* to describe a revolutionary structure that is boiling with explosive levels of collective energy and awesome in its potential for radical social change. We think of a charismatic structure in quantum terms: When it is successful, it can result in a radically new social order that represents a fundamental break with the past; or, if it fails, it may implode in a cataclysm of self-destructive energy.

These common usages of charisma represent three different concepts or levels of charisma: charisma as a social category, charisma as a social relationship, and charisma as a distinctive form of social organization (Bradley, 1987). Each corresponds to a separate level of social reality—the normative, the relational, and the organizational—nested in a hierarchical order so that each incorporates the preceding level. In addition to being grounded in our everyday notions of charisma, these concepts capture what is essential and clarify what is distinctive about the phenomenon in its different levels of manifestation.

Charisma as a Social Category. At the most elemental level, charisma is a social category—a social definition in a social system's normative framework that identifies and labels certain individual qualities as charismatic. Normatively, there are two elements in the attribution of charismatic qualities to an individual. The first is a belief that this person is endowed with extraordinary powers and abilities—extraordinary in that they are seen as exemplifying perfection and, accordingly, rare (Roth, 1975; Willner, 1984). Such qualities can be almost any highly refined talents or abilities that a group may project onto an individual (Schiffer, 1973; Schweitzer, 1974–1975). The second is the belief that there is a divine or supernatural basis to the exceptional powers, that they cannot be understood in everyday terms (Friedrich, 1961; Willner, 1984). Such powers, therefore, are not available to the ordinary person; they are perceived as a "gift of grace" (Weber, [1924] 1947).

Charisma as a Social Relationship. To move beyond this nominal level, charisma must be incorporated into a social relationship. This occurs when a relationship of "rule" has been established—when others submit to an individual as their leader because they believe that this person possesses charismatic qualities (Weber, 1946, p. 295). But, relationally, more than acknowledgment of authority is involved: This person's leadership is seen as the means to otherwise unattainable ends, which, experientially, engenders strong bonds of gratitude and love as well.

Building on the distinction between "leadership" and "authority" (Bierstedt, 1954), Bendix (1960) highlights the notion that Weber had two kinds of charismatic relationships in mind. One is Weber's pure type of charismatic rule in which "the exercise of power is bound up with a concrete person and his distinctive qualities" (Bendix, 1960, p. 307). Bendix labels this *charismatic leadership*. It is a personalized relationship between the leader and followers based on their recognition of the leader's qualities as a uniqe individual. Consequently, this charisma is not transferable to anyone else.

In order to be transferred, charismatic rule must undergo "routinization" and be transformed into a "depersonalized" quality. This second type of charismatic relationship is routinized charisma (charisma of an office), and it adheres to any incumbent of a position or office that is regarded as charismatic (see Chapter Two). As a result, it "may be transmitted to the members of a family or become the attribute of an office or institution regardless of the persons involved" (Bendix, 1960, p. 308). Bendix labels the second type of relational charisma *charismatic authority*.

Charisma as an Organizational Form. At the third level, charisma is more than a special bond between a leader and the led. As a system for radical social change, it liberates the energy from an established order and realigns it in a new mold. It is a transitional structure, a distinctive transformational mode of collective organization.

Consistent with this concept, Bradley's (1987) analysis of forty-six communal organizations shows that two relational patterns differentiate charismatic from noncharismatic structures. The first is communion, a highly charged, collective union of fraternal love. It is an intense emotional bonding of everyone with everyone else, and it generates strong feelings of collective affection and common identity.

Communion is the power plant in a charismatic system. It breaks down the roles and distinctions of established order to release social energy. It thus generates the extraordinary intensity and quantity of energy needed for social metamorphosis (see Bradley, 1987, Chapters 5 and 6). A group must generate, harness, and align this energy toward collective ends if it is to accomplish its desired radical change. But, as studies of collective behavior (Blumer, 1951; Turner and Killian, 1957; Smelser, 1962) and communes (Zablocki, 1971, 1980; Bradley, 1987) have shown, collective energy is negatively correlated with social stability.

To regulate collective and individual behavior, maintain stability, and institutionalize a new social mold, therefore, a charismatic group must implement mechanisms for social control. Accordingly, Bradley (1987, Chapter 6) has identified a second relational pattern characteristic of charismatic systems: a strong, coherent structure of collective power. As a single, densely interlocking power hierarchy connecting all and centralized under the charismatic leader, this structure is patterned to contain and realign the energy generated by communion. In short, at this third level charisma is conceptualized as a distinctive form of social organization—a complementary system of communion and collective power structured for the achievement of radical change (Bradley and Roberts, 1987).

Study Design and Method

The data for this study were drawn from multiple sources. Research collected at the district level began in 1983 in a midwestern suburban school district, at which time the leader was still a superintendent. Data consisted of archival material, participant observation of meetings and informal gatherings, and formal interviews with teachers, administrators, staff, parents, students, central office personnel, and school board members (see Roberts, 1985, for details).

At the state level, the research involved twenty-two formal taped interviews with the commissioner conducted from the fall of 1983 to September 1987. In addition, Roberts was a participant observer in the Governor's Discussion Group, an eighteen-month task force chaired by the commissioner. This group was charged with creating a "visionary proposal for state education." Roberts also accompanied the commissioner on speaking engagements, observing presentations to teachers and superintendents on both formal and informal occasions.

The commissioner was observed as she conducted meetings with her cabinet and staff and during legislative hearings, press conferences, and informal interactions with members of the Department of Education. Her personal schedule, notes, and calendar, as well as the department's plans and activities, were all open for this analysis. To supplement this information, official documents, interest group reports, and newspaper accounts about the commissioner and the Department of Education were examined. And, finally, to get a broader perspective on the commissioner—her programs, her impact, and her effectiveness—twenty-five formal interviews were conducted with state legislators and with representatives from the governor's office, the Department of Education, school boards and school district staffs, teacher unions, lobbyists, and other special-interest groups. Roberts also consulted colleagues who had conducted recent studies of the Department of Education's innovative legislative proposals.

Empirical Assessment

District-Level Analysis. At the school district level, all three levels of charisma were manifest during the superintendent's tenure in office. Charisma as a social category was evident in the descriptions of her made by school personnel, students, parents, and other community members. She was seen as a "mover," a "shaker," a "visionary"—a leader who had made a dramatic, unprecedented impact on the district. People believed that she had extraordinary talents. One administrator put it the following way: "I have told her many times there is no way [anybody] will fill your shoes. I have never met a soul like you; you have got to be one out of a million, and I doubt if we can find the second one."

In her relationships with district members, charisma also was evident in the special bond people felt with the superintendent and in the way they perceived her as their leader. For example, one teacher who had worked closely with her on several task forces and projects said that the superintendent had virtually a "cult-like" following in the district. In describing this special connection they experienced, people talked of mutual support, respect, and caring. Another associate captured it well: "I have never felt a closer relationship to a team of people that I work with. . . . I think [the superintendent's] enthusiasm is very contagious, and to know her is to love her, to work with her is to respect her. And because of that I would have to say she has the executive council pulling in her direction. Now, that does not mean that on every small issue or large issue that we all feel the same as she does. But she doesn't demand that of us; she demands loyalty, but she also respects our opinions. I feel that very strongly." According to evidence from interviews, observations, and archival records, this special relationship was not due to any charisma vested in the office of superintendent.

No attribution of charismatic qualities has been made to any superintendent who preceded her in the ten years prior to her arrival or who has followed her in the four years since her departure.

Charisma also was manifest in the school district at the structural level, as a collective force for social change. To mobilize the energies of district personnel, a number of communion-generating programs were implemented. Outside consultants were brought in to conduct workshops to facilitate the creation of a new vision of the future. Task forces to investigate district policy and budget problems were formed. And a process of participatory management was introduced to involve all interested people in district decision making. As one district member summed it up: "Well, it's the superintendent's style to make a lot of people involved. She brings the administration and teachers and people within the community all into task forces and seminars and workshops. . . . There aren't many things that are worked on in private. . . . Her philosophy is involvement with the greatest number of people. . . . Many superintendents are locked in a chain of command sort of thing. She seeks out input from people whom superintendents have traditionally ignored."

Results from these actions were impressive. Citizens' meetings attracted some 2,000 people to participate in a budget reduction process. Teachers in woodshop classes wanted to make buttons that read "I love kids and I love the superintendent." Staff in the district office displayed their enthusiasm with "I work for the superintendent" buttons. Other teachers wrote letters to her about how much she meant to them. Still others would respond with applause whenever she spoke. The superintendent called the experience "mind shattering"—a "marvelous experience."

One poignant event warrants special mention. After a scheduled forty-minute presentation to district staff, teachers besieged the superintendent, asking for more of her time to discuss the various initiatives the district was pursuing. Their request turned into a four-hour "dialogue" with 800 people, in which the superintendent shared her hopes, her dreams, her past, her disappointments. Many were moved to tears, including the superintendent. A critical point in the exchange came in answer to a question of how people could be certain that what she and the school board promised would indeed occur. The superintendent's response was, "Well, I guess you just have to trust us. I trust you." Dead silence followed as everyone drew in their breaths and held them for a moment or two. Later, upon being asked about the meaning of what had occurred, people responded that the superintendent had made her point: She had trusted them with her thoughts, hopes, and feelings; they, in turn, would trust her. That was what the "dialogue" and "honesty" were all about. Mutual trust had created a bond between the superintendent and the audience.

To channel the energy and enthusiasm that had been mobilized and keep the change effort focused, the superintendent instituted a number of formal and informal regulatory systems. Earlier in her tenure, she had removed a number of personnel from the district office, eliminated positions, reassigned people to local school sites, and redesigned jobs to capitalize on the talents of those she had recruited to work with her in the district. In addition, she had established clear, formal guidelines (policies, regulations, and procedures) so that people understood her expectations and were aware of strategies and options for action.

As one example, she and the district's principals had worked out a set of joint expectations for the principals' performance each year. The principals then developed action plans and time lines for implementation, and sent the superintendent weekly reports of their activities. In addition, they met with her at least once a week and pursued matters of mutual concern more deeply in a joint retreat every four to five months.

On an informal basis, the superintendent set up a number of temporary task structures to deal with the budget crisis facing the district. This loosely coupled system of groups and networks ran parallel to the formal organization and provided an important mechanism for generating districtwide recommendations for change. A highly participatory process, it introduced more flexibility and responsiveness than could be provided by the protocols and routines of the formal structure.

The charismatic structure that evolved resulted in some dramatic changes in the district. Budget reductions were scheduled without acrimonious debate. The school board unanimously approved the superintendent's budget reductions after only a brief discussion. Teachers awarded her a standing ovation, despite her recommendations to cut support jobs and program funding. Innovative ideas poured in from district personnel during in-service programs. At the end of her two years as superintendent, the district had catalogued over 300 suggestions for innovative ventures. Many of these came from teachers who now felt "empowered" to be creative.

Transfer of Charisma: The State Level. The commissioner took over as head of the Department of Education in the summer of 1983. Her model of change for the state educational system was identical to the one she had used for the district: Begin with a mission and a vision that outline where one wants to go; generate enthusiasm and support for the vision at the grass-roots level, with district visits, task forces on various educational topics and issues, and a "dialogue" among the citizens; create a structure for change at the Department of Education that will serve to channel the interest and energy into innovative programs; and, finally, institutionalize the programs through the legislative process.

The commissioner's progress in implementing her change model during the first year was impressive. The commissioner and her "team" personally visited almost all of the 435 districts in the state—something no commissioner had ever done before. This visibility gave the commissioner and her ideas wide exposure in both the local and the state media. Having known almost all 800 teachers and staff by name during her superintendency, she was eager to see firsthand what was happening throughout the state and to make personal contact with as many educators as possible. Building a network of support for her restructuring ideas and her new vision of education was a major goal.

To broaden the interest and participation in education, the commissioner initiated a series of "town meetings" with community groups in school districts throughout the state. She called it the "[state] dialogue." The purpose was to give everyone a chance to say what "he or she thinks the public schools should accomplish." The meetings, held in 388 public school districts, drew almost 15,000 citizens.

In conjunction with the dialogue, 250,000 questionnaires were distributed to poll public opinion on a number of issues, such as achievement-based (rather than age-based) student advancement, statewide student testing, a greater instructional role for parents, and changes in the school day and the school year. Some 173,000 public school students in kindergarten through twelfth grade joined these activities to give their opinions about education. Survey responses from 191,400 people were compiled by the Department of Education. The commissioner's objective was to time the survey results for the 1984 legislative session and use the findings to develop proposals for the 1985 session.

The structure for channeling and focusing this grass-roots activity had been put in place when the commissioner assumed office. Among her first actions was a "major management shuffle," the first in a decade. She replaced the top five assistant commissioners with her own team of nine people, all from outside the Department of Education. Her intent was to bring in new experts with hands-on experience—people "who had been in the field"—rather than to rely on those whose knowledge and involvement were primarily bureaucratic. Also, having a loyal administrative staff that supported her vision was imperative. This team was to keep the change program alive—to prevent it from becoming stalemated by a bureaucracy that traditionally maintained a "low profile" and rarely attempted educational leadership. These and other "firsts" during her four-year term in office generated much visibility, interest, and activity (see Roberts, 1987, for a complete overview).

But even with this success, the question here is whether there is any evidence of charisma. While all three kinds of charisma were apparent at the district level, had this occurred at the state level? Did the commissioner's charisma transfer? At this point, the data are clear. Thus far, there is no evidence of charisma associated with the commissioner at the state level.

In hundreds of hours of interviews, observations, and interactions, nothing has been found to link charisma in any form with the commissioner—not charisma as a social category, as a social relationship, or as a distinctive pattern of social organization.

As commissioner, people described her as "hard driving," "creative," "innovative," and "committed"—comments that reflected the high regard with which she was held as a leader. But she was not seen as possessing extraordinary abilities; nor was she characterized in the awestricken terms that had been used to describe her as superintendent. She was no longer viewed as endowed with charismatic qualities.

Regarded thus, in much more ordinary terms, her relationships with people varied, reported as "fairly good," "satisfactory," or, in some cases, "poor." While some peers praised her innovative efforts, others voiced criticism (some complaining that more respect for "how things are done" at the state level was necessary). A similar variation was observed in her relationships with subordinates, which ranged from formalized cordiality or discomfort to warm, mutually satisfying, cooperative exchanges. However, the governor's view of his commissioner was consistent throughout her first term and into the first year of her reappointment: "She's been doing an excellent job." But none of these relations were charged with the intense affection, loyalty, and trust that uniformly had characterized her relationships during her superintendency.

Her programs, such as the "dialogue," state-wide survey, task forces, and district visits, were all intended to focus public attention on the schools and build a common union of interest among citizens. And while these initiatives did succeed in gathering and disseminating important data on public education, they did not generate a broad-based groundswell of enthusiasm for the commissioner and her ideas—certainly not in any way comparable to that of the district. In fact, some of her programs had to be rescued from gridlock with the finance department and the legislature by sympathetic policy entrepreneurs (change agents in government), who had engineered a direct access to the governor and his staff (Roberts and King, 1987).

Accounting for the Limits

Charisma did not transfer with the commissioner as she moved from district to state-level office. The key question is why? What are the limits to this leader's charisma? What prevented a transfer of charisma from one setting to another? In terms of our framework, what aspects of charisma—as a social category, as a social relationship, as a structure for social transformation—were missing?

From the perspective of charisma as a *social category,* some crucial elements were missing at the state level (Table 1). Previous work has identified extreme social stress in the form of threat or crisis as a necessary contextual condition for the emergence of charisma (Friedland, 1964; Schweitzer, 1984). While a collective perception of "crisis" fueled the unfolding of events at the district level, this was lacking during the commissioner's tenure at the state level. And although there were alarmed reports of "a nation at risk"—a nation threatened by a "rising tide of mediocrity" in its public schools (National Commission on Excellence in Education, 1983)—only a minority in the state heeded these warnings.

Most citizens wanted to improve their schools, not restructure them (Mazzoni, 1986b). People felt that their schools were basically sound. Improvements rather than radical changes were needed to regain momentum lost during the severe budget cuts of the early 1980s (Roberts and King, 1987). As a result, no real groundswell of support materialized for major changes in public education. Without a crisis to focus attention and provide the rationale for a fundamental restructuring of the schools, it was difficult for the commissioner to gain agreement on her vision for state education. And, most importantly, without a crisis to define the times as extraordinary, there was no call for "extraordinary leaders" and, therefore, no rationale for unorthodox proposals for radical change.

From the perspective of charisma as a *social relationship,* other key elements were missing at the state level. The authority and personal power of the superintendent/commissioner differed markedly in the two positions. Structurally, as a superintendent,

Table 1. Empirical Assessment of Charismatic Elements,
Comparing District and State Levels.

Analytical Dimensions of Charisma	Requisite Theoretical Elements	District Level	State Level
Normative:			
Charisma as a social category	Definition of situation as crisis	Public consensus of budget crisis	No consensus that state education is in crisis
	Attribution of extraordinary abilities to person or position	Collective perception of superintendent as exceptional	No collective perception of commissioner as exceptional
Relational:			
Charisma as a leadership relationship	Acknowledgment of the charismatic as leader	Perception of superintendent as empowering, virtually unlimited authority	Limited authority: accountable to governor and others
	Bond of intense mutual affection between leader and led	Widespread, intense mutual affection	Limited mutual affection
Organizational:			
Charisma as a structure for social transformation	Strong, consensual structure of collective power to align energy for transformation	Establishment of highly coordinated team	Inability to establish highly coordinated team
	Highly charged bonds of communion to generate social energy	Visits and meetings created collective affect and unity	Failure of attempts to create affective bonds of collective unity

Note: 1. The position of superintendent in the school district, by its very nature, involves a high degree of autonomy for the incumbent.
2. The size of the unit may change the nature of the relationship between the charismatic leader and the led. Larger units require moving from interpersonal face-to-face communication channels to the more impersonal channels of mass media. Observational evidence suggests that the commissioner had yet to master the necessary skills for the latter.

she had had much more control (and more autonomy) over educational matters than she was able to claim as commissioner. Furthermore, the close working relationships established at all levels of the district inspired a deep affection and trust in her leadership: She was viewed with awe.

However, there were a number of inherent constraints to the office of commissioner. Being the governor's political appointee meant acquiescing to established authority. Her first concern, therefore, was political loyalty—not to do ''anything to embarrass the governor.'' She was no longer free to initiate action as she saw fit. Now her agenda for action had to be cleared with the governor's executive office. Moreover, her stakeholder map revealed that, as commissioner, she was embedded in a much more complex web of relations among the legislature, state executive departments, constituents, interest groups and networks, and state and national educational communities (Roberts and King, 1985). Conflicting demands from the various stakeholders put her in a situation of structural ''ambivalence'' (Merton and Barber, 1976). It required a delicate, energy-consuming balancing act to mediate between competing political interests. As commissioner, she was not able to transcend the relational constraints of the existing political structure.

From the perspective of charisma as a *structure for radical social change,* other elements were missing. The communion-building programs the commissioner initiated throughout the state—the visits, the ''dialogue,'' the problem-solving task forces—were quite successful in obtaining and distributing information for program development and district needs. But these activities did not fire up the state community as they had the district community. The same mechanisms that had energized personal and program support were not effective at the state level. Missing was the commissioner's personal touch and involvement. The size of the agency, the complexity of state government, and the various committees, groups, and associations in which she participated all required that she delegate as much as possible to others. There was not enough time in her eighteen-hour day to build and maintain the close, personalized bonds that had fired her charisma as superintendent. These factors insulated her affect; her impact remained impersonal.

This lack of affective impact was particularly evident in her public speaking appearances. Required to address much larger audiences, often with full media coverage, her speeches were dry, often lacking spark and vitality. They were devoid of evocative symbols, graphic language, and inspiring metaphors—devoid of mechanisms to captivate and excite a public's imagination. The warmth, spirit, enthusiasm, and high energy that were characteristic of her one-to-one spontaneous exchanges and small group interactions did not materialize when she spoke to these larger crowds. The commissioner was not able to mobilize the intense affective energy of "communion" at the state level.

The commissioner also had problems in building the organizational system necessary to align activity and guide efforts toward educational innovation. Her attempts to restructure and restaff the Department of Education were embattled and weakened virtually from the outset. Five of her new assistant and associate commissioners, jocularly branded the "A Team" (since, as new "outside" talent, they were expected to be more effective catalysts for change than the career administrators they displaced had been), either were fired or resigned from office within the first year. Reports of morale problems over the restructuring of the department, departures of key middle managers, confusion over routine tasks and job assignments, and the demotion of career administrators reached the press. These and other internal departmental problems put the commissioner on the defensive. In addition, much of her time in the first two years went into "learning the ropes" of state government and "putting out fires" (challenges to her leadership) in the department. In short, rather than being able to build a structure that would transcend the routines of the department and free her to focus on the long-range goals of change, she found herself embroiled in the day-to-day details of established bureaucratic order.

The commissioner's charisma thus did not transfer from one setting to another. Although much was accomplished during her four years in office at the state level (Roberts, 1987), she was not able to build a charismatic organization, establish a relationship as a charismatic leader, or even effect the perception of being charismatic. The requisite mix of contextual, structural, and personal factors was missing.

Theoretical and Practical Implications

To understand why charisma was not transferred, we have used Bradley's (1987) conceptual framework. By identifying the distinctive elements of three levels of charisma, this framework provides the theoretical basis for a systematic comparison of data from the district and state settings. As summarized in Table 1, the framework brings into sharp relief the contrast between the two contexts and thus provides an understanding of why charisma, in any form, did not emerge in the state setting.

The framework also has theoretical utility as a dynamic model of the evolution of charismatic processes. It postulates a determinate sequence of movement through the three levels as charisma unfolds from its nominal manifestation, as a socially acknowledged potential for radical change, to its full-blown development organizationally, as a powerful collective force for social transformation. Specifically, the model predicts that charisma appears first as a social category and then must develop into a leadership relationship in order, finally, to evolve to its most complex social manifestation as a purposeful organization. This developmental sequence was borne out by the order in which events occurred in the district (for specific details, see Roberts, 1985).

At a general level, we can use the model to specify the necessary and sufficient conditions for the occurrence and development of charisma in other settings. It identifies the requisite ingredients for each level of charisma and explicates the developmental logic of their interrelationship.

At the normative level, the necessary condition for charisma as a social category (level one) is collective perception of crisis—the belief that some problem or challenge is so great and of such proportion that extraordinary measures (means that depart from ordinary practice) are necessary. Following from this, the sufficient condition is the identification of a particular individual who is seen as capable of resolving the crisis: This person is perceived as endowed with extraordinary, "super-human" qualities.

These elements, extreme social stress and the attribution of exceptional powers, are the necessary conditions for the development of charisma as a leadership relationship (level two). Relational charisma is built on the acknowledgment of the charismatic's special powers as the basis of authority for leadership. These awe-inspiring qualities engender strong feelings of love, optimism, and excitement, as well. Together, therefore, the dual bonds of affect and power are the sufficient conditions for relational charisma.

Movement to the third level, charisma as a structure for radical social change, requires that both normative and relational charisma be present. In other words, transformational charisma cannot develop unless (1) crisis is believed to exist and a person of extraordinary powers has been identified and (2) strong bonds of power and affection are established between this leader and the led. Given these conditions, highly charged bonds of communion and a strong collective order of power can be structured to mobilize and align the extremely high levels of energy required for social transformation. In sum, the three levels of charisma are nested in a hierarchical order in which each incorporates the level preceding it.

From this perspective, then, we view charisma as an emergent process—the consequence of a complex set of interactions among its requisite elements. It is clear from the results of this analysis that the interdependencies among contextual, structural, relational, and personal factors are so subtle and tightly interwoven that the emergence and development of charisma are not the result of any one of these factors alone. Rather, they are due to a series of reciprocal and recursive interactions among these elements—a process of co-evolution among complementary ingredients (Jantsch, 1980). Thus, according to this analysis—and contrary to Willner's (1984) position—it is certain that charisma will not result from a leader's talents and actions alone: Charisma cannot be created at will. This is strikingly apparent from the commissioner's inability to transfer charisma—her failure to recreate charisma at the state level.

This means that there are severe limits to efforts aimed at the deliberate creation of charisma. Charisma lies beyond the reach of purposeful, "rational" action: It cannot be manufactured by a leader or an organization, as Bass (1987) maintains; neither can it be simulated or fabricated in a laboratory, as Howell (1987) believes. Charisma is not something that we can "train for" or schedule; it is not something we know how to "switch on" or "switch off."

But even if charisma, or something like a "charismatic effect," could be deliberately created—that is, manufactured or trained for—there is still the ethical question: Is charisma a desirable way of doing things in this world? Charisma is a response to demanding and extraordinary times. It requires extreme social stress and crisis—at the least, the perception of crisis. It also demands a rejection of established rationality and the suspension of existing moral order. Such unusual circumstances not only mean a subjective perception of great peril; objectively, they also mean that there is, in fact, a real risk of expunging a given established order. Are the times so extraordinary that we should take such a risk and turn to charisma as a means of solving our problems? Should we not explore other processes of leadership, other means of facilitating peak performance and change, instead of surrendering to a "spellbinder" or a "pied piper"? And, if the times are not truly extraordinary and we manufacture crisis to increase the probability that someone will be viewed as charismatic, then charisma is nothing but a "con"—a manipulative deception aimed at exploiting the collective.

Conclusion

Charisma is an awesome catalyst for extraordinary collective action and change. Once triggered and manifested, its future development and consequences are unpredictable. Mobilizing enormous quantities of social energy, it can evolve (or devolve) rapidly in virtually any direction, often leaving a legacy of irreversible social implications that may continue to unfold long into the future. At present, we have neither a theory to

predict outcomes nor any practical understanding to ensure
"good" charisma and prevent "bad." We cannot say, for example, that in seeking to harvest a charisma like Iacocca's we
will not end up with a yield of destruction and violence like
Jonesville. Despite all of our efforts, we simply do not know
that much about charisma: It is still very poorly understood.
But what is known and well established by historical record is
that, as a transforming force, charisma is charged with explosive,
unpredictable potential that, like the genie when released from
the bottle, is beyond our control. Do we really want to deliberately risk unleashing its darker side?

References

Bass, B. "Charismatic and Inspirational Leadership: What's
the Difference?" Paper presented at the International Symposium on Charismatic Leadership in Management, McGill
University, Montreal, May 1987.

Bendix, R. *Max Weber: An Intellectual Portrait.* New York: Anchor
Books, 1960.

Bierstedt, R. "The Problem of Authority." In M. Berger, T.
Abel, and C. Page (eds.), *Freedom and Control in Modern Society.*
New York: D. Van Nostrand, 1954.

Blumer, H. "Collective Behavior." In A. M. Lee (ed.), *Principles of Sociology.* New York: Barnes & Noble, 1951.

Bradley, R. T. *Charisma and Social Structure: A Study of Love
and Power, Wholeness and Transformation.* New York: Paragon
House, 1987.

Bradley, R. T., and Roberts, N. C. "The Dynamics of Charismatic Transformation: The Paradox of Love and Power."
Paper presented at annual meeting of the International Society
of Political Psychology, San Francisco, July 1987.

Friedland, W. H. "For a Sociological Concept of Charisma."
Social Forces, 1964, *43,* 18-26.

Friedrich, C. "Political Leadership and the Problem of Charismatic Power." *Journal of Politics,* 1961, *23,* 3-24.

Howell, J. "The Socialized and Personalized Faces of Charismatic Leadership." Paper presented at the International

Symposium on Charismatic Leadership in Management, McGill University, Montreal, May 1987.

Jantsch, E. *The Self-Organizing Universe: Scientific and Human Implications of the Emerging Paradigm of Evolution*. Elmsford, N.Y.: Pergamon Press, 1980.

Mazzoni, T. "The Choice Issue in State School Reform: The Minnesota Experience." Paper presented at the annual meeting of the American Educational Research Association, Apr. 1986a.

Mazzoni, T. "Educational Choice and State Politics: A Minnesota Case Study (1983–1985)." Unpublished manuscript, School of Education, University of Minnesota, 1986b.

Mazzoni, T., and Sullivan, B. "State Government and Educational Reform in Minnesota, 1983–1984." Unpublished manuscript, School of Education, University of Minnesota, 1985.

Merton, R. K., and Barber, E. "Sociological Ambivalence." In R. K. Merton, *Sociological Ambivalence and Other Essays*. New York: Free Press, 1976.

National Commission on Excellence in Education. *A Nation at Risk: The Imperative for Reform*. Washington, D.C.: U.S. Government Printing Office, 1983.

Nicolis, G., and Prigogine, I. *Self-Organization in Nonequilibrium Systems: From Dissipative Structures to Order Through Fluctuations*. New York: Wiley-Interscience, 1977.

Prigogine, I., and Stengers, I. *Order out of Chaos: Man's New Dialogue with Nature*. New York: Bantam Books, 1984.

Roberts, N. C. "Transforming Leadership: A Process of Collective Action." *Human Relations*, 1985, *38* (11), 1023–1046.

Roberts, N. C. "Transforming Leadership: A Process of Collective Action, Part II." Unpublished manuscript, Naval Postgraduate School, Monterey, Calif., 1987.

Roberts, N. C., and King, P. J. "The Stakeholder Audit: A Key Political Tool in the Change Process." Paper presented at the annual Academy of Management meeting, San Diego, Calif., Aug. 1985.

Roberts, N. C., and King, P. J. "The Dynamic Process of Policy Innovation: The Catalytic Function of Policy Entrepreneurs." Paper presented at the Minnesota Innovation Research Project Symposium, Minneapolis, May 1987.

Roth, G. "Socio-Historical Model and Development Theory: Charismatic Community, Charisma of Reason, and the Counter Culture." *American Sociological Review,* 1975, *40,* 148–157.

Schiffer, I. *Charisma: A Psychoanalytic Look at Mass Society.* New York: Free Press, 1973.

Schweitzer, A. "Theory of Political Charisma." *Comparative Studies in Society and History,* 1974–1975, *16,* 150–181.

Schweitzer, A. *The Age of Charisma.* Chicago: Nelson-Hall, 1984.

Smelser, N. J. *Theory of Collective Behavior.* London: Routledge and Kegan Paul, 1962.

Trice, H. M., and Beyer, J. M. "Charisma and Its Routinization in Two Social Movement Organizations." *Research in Organizational Behavior,* 1986, *8,* 113–164.

Turner, R., and Killian, C. *Collective Behavior.* Englewood Cliffs, N.J.: Prentice-Hall, 1957.

Weber, M. *From Max Weber: Essays in Sociology.* (H. Gerth and C. W. Mills, trans.) New York: Oxford University Press, 1946.

Weber, M. *The Theory of Social and Economic Organization.* (A. M. Henderson and T. Parsons, trans.; T. Parsons, ed.) New York: Free Press, 1947. (Originally published 1924.)

Willner, A. R. *The Spellbinders: Charismatic Political Leadership.* New Haven, Conn.: Yale University Press, 1984.

Zablocki, B. D. *The Joyful Community.* New York: Penguin Books, 1971.

Zablocki, B. D. *Alienation and Charisma: A Study of Contemporary American Communes.* New York: Free Press, 1980.

10

Developing Transformational Leaders: A Life Span Approach

Bruce J. Avolio
Tracy C. Gibbons

"In archaic societies, the appropriate way to honor progenitors, mythical or actual, is to repeat their gestures and their sacred words. In 'modern societies,' the way to show esteem and honor is not to repeat but to build on; not ritually to invoke but productively to extend; not to follow in the footsteps but to widen the path" (Wapner and others, 1983; p. 111).

Much of the discussion in the previous chapters of this book has concentrated on the nature and the limits of charismatic leadership. In this chapter, our intent is to expand the discussion of charisma in the context of transformational leadership within a framework of developmental theory. Our primary objective is to explain how charismatic leaders develop themselves and their followers.

In introducing the idea of development into an analysis of charismatic leadership, we make several assumptions. First, the development of charismatic leadership is assumed to be a transformational leadership process. Second, transformational leaders are assumed to be charismatic as well as intellectually stimulating, inspirational, and so forth; thus, to understand how charismatic leaders develop or transform others, we must broaden our scope of analysis to include all relevant facets of transformational leadership. Third, we assume that "pure" charismatics are not concerned with the development of others. Optimally, the pure charismatic has attracted followers' attention, convinced them of the merits of his or her vision, and established a strong following. Yet the pure charismatic does not focus on developing followers into leaders. At the extreme, charismatic leaders may fail to develop themselves, and in turn their missions may fail from a lack of sensitivity to environmental demands (Avolio and Bass, 1987). Our own conceptualization of the pure charismatic is similar to Howell's discussion of personalized charisma (Chapter Seven), while her socialized charisma is more in line with our conception of charismatic/transformational leadership. Finally, we view the charisma of the transformational leader as the emotional fuel that energizes and transforms followers into leaders.

We begin our discussion by examining the construct of leadership with respect to developmental theory. A discussion of transformational leadership follows, with an emphasis on explaining how development occurs. Findings from preliminary work on the developmental antecedents of charismatic/transformational leadership are also included, as well as recommendations for future research and training.

A One-Minute Critique

Leaders are by definition change (developmental) agents in organizations. Yet we know very little about how leaders develop followers (the process), how individual differences affect the time it takes a leader to develop one follower rather than another, and how specific life events moderate the influence a leader has on his or her followers. And while thousands of studies have examined the content, process, and impact of leadership, most of the literature has portrayed leadership as a "timeless" dimension rather than as an ongoing process (McCauley, 1986; Gordon and Rosen, 1981). Although there are exceptions, the majority of leadership studies have not examined leadership within life-span and developmental frameworks.

As such, research has yet to produce a strong developmental theory of leadership. By "strong" theory we mean one that attempts to explain changes in human behavior in terms of its form, the conditions contributing to behavioral change, and the time interval required for change to take place. Weak developmental theories note the occurrence of change but fail to explain the form and the conditions that contribute to or inhibit the change process.

Instead, the leadership literature is largely composed of research that has been collected cross-sectionally, whereby leadership and such outcome measures as effort, performance, and satisfaction are obtained at similar points in time. Yet using such cross-sectional research designs results in a single, static estimate of the leader's effect on followers' motivation and performance and inhibits researchers from effectively evaluating the developmental role that leaders take on in organizational settings.

Before we can begin evaluating developmental and transformational changes in followers that are attributed to charismatic leaders, we must first determine the appropriate time intervals within which to measure leadership and its effect(s) on followers. Deciding on appropriate intervals is essential to a model that describes how leaders influence higher- and lower-order needs in followers, as suggested by the transformational leadership model (Bass, 1985). Since development proceeds at different rates for different individuals, it is also essential to determine the time intervals in which to examine whether change correctly (or incorrectly) attributed to a leader has occurred. Building such parameters into our analysis of leadership is a prerequisite for testing the construct validity of a leadership model that depicts how charismatic leaders develop and transform situations and followers. A possible strategy is to operationalize expected changes due to leadership and then estimate the time interval necessary to assess the full impact of leadership on the relevant process and outcome variables.

An appropriate time interval will depend on the type of change that is expected, the individuals involved, and the organizational context in which change (higher- or lower-order) will occur. Estimating these intervals in which change is expected to occur will, however, require a closer look at both leader and follower interactions. A useful framework for analyzing leader-follower interactions is the vertical dyad linkage model (Graen and Cashman, 1975; Dansereau, Alutto, and Yammarino, 1985).

A Developmental Perspective

Before discussing our additions to Bass's (1985) model of transformational leadership, an appropriate framework for discussing developmental change and leadership is required. One of our primary assumptions is that developmental change should be viewed as a continuous process accumulated, for the most part, gradually and incrementally over time. As such, and contrary to popular crisis-stage models of development (Levinson, 1978), individual development results from smaller and less obvious incremental changes involving the circumstances of daily events and the individual's interpretation of those events. Development is not necessarily due to a crisis or abrupt change (Brim and Ryff, 1980; Campbell, 1980). Whereas crisis theories posit the resolution of a life crisis as the impetus for individual development, it is equally plausible that, for many, crisis is simply a reaction to the awareness of change or the need for change and not necessarily the driving force behind development.

Development, then, entails the accumulation of both minor and major events across one's life span resulting in what Whitbourne (1985) refers to as the life span construct. The life span construct is the script of an individual's past and present. It establishes a basic framework for interpreting future events and is the mechanism used to organize an individual's life experiences into an integrated and interpretable whole (Whitbourne, 1985). Explaining development, leadership or otherwise, using the life span construct also assumes that people play an active role in structuring their own development.

Development is also seen as a continuous process of change and reaction to life events that occur over time. For example, Campbell (1980) concludes that most adults do not partition their life spans into major age-related shifts or stages but rather see them as a continuous process of change and development without abrupt stages or crisis. The delineation of broad stages of development most likely underestimates the continuity, as well as the numerous transitions, associated with individual development (Gubrium and Burkholdt, 1977).

Some may argue, however, that there are common or universal developmental events or stages that are culturally determined and that occur at standard points in time for most, if not all, individuals. We, however, would argue that such constructs underestimate many areas of life span development. The three-stage model framework is too simplistic a classification system for capturing the dynamic nature of life span development and too simplistic to explain charismatic/transformational leadership.

The mode of analysis we recommend for studying charismatic/transformational leadership focuses on transitions (critical or not) using a longitudinal framework. The unit of analysis is the interaction of the leader with his or her environment over a specific time interval. A similar framework for studying human development was recommended by Murray (1938) and, more recently, by Stokals (1982). Both recommended an analysis of life span development that is unique to the individual but does not disregard historical events common to a particular individual or group.

Our framework is also tied to Werner's (1926, 1940) thesis on comparative developmental psychology—an organismic developmental systems approach. Werner discusses two key elements for studying change: the structural components (in our case, the leader, follower, and context) and the dynamic components (the interactions of the structural components). The components of systems, the relations among those components, and the interaction of the personal system with the environmental system are assumed to have a developmental order (Wapner and others, 1983; Werner, 1957). Over time, they become more differentiated. At the upper endpoint of the developmental continuum, optimal development was operationalized by Kaplan (1966) as "a differentiated and hierarchically integrated person-in-environment system with capacity for flexibility, freedom, self-mastery and ability to shift from one mode of person-in-environment relationship to another as required by goals, by the demands of the situation, and by the instrumentalities available" (p. 11). Kaplan's definition of optimal development comes close to describing several popular definitions of charismatic/transformational leaders (see Avolio and Bass, 1987).

The developmental lens we have proposed for analyzing charismatic/transformational leadership has several important characteristics, which are summarized in Figure 1. First, critical and noncritical transitions of development are dependent on an individual reaction to major and minor life events, which in turn depend upon the life span construct developed by each individual. Second, developmental transitions associated with transformational leadership should be interpreted with respect to the time period in which they occur, such as individual or historical time. Third, the time interval selected in which to study developmental changes associated with charismatic/transformational leadership will vary depending on the phenomenon being studied—for example, the leader's own development, the followers' development, the development of the environmental/organizational context, and/or some interaction of the three.

Figure 1. How Transformational Leaders
Develop and How They Develop Others.

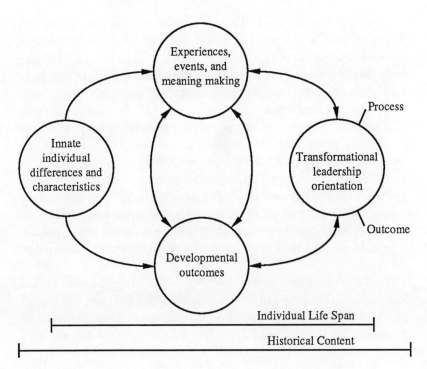

To summarize, experiences and events are accumulated over personal and historical time and result in a meaning-making system that offers each individual a unique perspective of his or her stimulus world. The way in which life events are interpreted is a function of such individual characteristics as intelligence and cultural upbringing. The meaning-making lens used to interpret life events affects an individual's pattern of development. Development, in turn, affects the meaning-making system utilized by the individual to interpret his or her world. They feed into each other. Taken together, personal characteristics, developmental experiences and outcomes, and the individual's meaning-making system built up over time and used to interpret life events affect the leadership orientation exhibited by that individual at a particular time. The process shown in Figure 1 is continuous and interactive, and takes place across an individual's life span.

Overview of Transformational Leadership

Since Bass's (1981) discussion of transformational leadership in *Stogdill's Handbook of Leadership,* considerable data have accumulated regarding the factors that comprise transformational leadership, some of its effects on follower effort and performance, and certain developmental antecedents that instill leaders with transformational qualities. While these are discussed by Bass and by other chapter authors in this volume, it is important to note that charismatic leadership is central to the transformational process and accounts for the largest percentage of common variance in transformational leadership ratings. Followers want to emulate their charismatic leader, they place a great deal of trust in their leader's judgment, as well as in his or her mission, they support the leader's values and typically adopt them, and they frequently form strong emotional ties to the leader.

Charismatic/transformational leadership, however, differs from earlier conceptualizations of charisma (see, for example, House, 1977) in that the leader is also seen as demonstrating a concern for the individual needs of followers (treating followers on a one-to-one basis) and encouraging followers to look at old problems in new ways through intellectual stimulation. This is unlike purely charismatic leaders, who may intentionally or unintentionally fail to transform followers. Pure charismatics may find followers' desire for autonomy a threat to their own leadership and hence intentionally keep followers from developing. They may also unintentionally fail to recognize followers' needs (Avolio and Bass, 1987). And in regard to intellectual stimulation, we see a fundamental difference between the purely charismatic leader, who has trained followers to blind obedience or habituated subordination (Graham, 1987), and the transformational leader, who encourages followers to think on their own.

Understanding the antecedents to charismatic/transformational leadership theory comes at an appropriate time in the development of this construct. The concept of transformational leadership did not formally appear in the literature until Burns's 1978 book entitled *Leadership* was published. Since its introduction of this concept to the field of leadership, the focus in the literature has been primarily on operationalizing what transformational leadership is, who has it, what it can do, and how it differs from other conceptualizations of leadership. Although some disagreement still remains in the literature concerning these fundamental issues, it seems appropriate to turn our attention to analyzing transformational leadership using a life span orientation. The justification for a developmental analysis comes from the consensus in the field that transformational leaders change and develop followers. Equally important, transformational leaders also change and develop themselves.

Gibbons (1986) summarized and integrated three theories of human development to explain the origin, acquisition, and development of transformational leadership. Figure 2 provides an overview of those antecedent events and conditions that previously have been linked to the development of charismatic/transformational leadership. The three theories are the psychoanalytical, the humanistic, and the constructivist. All three theories lean toward explaining transformational leadership as having its primordial roots in childhood. For example, Bass (1960) identified several family factors, such as birth order, sibling relationships, the home environment, parental ambitions, and attitudes toward the child as having a significant influence on leadership development. He also credited peer group relationships and the nature of an individual's school environment with having an impact on leadership potential.

Figure 2. A Model of Life Span Events That Contribute to Leadership.

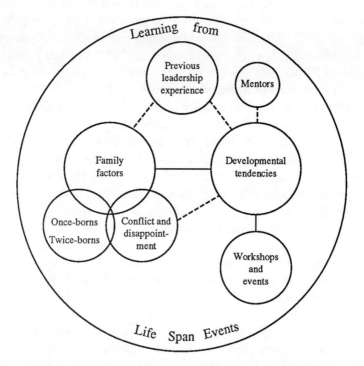

Psychoanalytical Theory. From a psychoanalytical perspective, Zaleznik (1977) attributed the development of charismatic leadership to early childhood experiences, although he assigned greater importance to crisis experiences, such as when an individual separates from his or her parents. His "twice-born" charismatic leaders experienced early development and separation from their parents as a crisis and a painful experience, which resulted in a sense of isolation, of being different (perhaps special), and in a turning away from the outer world. Corresponding with a shift inward, the twice borns became more dependent on their own beliefs and thoughts as their standard of reference for making decisions. They developed an inner strength and sense of resolution.

Through this resolution of inner conflict, disappointment, and problems, the leader moves to a level of development at which he or she can be responsible for resolving the conflicts, disappointments, and problems of others (Bass, 1985). According to the psychoanalytical model, higher-level stages of development are only possible through the resolution of early inner conflict (Zaleznik, 1963). Zaleznik (1984) portrayed development as a crusade for "self-mastery" through a field of internal conflicts. By learning how to deal with and resolve (master) personal conflict and disappointment in childhood, leaders can turn their attention to more substantive, far-reaching issues. Bass (1985) referred to the visionary qualities of charismatic/transformational leaders as a function of the leader's freedom from inner conflict. After getting their personal shops in order, charismatic/transformational leaders are free to look outward and beyond the time period in which they operate to solve significant problems (Zaleznik, 1984).

Humanistic Theory. The humanistic model of development stems from the work of Allport (1961), Rogers (1961), and Maslow (1970). Allport felt that all behaviors and thoughts were unique to the individual and could be understood by examining the individual's developmental history or what he called the life script. Maslow focused on the individual's innate potential. According to Maslow, environments shape an individual's development only to the degree that they help, permit, and encourage the potential that is already there to become actualized (Maslow, 1968). Similar to Maslow and Allport, Rogers viewed the optimum level of development as the "fully functioning" person. Rogers described such an individual as having characteristics similar to those in Maslow's stage of self-actualization: accepting of one's feelings, more creative than average, and more accepting of others. Rogers's point of departure with other humanistic theorists was in the variance in development he attributed to interactions with significant others, such as with one's parents. Human qualities, such as personal self-regard and inner self, were viewed by Rogers as dependent on the approval (or disapproval) received from one's parents in early childhood development (Rogers, 1951). Rogers's view of human development also differed from Maslow's and Allport's to the degree that he felt that interventions later in life, such as psychotherapy, could lead to overdue adjustments in development—that is, get the individual back on his or her optimal developmental track.

The views of humanists and psychoanalysts overlap with respect to the relevance of the inner self to an individual's personality and to transformational leadership development. While both humanistic and psychoanalytical theories can contribute to our understanding of charismatic/transformational leadership development, we consider them weak developmental theories in that each does not adequately explain changes in leadership development across the life span.

Constructivist Theory. The constructivist view of development, however, focuses on explaining how individuals perceive or make meaning of the world around them (Kegan, 1982; Kegan and Lahey, 1984). Kegan and Lahey's theory has more of a life span orientation than either the psychoanalytical or the humanistic model. Significant to our earlier discussion regarding the life span construct is the idea that people respond to change and life events according to their individual world view or meaning-making system (Kegan and Lahey, 1984).

Kegan and Lahey suggest that development is a function of the way people make meaning out of their experiences, regardless of their age. People at the same point in their life spans may experience events differently based on their interpretation of those events. The interpretation of an event is dependent upon an individual's life construct and his or her cognitive development level. Basing their discussion on Piagetian stages of cognitive development, Kegan and Lahey view leadership development as a function of "the qualitative change in the meaning system which occurs as one's cognitive complexity level increases" (Kegan and Lahey, 1984, p. 202). The meaning system employed by an individual to interpret events, in turn, is tied to his or her prior experiences and how those experiences were interpreted.

Kegan and Lahey refer to three cognitive stages or levels of adult development to explain three developmental phases of leadership—interpersonal, institutional, and interindividual. The three levels represent different stages of one's identity or ego development. At the primary level, the leader is able to switch back and forth between concern for others and concern for him- or herself. The individual's identity is codetermined based on other people's needs, the situation, and so forth. The interpersonal leader is seen shifting with the wind and is often labeled inconsistent. In stage two, the leader becomes more autonomous and self-directing; however, the identity he or she develops may be too rigidly adhered to with no built-in mechanism for alteration or self-correction. The leader's identity is inextricably linked to the organization's identity. Rather than being the shaper, such leaders are the shaped. In stage three, the individual's identity is more firmly established and independent. There is a capacity for self-reflection and correction not observed in stage two. In stage three (or interindividual), the leader is more concerned about development of systems and people than about their maintenance. The leader's identity transcends the present demands placed on him or her; thus, he or she is more willing and able to change and develop others as well as him- or herself.

Lewis and Kuhnert (1987) have generalized the constructivist view to describe the development of transformational leaders. Viewing development hierarchically and in stages, Lewis and Kuhnert discuss four qualitatively different stages or levels of leadership. At the lowest level (stage one), leaders are developmentally incapable of transcending their own self-interests and needs, while at the highest developmental level (stage four), transformational leaders operate out of a personal value system that transcends immediate transactions, goals, and individual loyalties. Leaders at stage four construct or make meaning out of the world through their end values. Stage four leaders have a self-determined sense of identity. As suggested by the psychoanalytical view, the leader is more inner-directed and therefore more able to transcend the interests of the moment. This inner-directedness provides a transformational view as an unusual energy for pursuing goals, missions, and, ultimately, the leader's vision. The leader's enthusiasm for an objective can become infectious. The sense of inner-direction, if translated properly by the leader, will attract followers who agree with the leader's end values. How effectively those end values are communicated and the degree to which followers identify with the leader's end values both result in what House (1977) described as charismatic leadership. The values of the leader and their expression become the foundation for higher-order change in followers (Bass, 1985; Waldman, Bass, and Einstein, 1987).

A Retrospective Study of the Developmental Life Events of Transformational Leaders

Gibbons's (1986) investigation represents the most comprehensive attempt to combine the three models of leadership development previously discussed in this chapter. Gibbons used the Multifactor Leadership Questionnaire (MLQ) to differentiate transformational leaders from other types of leaders—transactional, laissez-faire, and management-by-exception—in a sample of top-level corporate executives. Her analysis of leadership development was based primarily on retrospective life histories generated from in-depth clinical interviews with sixteen individuals whose MLQ scores showed them to be transformational and transactional, pure transformational, pure transactional, or laissez-faire leaders. Gibbons's analysis of the qualitatively generated data resulted in the identification of seven key elements that encompass some of the significant antecedents to the development of transformational leadership. The seven factors, which, when present, appear to result in transformational leadership, are shown in Figure 3. (Note that the size of the circle presented in Figure 3 denotes the importance attributed to that factor in the development of transformational leadership.) These seven factors are:

Figure 3. A Model of Life Span Events That Contribute to Leadership.

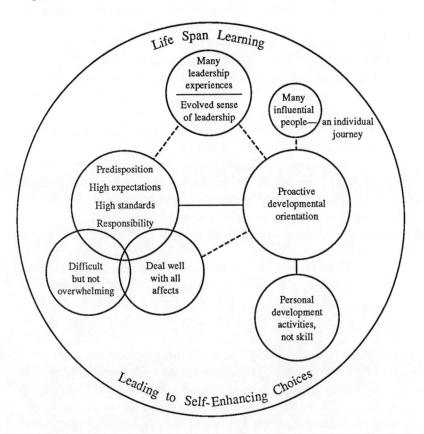

1. A predisposition is established as a result of parental encouragement and expectation to set high standards for achievement, which extends to many arenas of life. As children, these leaders are expected to be the best and are given a moderately high amount of early responsibility in the family.

2. The family situation, conditions, and circumstances may be difficult and often demanding, but sufficient resources, both individual and systemic, are available to avoid being overwhelmed. Balance is the important condition and is relative to each family situation.

3. The individual learns how to deal with his or her emotions, including conflict and disappointment and their effects, as well as other emotions and feelings. If this condition is not learned within the family, then it is learned by choice or necessity at a later point in the leader's life span.

4. The leader has had many previous leadership opportunities and experiences in a variety of settings. (The transformational leaders studied often reflected on those experiences that helped shape them for the leadership position they occupied at the time of Gibbons's study.)

5. The leaders have a strong desire to engage in developmental work, especially as adults. Such work is undertaken in a conscious, deliberate way, and it becomes so much a part of transformational leaders that it appears automatic. Development is an orientation or way of being, not a role transformational leaders take on. The same high standards and expectations that were learned as a child are applied to other areas of work and life. There is a willingness to take risks on behalf of one's personal development. Personal development is a primary work goal, as well as life goal.

6. Workshops, events, other more formal, structured developmental activities, and relationships with influential people who may also have been role models are used to augment and enhance the developmental orientation and process. The activities selected are related to personal development and are not specifically confined to skill training in leadership. Short-term workshops are not viewed as being critically important to the development of transformational leadership.

7. The leader views all experiences as learning experiences and demonstrates a strong tendency to be self-reflective and to integrate learning. The integrated learnings are more often than not used to make self-enhancing rather than self-limiting choices.

In sum, Gibbons's findings provided support for all three models of leadership development previously discussed. Moreover, her conclusions highlight the importance of using a developmental lens to study leadership, a lens that focuses on continuous and incremental life span changes. Finally, supporting earlier research by Campbell (1980) and Whitbourne (1985), Gibbons's results did not present consistent evidence that necessarily supports a "critical life events" model of leadership development.

Gibbons's findings affirm our earlier argument that there are commonalities across leaders with respect to developmental life experiences but there is no evidence for specific and/or universal stages of development that culminate in producing a charismatic/transformational leader. Rather, development of charismatic/transformational leaders is best characterized as a life span process of change with early, as well as later, life events affecting the development of leadership potential.

It suffices to say that companies and/or individuals who rely principally on one or even a few developmental strategies for building transformational leaders will probably be disappointed, since the most successful developmental programs are those that reflect the individual and his or her unique needs and strengths. The critical elements making up the chemistry of a charismatic/transformational leader appear to vary across individual leaders.

Gibbons's work does represent one of the most comprehensive studies to date of the antecedents to charismatic/transformational leadership. However, her conclusions are based on a retrospective analysis and reconstruction of the leader's life history and events and therefore are subject to errors of omission and intrusion. People remember events on the basis of their reconstruction of those events in recall, not necessarily the actual events or facts (Cantor and Mischel, 1977; Phillips and Lord, 1982). For example, one may initially classify an experience as unpleasant but later in his or her life span go back and reclassify the experience as developmental—seeing the experience as having made a positive contribution to development. The key question is how much of anyone's inner self is a composite of reconstructed prior events and experiences? Also, to what extent are the developmental stages referred to in the literature actually an explanation of developmental processes rather than merely a convenient system of classification for recalling events? Nevertheless, while criticizing retrospective accounts as a means of conducting life span leadership research, one must realize that at present there are no ongoing longitudinal research studies of charismatic/transformational leadership. The type of data needed to build a strong developmental theory of leadership is still many years away from being collected.

Although there are no longitudinal research programs currently studying charismatic/transformational leadership, the Management Potential Study conducted at AT&T has produced some interesting parallels to Gibbons's findings (see Bray, Campbell, and Grant, 1974; Bray and Howard, 1983). Specifically, the overlap between the characteristics associated with transformational leaders and what Bray, Campbell, and Grant (1974) called the "enlargers" in their study of managers at AT&T is rather direct. Enlargers are attracted to challenges and to extending themselves, demonstrate greater than average emotional and intellectual independence (inner self), desire more responsibility and autonomy than others, and have developed a more sophisticated framework for making meaning out of reality (Lewis and Kuhnert's [1987] stage four leaders). Also, supporting Gibbons's conclusions, intrapersonal development over the two decades of data collection in the Management Potential Study was seen as a key factor in the success (rate of promotion) of the enlargers at AT&T (Bray and Howard, 1983).

In sum, our analysis of the models presented in this section argues in favor of looking at leadership as a continuous developmental process. Up to this point, based on the focus of previous literature, the emphasis in our discussion has been on the leaders' development and in particular on their personality/cognitive development. Each of the models reviewed has made a contribution to our understanding of how charismatic/transformational leaders develop. Our primary criticism of all three models, however, is that they all fall into the category of weak developmental theories. The strongest of the developmental theories—the constructivist view—still falls short of explaining how developmental change and transitions occur. Moreover, the central focus of the constructivist's explanation of change is based on developmental stages. Unfortunately, the stage theories cited do not explain how transitions between and within stages occur or whether passing through each of the stages in a prescribed order is necessary to achieve the highest level of development. However, the classification system proposed by Lewis and Kuhnert (1987) is useful in helping us capture leadership development as an orderable process of increasing complexity and differentiation (the orthogenetic principle). Its fundamental flaw is the idea that leaders need to be at the highest stage of cognitive development in order to be charismatic and transformational. Our view is that charismatic/transformational leadership occurs relative to the group with which the leader interacts and that transformational leadership can occur even at lower levels of cognitive development.

Emotional and Cognitive Development of Transformational Leaders and Their Followers

Most of the prior research on charismatic/transformational leadership has been conducted with top organizational leaders, with the exception of the work of Bass and his colleagues. Therefore, we have a theory of charismatic/transformational leadership that is bounded by the sample characteristics of the population upon which it has been construct validated.

There are two important distinctions to be made here. First, in terms of the individual, transformational leadership can occur at different levels of cognitive and emotional development. There is no empirical evidence that a certain stage of development or specific cutoff must be reached before one can be a charismatic/transformational leader. The level of individual development required to be transformational is, in part, relative to the developmental level of the individual or group being led. Raising the needs of followers who are at the lowest developmental level to a qualitatively higher level is transformational. However, previous authors have often referred to charismatic/transformational leadership as a dichotomous condition—that is, one either is or is not transformational—when in fact it is a matter of degree.

The second distinction involves the level within an organization at which charismatic/transformational leadership is observed. Recent evidence summarized by Avolio and Bass (1987) shows that charismatic/transformational leadership can occur at *all* organizational levels in varying degrees. The charismatic/transformational leadership qualities we commonly associate with top corporate leaders appear to also be present in leaders at lower levels of the organizational hierarchy. In this case, the degree of charismatic/transformational leadership observed is relative to the organizational level. At different levels, as well as in different organizational settings, the likelihood of observing some charismatic/transformational leadership varies.

One assumption about a charismatic/transformational leader's developmental level is clear: A leader who operates at a lower developmental level than his or her followers cannot transform followers to a level higher than his or her own. Conversely, a leader who views the world from a developmental level that is not understood by his or her followers will also have difficulty transforming followers to his or her way of thinking. Tichy and Devanna (1986), in their summarization of transformational leaders, suggest that the more successful transformational leaders are able to "dumb down" their vision to grab followers' interest, attention, and understanding. We hope that our discussion here puts a new light on the relativity of "dumbing down" the leader's message.

After interviewing ninety leaders, Bennis and Nanus (1985) reported that what differentiates leaders from nonleaders is a commitment to personal development as well as to the development of others. Similarly, Burns (1978), in his analysis of world-class political leaders, concluded that transformational leaders are characterized by a desire and intrinsic drive to engage in growth and development of the self. Bass (1985) similarly described transformational leaders as continually developing to higher levels and to developing followers into leaders. Gibbons (1986) concluded that transformational leaders are eager to develop and challenge themselves consciously throughout their careers. Similarly, providing challenges is also a key factor in the development and transformation of their followers.

Berlew and Hall (1966) reported that the more challenging one's first job with a company, the greater one's advancement rate will be within the company. Early job challenge also has been correlated with developmental career success in several other research investigations (Bray, Campbell, and Grant, 1974; Broderick, 1983; Davies and Easterby-Smith, 1984; Digman, 1978; Vicino and Bass, 1978). If we assume that these results are not totally attributable to methodological artifacts, such as more able people being selected for more challenging jobs or more challenging jobs increasing the visibility of an individual in his or her organization (Kanter, 1977), then there are two developmental connections that can be drawn to charismatic/transformational leadership. First, providing intellectual challenges for followers can affect the followers' cognitive development by encouraging the development of new information structures or cognitive scripts to address the impending challenge. The developmental process is analogous to our earlier discussion of how life events shape an individual's life construct. Second, job challenges can—and usually do—result in increased levels of emotional stress. The increased stress results in a need to seek ways to cope effectively with the challenge. If the challenge is appropriate for the individual's current developmental level (or potential), then challenge can result in emotional development as well. This situation is similar to our earlier discussion of overcoming early life conflicts/transitions and the impact of those events on the development of the inner self. If we expand on Zaleznik's (1977) concept of the twice-born leader, challenges throughout life, job or otherwise, can potentially stimulate a partial (or total) reevaluation of the inner self each time a minor (or major) challenge is confronted.

Providing intellectual challenges to followers promotes a key facet of individual development—the evolution of meaning-making systems to higher levels of cognitive complexity (Kohlberg, 1969; Loevinger, 1966; Merron, Fisher, and Torbert, 1986). Developing an ability in followers to see problems through a more sophisticated and creative lens reduces the use of more dogmatic approaches to problem solving on the job (Costa and McCrae, 1980). Merron, Fisher, and Torbert (1986) found that

managers at higher developmental levels see problems as opportunities to observe and learn; managers at lower developmental levels see problems as fires to be put out.

Intellectual stimulation is also an important component
of building autonomy in followers or developing followers into
leaders. Intellectual stimulation may encourage the acceptance
of others who have different points of view (Bartunek, Gordon,
and Weatherby, 1983), which ties into an important facet of
emotional development—one's level of empathy for other people's needs. Transformational leaders show empathy toward
followers through individualized consideration (Bass, 1985).
Development leads to higher forms of empathy, such as those
described by Kohlberg in his moral development stage (Kohlberg, 1969). Part of developing followers' individualized consideration (empathy) is to move them developmentally from being able to recognize affective states in others to being able to
assume the perspectives of others and ultimately to be respon-
sive to them. How much empathy followers are capable of depends on their view of the world (or meaning-making system)
and their level of emotional development (Feshbach, 1978, 1982;
Parke and Asher, 1983). Leaders must concentrate on the cognitive *and* emotional development of followers if the followers
are to lead themselves as well as others and ultimately transform.

The presentation of challenges to followers provides opportunities—for those who are developmentally ready to accept
them—to learn and develop from the challenges. Lessons learned
from a challenge, whether it was handled successfully or not,
can be used as a basis for creating future opportunities in an
individual's life span. All problems can be viewed as learning
experiences, both cognitively and emotionally; to do so is to be
seen as a transformational leader (Gibbons, 1986).

Of course, challenges can also lead to regression or the
institutionalization of nondevelopment. Salaman (1978) described
how nondevelopment became institutionalized in an organizational case study of an autocratic leader. The autocratic leader
described by Salaman institutionalized his power base, as well
as nondevelopment, by overseeing all decisions, personally select-
ing all of his subordinates, ambiguously describing all jobs, and
keeping to himself information necessary for making even the

lowest-level decision. Eventually, no one in the organization would undertake new initiatives without explicit permission from the leader. Self-doubt and the doubting of co-workers' competence cascaded throughout the organization. Everyone became convinced that everyone else was incompetent, which led to over-regulation and increasing levels of institutional controls. When the leader was finally removed, the controls became *worse:* Nondevelopment had become institutionalized.

Challenge, as we have already seen from Gibbons's (1986) results, can be developmental and transformational. Unlike the challenges confronting the transformational leaders in Gibbons's sample, the people in the autocratically run organization described by Salaman (1978) felt no sense of balance between the challenge and the support and other resources made available to them. Obviously, both support and resources were intentionally withheld by the autocratic leader, which led to increased dependence on the person in charge and less desire for growth and individual development. Charismatic/transformational leadership thrives in an environment in which some sort of balance is maintained. Transformation and development also can become institutionalized and have been shown to cascade from one level of an organization to the next (Bass, Waldman, Avolio, and Bebb, 1987).

In sum, charismatic/transformational leaders provide challenges to both followers and themselves to move to higher levels of development. By addressing those challenges and building some record of successful achievement, the leader develops to a higher level of emotional and cognitive development. A leader's level of success in overcoming challenges has a direct bearing on his or her level of perceived self-efficacy (Bandura, 1977). Self-efficacy, or the confidence an individual has in his or her ability to overcome a challenge, is an integral component of the development of transformational leadership.

Self-Efficacy, Self-Management, and Self-Development

A useful model for evaluating individual development, particularly development linked to personal challenges, is provided by Bandura's (1977) discussion of social learning theory.

According to social learning theorists, behavior is a function of both internal and external events. Self-efficacy represents one's belief that a certain amount of effort will result in the achievement of a desired outcome. The internal mechanism to which Bandura refers is represented by feelings of self-efficacy, while the external event is the challenge and the risk that goes along with that challenge. A significant part of developing or transforming followers is developing their feelings of self-efficacy. The four primary contributors to self-efficacy through which transformational leaders can affect followers' development are acknowledging previous accomplishments, providing emotional challenges, conveying high expectations, and modeling appropriate strategies for success. Charismatic/transformational leaders can develop a follower's self-efficacy in the following manner:

1. The leader provides for followers tasks that result in experiences of success. Incremental successes encourage followers to pursue more difficult objectives. As feelings of self-efficacy develop, the probability assigned by followers to the risk of failure decreases. Explicit challenges also provide for the development of an alteration in an individual's meaning-making system.
2. The leader gets the followers appropriately involved by providing emotional challenges, which results in higher intrinsic motivation and an increase in feelings of self-efficacy.
3. The leader's ability to convey the importance of completing a task (verbal persuasion) for the leader's and follower's goals, values, mission, or even their vision increases the probability that the follower will attempt to accomplish the task.
4. The leader models for the follower appropriate strategies for achieving success.

By raising followers' self-efficacy levels, the charismatic/transformational leader enables those followers to address more challenging problems. A further logical extension of developing self-efficacy in followers is the institutionalization of self-control and self-development.

Manz and Sims (1980) have used social learning theory as a framework for discussing the development of self-management skills. They recommend that, in order to develop self-management skills (or to transform followers into leaders), we need to concentrate on both environmental planning and behavioral change. Based on social learning theory, the simplest suggestion for developing followers into leaders and/or raising personal standards is to have leaders model self-management techniques (Bandura and Cervone, 1986). However, Manz and Sims (1986) recently found that simple modeling does not result in the desired behavioral effects. Their research showed that followers who observed specific behaviors modeled by a leader (simple modeling) did not adopt those behaviors beyond chance levels. These results demonstrate that there are more complex linkages between behavioral modeling and the behaviors we are attempting to develop than a simple imitation-demand effect model would indicate. In order to change and develop followers into leaders, we will have to do more than simply model desirable behaviors.

Another primary goal of transformational leadership is to develop in followers mechanisms for self-confidence and self-development. The leader transforms followers into leaders who are responsible for their own actions, behaviors, performance, and development. For some followers, this is represented by a gradual developmental process in which the leader reduces external reinforcement for specific behaviors as internal self-control mechanisms come into place; for others, the process may be accelerated if they are developmentally able and willing to take on more responsibility. Social learning theory is useful for understanding how transformational leaders both shape behaviors to desired end states and affect the cognitive scripts or mental road maps followers use to interpret the world around them.

In addition to social learning theory, we have put forth a life span orientation to help examine the events that move people to developmental levels at which they are able to handle more responsibility for their own behavior and eventually, for some, the behavior of others. The development of our understanding of how self-management comes about and the effects that charismatic/transformational leadership can have on the process of shifting from external to internal controls should provide a more comprehensive view of individual development of leaders in organizational settings. The biggest contributor to understanding how development takes place is understanding how the personal history of an individual has contributed to his or her current developmental level (Bandura and Cervone, 1986).

Conclusion

Our discussion has focused primarily on the dynamic components and processes underlying a form of leadership concerned with the development of followers. The model of transformational leadership presented by Bass (1985) has been used as a basis for discussing leadership development as a transformative process—a process that entails a progressive reorganization and reformulation of frames of reference and that results in higher levels of development. Heeding the advice of Weick (1979), we have attempted to blend together different theoretical views and perspectives (Weick's theory of complementarity) into a broader understanding of a complex phenomenon called charismatic/transformational leadership.

Some of the groundwork has been established to move the field a step closer to a strong developmental theory of leadership. A significant amount of work still needs to be accomplished before that goal is realized. In the interest of molding the frame of reference for studying charismatic/transformational leadership further, we have outlined some additional ideas for future research to consider. First, Bandura and Cervone (1986) have indicated that the single most important contributor to self-efficacy is the individual's personal history. Since self-efficacy plays such an integral role in the development of followers, greater attention needs to be paid to the connection between life events, self-efficacy, and developmental leadership. Individually perceived self-efficacy does directly relate to perseverance, level of effort, and eventual task accomplishment. Charismatic/transformational leaders can affect self-efficacy through their charisma or by providing a common vision for followers to make them feel stronger and more in control of their own destinies; through intellectual stimulation by providing a different frame of reference to overcome any impediments; and through individualized consideration or elevation of follower needs to accomplish more and to take more personal responsibility for their self-development. Second, we need to explore in greater detail the developmental antecedents to charismatic/transformational leadership. This will involve a reorientation of our approach to studying leadership—moving away from a timeless orientation to one that recognizes the importance of life events in the shaping of individual life constructs. It will also require the following assumption: The developmental experiences of individuals that result in charismatic/transformational leaders are orderable but not necessarily universal. And third, it will be worthwhile for leadership researchers to develop some guidelines for determining the length of time necessary for a leader to have some influence on followers in terms of development, effort levels, and also performance.

One specific reason for incorporating time intervals into our study of leadership relates to what Bass (1985) referred to as higher- and lower-order change in followers. With lower-order change, a charismatic/transformational leader is attempting to identify a follower's current material and psychic needs and to help provide a job environment that can satisfy those needs. The time interval necessary for achieving lower-order change should be shorter than the interval necessary for a leader to influence higher-order change—change in which a follower's needs, goals, desires, and values are qualitatively elevated and altered. Looking at higher- and lower-order change along a continuum regarding the degree of change expected should help determine when and where measurement of the effects of charismatic/transformational leadership should take place.

A second advantage of studying leadership with respect to time concerns the information it will provide about leadership itself. Assuming as we have that leadership is a continuous, progressive, developmental process, knowing how certain leaders' actions effect more or less immediate change in followers should offer some insights into the leadership process itself.

Specifically, we can learn which leadership actions are more (or less) effective, which leadership actions take more time to incubate before change can be observed, and what type of follower responds more or less readily to those actions. By examining leadership according to time and inter- and intraindividual change, we can begin to build a model of leadership that more accurately predicts a leader's ability to influence individual as well as group behavior within appropriately defined time intervals.

Evaluating effects of charismatic/transformational leadership will require some additional changes in research strategy. A combination of longitudinal and cross-sectional research designs seems appropriate. A cross-sequential design may be the most appropriate model for maximizing the amount of information one can obtain in the shortest possible time. With a cross-sequential design, we start by collecting data cross-sectionally at the first period of measurement, then we follow respective cohorts over time longitudinally. Using this design, we can examine both inter- and intraindividual change while also looking at the effects of time, of measurement, and of cohort membership on the dependent variables of interest.

Short-term experimental simulations are appropriate when used to establish preliminary groundwork on the rate and direction of change expected due to certain leadership actions and behaviors. However, analyzing higher-order changes in followers will require a longer-term strategy to capture the phenomenon under investigation.

Given what we already know about charismatic/transformational leaders, we can offer the following recommendations for developing such leaders in organizations:

1. The MLQ survey developed by Bass and his colleagues can be used initially to help identify charismatic/transformational leaders and also to make individuals aware of where they stand with respect to being charismatic/transformational leaders.

2. Building on self-awareness, a developmental plan can be constructed that incorporates the strengths and weaknesses of the leader. The plan should have a life span orientation with

respect to how the individual leader will build on his or her strengths while reducing his or her weaknesses. The plan must be individually oriented, keyed to earlier life events that can be obtained through interviews or biographical surveys, and flexible enough to accommodate changes in the individual and in the context in which he or she operates.

3. Behavior and skills exhibited by charismatic/transformational leaders can be taught in workshops focused on intrapersonal (self-) development. Much of what we already know concerning self-development and confidence building can be used in the development of the charismatic/transformational leader.

4. Emphasis needs to be placed on transferring skills and behaviors learned in workbooks back to the job. A careful analysis of potential ''roadblocks'' in the development of a charismatic/transformational leader should be identified. Optimally, training can take place on the job, making appropriate changes in context and culture to accommodate the developmental aspirations of the leader.

5. All of our previous recommendations lead to one basic conclusion: The program of intervention should focus on changing the meaning-making system of the individual to approximate the framework that would be used by a charismatic/transformational leader.

This chapter has discussed charismatic/transformational leadership as a developmental process that unfolds across the life span. Empirical work is now needed to evaluate in a more systematic manner the developmental factors that result in what Bass and his colleagues refer to as the optimal form of leadership. We hope that our discussion has established a new frame of reference for studying leadership as it must be studied—using a developmental perspective.

References

Allport, G. W. *Pattern and Growth in Personality*. New York: Holt, Rinehart & Winston, 1961.

Argyris, C., and Schön, D. *Organizational Learning.* Reading, Mass.: Addison-Wesley, 1978.

Avolio, B. J., and Bass, B. M. "Charisma and Beyond." In J. G. Hunt (ed.), *Emerging Leadership Vistas.* Elmsford, N.Y.: Pergamon Press, 1987.

Bandura, A. *Social Learning Theory.* Englewood Cliffs, N.J.: Prentice-Hall, 1977.

Bandura, A., and Cervone, D. "Differential Engagement of Self-Reactive Influences in Cognitive Motivation." *Organizational Behavior and Human Performance,* 1986, *38,* 92–113.

Bartunek, J. M., Gordon, J. R., and Weatherby, R. P. "Developing Complicated Understanding in Administrators." *Academy of Management Review,* 1983, *8,* 273–284.

Bass, B. M. *Leadership, Psychology and Organizational Behavior.* New York: Harper & Row, 1960.

Bass, B. M. *Stogdill's Handbook of Leadership.* New York: Free Press, 1981.

Bass, B. M. *Leadership and Performance Beyond Expectations.* New York: Free Press, 1985.

Bass, B. M., Waldman, D. A., Avolio, B. J., and Bebb, M. "Transformational Leadership and the Falling Dominoes Effect." *Group and Organizational Studies,* 1987, *12,* 73–87.

Bennis, W., and Nanus, B. *Leaders: The Strategies for Taking Charge.* New York: Harper & Row, 1985.

Berlew, D. E., and Hall, D. T. "The Socialization of Managers: Effects of Expectations on Performance." *Administrative Science Quarterly,* 1966, *11,* 207–233.

Bray, D. W., Campbell, R. J., and Grant, D. L. *Formative Years in Business.* New York: Wiley, 1974.

Bray, D. W., and Howard, A. "The AT&T Longitudinal Studies of Managers." In K. W. Schaie (ed.), *Longitudinal Studies of Adult Psychological Development.* New York: Guilford Press, 1983.

Brim, O. G., and Ryff, C. D. "On the Properties of Life Events." *Lifespan Development and Behavior,* 1980, *3,* 367–388.

Broderick, R. "How Honeywell Teaches Its Managers to Manage." *Training,* Jan. 1983, pp. 18–22.

Burns, J. M. *Leadership.* New York: Harper & Row, 1978.

Campbell, A. *The Sense of Well-Being in America.* New York: McGraw-Hill, 1980.

Cantor, N., and Mischel, W. "Traits as Prototypes: Effects on Recognition Memory." *Journal of Personality and Social Psychology,* 1977, *35,* 38–48.

Costa, P. T., Jr., and McCrae, R. R. "Still Stable After All These Years: Personality as a Key to Some Issues in Aging." In P. B. Baltes and O. G. Brim (eds.), *Lifespan Development and Behavior.* Vol. 3. Orlando, Fla.: Academic Press, 1980.

Dansereau, F., Alutto, J. A., and Yammarino, F. J. *Theory Testing in Organizational Behavior: The Varient Approach.* Englewood Cliffs, N.J.: Prentice-Hall, 1985.

Davies, J., and Easterby-Smith, N. "Learning and Developing from Managerial Work Experiences." *Journal of Management Studies,* 1984, *2,* 1969–1983.

Digman, L. A. "How Well-Managed Organizations Develop Their Executives." *Organizational Dynamics,* 1978, *1,* 63–79.

Feshbach, N. D. "Studies of Empathic Behavior in Children." In B. A. Maher (ed.), *Progress in Experimental Personality Research.* Vol. 8. Orlando, Fla.: Academic Press, 1978.

Feshbach, N. D. "Sex Differences in Empathy and Social Behavior in Children." In N. Eisenberg-Berg (ed.), *The Development of Prosocial Behavior.* Orlando, Fla.: Academic Press, 1982.

Gibbons, T. C. "Revisiting the Question of Born vs. Made: Toward a Theory of Development of Transformational Leaders." Unpublished doctoral dissertation, Human and Organization Systems, Fielding Institute, 1986.

Gordon, G. E., and Rosen, N. "Critical Factors in Leadership Succession." *Organizational Behavior and Human Performance,* 1981, *27,* 227–254.

Graen, G., and Cashman, J. F. "A Role-Making Model of Leadership in Formal Organizations: A Developmental Approach." In J. G. Hunt and L. L. Larson (eds.), *Leadership Frontiers.* Kent, Ohio: Kent State University Press, 1975.

Graham, J. W. "The Essence of Leadership: Fostering Follower Autonomy, Not Automatic Followership." In J. G. Hunt (ed.), *Emerging Leadership Vistas.* Elmsford, N.Y.: Pergamon Press, 1987.

Gubrium, J. F., and Burkholdt, D. R. *Toward Maturity: The Social Processing of Human Development.* San Francisco: Jossey-Bass, 1977.

House, R. J. "A 1976 Theory of Charismatic Leadership." In J. G. Hunt and L. L. Larson (eds.), *Leadership: The Cutting Edge.* Carbondale: Southern Illinois University Press, 1977.

Kanter, R. M. *Men and Women of the Corporation.* New York: Basic Books, 1977.

Kaplan, B. "The Comparative Developmental Approach and Its Application to Symbolization and Language in Psychopathology." In S. Arieti (ed.), *American Handbook of Psychiatry.* Vol. 3. New York: Basic Books, 1966.

Kegan, R. *The Evolving Self: Problem and Process in Human Development.* Cambridge, Mass.: Harvard University Press, 1982.

Kegan, R., and Lahey, L. L. "Adult Leadership and Adult Development: A Constructivist View." In B. Kellerman (ed.), *Leadership: Multidisciplinary Perspectives.* Englewood Cliffs, N.J.: Prentice-Hall, 1984.

Kohlberg, L. "Stage and Sequence: The Cognitive-Developmental Approach to Socialization." In D. A. Goslin (ed.), *Handbook of Socialization Theory and Research.* Skokie, Ill.: Rand McNally, 1969.

Levinson, D. *The Seasons of a Man's Life.* New York: Ballantine Books, 1978.

Lewis, P., and Kuhnert, K. "Post-Transactional Leaders: A Constructive Developmental View." Paper presented at the second annual conference of the Society for Industrial and Organizational Psychology, Atlanta, Aug. 1987.

Loevinger, J. "The Meaning and Measurement of Ego Development." *American Psychologist,* 1966, *21,* 195–206.

McCauley, C. D. *Developmental Experiences in Managerial Work: A Literature Review.* Technical Report No. 26. Greensboro, N.C.: Center for Creative Leadership, 1986.

Manz, C. C., and Sims, H. P., Jr. "Self-Management as a Substitute for Leadership: A Social Learning Theory Perspective." *Academy of Management Review,* 1980, *5,* 361–367.

Manz, C. C., and Sims, H. P. "Beyond Imitation: Complex Behavior and Affective Linkages Resulting from Exposure to Leadership Training Models." *Journal of Applied Psychology,* 1986, *71,* 571–578.

Margerison, C., and Kakabadse, A. *How American Executives Succeed.* New York: American Management Association, 1984.

Maslow, A. H. *Toward a Psychology of Being.* (2nd ed.) New York: D. Van Nostrand, 1968.

Maslow, A. H. *Motivation and Personality.* (2nd ed.) New York: Harper & Row, 1970.

Merron, D., Fisher, D., and Torbert, W. R. "Meaning Making and Managerial Effectiveness: A Developmental Perspective." Paper presented at the national meeting of the Academy of Management, Chicago, Aug. 1986.

Murray, H. A. *Explorations in Personality.* New York: Oxford University Press, 1938.

Parke, R. D., and Asher, S. R. "Social and Personality Development." *Annual Review of Psychology,* 1983, *34,* 465–509.

Phillips, J. S., and Lord, R. G. "Schematic Information Processing and Perceptions of Leadership in Problem-Solving Groups." *Journal of Applied Psychology,* 1982, *67,* 486–492.

Rogers, C. R. *Client-Centered Therapy.* Boston: Houghton Mifflin, 1951.

Rogers, C. R. *On Becoming a Person: A Therapist's View of Psychotherapy.* Boston: Houghton Mifflin, 1961.

Salaman, G. "An Historical Discontinuity: From Charisma to Routinization." *Human Relations,* 1978, *30,* 373–388.

Stokals, D. "Environmental Psychology: A Coming of Age." In A. Kraut (ed.), *G. Stanley Hall Lecture Series.* Vol. 2. Washington, D.C.: American Psychological Association, 1982.

Tichy, N. M., and Devanna, M. A. *The Transformational Leader.* New York: Wiley, 1986.

Vicino, F. L., and Bass, B. M. "Lifespace Variables and Managerial Success." *Journal of Applied Psychology,* 1978, *63,* 81–88.

Waldman, D. A., Bass, B. M., and Einstein, W. O. "Effort, Performance and Transformational Leadership in Industrial and Military Service." *Journal of Occupational Psychology,* 1987, *60,* 1–10.

Wapner, S., and others. "An Examination of Studies of Critical Transitions Through the Life Cycle." In S. Wapner and

B. Kaplan (eds.), *Toward a Holistic Developmental Psychology.* Hillside, N.J.: Erlbaum, 1983.

Weick, K. *The Social Psychology of Organizations.* (2nd ed.) Reading, Mass.: Addison-Wesley, 1979.

Werner, H. *Einfuhrungindie Entwicklungs-Psychologie.* Leipzig, E. Germany: Barth, 1926.

Werner, H. *Comparative Psychology of Mental Development.* New York: Harper & Row, 1940.

Werner, H. "The Concept of Development from a Comparative and Organismic Point of View." In D. B. Harris (ed.), *The Concept of Development.* Minneapolis: University of Minnesota Press, 1957.

Whitbourne, S. K. "The Psychological Connection of the Life-span." In J. E. Birren and K. W. Schaie (eds.), *The Psychology and Aging Handbook.* New York: Van Nostrand Reinhold, 1985.

Zaleznik, A. "The Human Dilemmas of Leadership." *Harvard Business Review,* 1963, *41,* 49–55.

Zaleznik, A. "Managers and Leaders: Are They Different?" *Harvard Business Review,* 1977, *15,* 67–78.

Zaleznik, A. "Charismatic and Consensus Leaders: A Psychological Comparison." In M.F.R. Kets de Vries (ed.), *The Irrational Executive: Psychoanalytic Explorations in Management.* New York: International Universities Press, 1984.

11

Training
Charismatic Leadership:
A Risky and Critical Task

Jay A. Conger
Rabindra N. Kanungo

At this point in the book, it seems quite natural to raise the important question of whether we can train charismatic leaders. For by now, we would hope that much of the mystery surrounding charisma has been stripped away and that the reader has formed some idea of the ingredients of charismatic influence. As one can see from the previous chapters, there is an emerging consensus that manifestations of charismatic leadership depend significantly on the leader's expression of certain abilities, skills, and behaviors in specific organizational contexts. Furthermore, these manifest abilities and behaviors tend to have a strong impact on the motivation and performance of organizational members. As a result, charismatic leadership may have important consequences for organizational effectiveness.

   As we mentioned in our Introduction, many of the charismatic's qualities of strategic vision, entrepreneurship, commitment to and passion for making things better, communication skills, and environmental sensitivity are qualities desperately needed by business today. And while it is naive to assume that managers everywhere can be transformed into Iacoccas, it is quite reasonable to assume that through teaching more creative strategy making, more effective speaking skills, greater use of empowering management practices, and more unconventional approaches to problem solving, we can enhance the effectiveness of managers in leadership roles. Organizations then may wish to develop certain of these leadership qualities among their managers.

While as the authors of this chapter we feel strongly that charismatic leadership qualities can be trained, it is important to acknowledge the range of perspectives on this issue. Some share our view; others do not. Behaviorial scientists such as Bass, House, Howell, and ourselves analyze charisma in terms of a set of manifest abilities and behavior in a given organizational context. Many of the abilities and behaviors associated with charisma are perceived to be acquired through training and experience rather than through genetic inheritance or solely as a result of contextual forces. In other words, from a behavioral perspective, many of the charismatic qualities identified in earlier chapters can be learned. Armed with such beliefs, several researchers (for example, Bass) have already initiated leadership training designs that incorporate several of the behavioral components of charisma.

From a developmental perspective, Kets de Vries (Chapter Eight) and Avolio and Gibbons (Chapter Ten) argue that there may be important antecedents of charisma over which we have no control. If they are correct, it may be difficult to alter the impact of early family dynamics and socialization experiences that determine a manager's disposition to become charismatic. The effectiveness of a training program will then vary across individuals because of different dispositions and varying levels of personal development. This implies that, to be effective, training programs must, at the least, take into account the socialization influences and dispositions of the trainees. For this reason, Avolio and Gibbons suggest individually oriented training programs "keyed to earlier life events." In many ways, developmental and psychoanalytical perspectives view training in charisma as a therapeutic and self-development device for managers.

Other social scientists, such as Roberts and Bradley (Chapter Nine), seriously question whether charisma can actually be taught. Instead, they argue that context plays a pivotal role and

that individuals may have no control over the important contextual variables that foster charisma. In addition, they raise
the ethical question of whether it is morally defensible to train
charisma. They fear that training in charisma may lead to
deception and exploitation of followers—for example, by manufacturing crises when there are none. In addition, they see
charismatic followings as unpredictable and fear the possibility of negative outcomes. Training, in the eyes of Roberts
and Bradley, entails risks that are potentially too costly to undertake.

While we agree with the assertion made by Roberts and
Bradley that charisma as an emergent process results from an
interaction of contextual, relational, and personal factors, we do
not share their pessimism with respect to the trainability of charisma. If the elements of the charismatic influence process are
identified (in the nature of the context, in the characteristics of
leaders and followers, and in the nature of their relationship)
in clear operational terms, then it is possible to train leaders
to become more effective influence agents. We further believe
that increasing the self-efficacy of managers in leadership roles
is morally defensible in terms of increasing both organizational effectiveness and followers' motivation and competence.

Our own position on the issue of charisma's trainability
is eclectic. We identified in Chapter Three a number of the
behavioral components of charismatic leadership, and believe
that these can be acquired by managers through appropriate
training programs. However, we recognize the fact that certain
contextual factors within the organization (and in its external
environment) and/or certain developmental antecedents in the
life history of a manager may act as barriers to the effectiveness
of these programs. As such, it may be more difficult to train
some managers in some contexts than other managers in other
contexts. For example, managers with high power and esteem
needs may be more easily trained than managers with low power
and esteem needs. Additionally, it may be more difficult to
train managers to acquire the entire constellation of charismatic
behaviors.

We also feel that transforming ordinary managers into

highly charismatic leaders may sometimes be dysfunctional for organizations. For example, certain managers may attempt to engender a greater dependence on themselves than is necessary. Or, in more stable situations, charismatic leadership may not be needed. However, under appropriate organizational conditions (for example, when there is need for organizational renewal or change), it may be possible to train a corps of managers who possess the potential to become charismatic leaders. And we feel that training managers to improve their charisma-related skills will improve their personal effectiveness and influence over others and in turn facilitate the achievement of organizational objectives. It is also our belief that the training of these skills is no different from the training of skills in other leadership programs, such as the Managerial Grid (Blake and Mouton, 1964), or participative leadership training (Vroom and Yetton, 1973). Certainly Howell's laboratory study (cited by Bass in Chapter Two) suggests this possibility. Drawing on his experience with leadership training, Harvard psychologist David McClelland (1975) confirms our perspective: "Repeatedly we have discovered that leaders are not so much born as made. We have worked in places where most people feel there is not much leadership potential. . . . Yet we have found over and over again that even among people who have never thought of themselves as leaders or attempted to influence in any way, real leadership performance can be elicited by specialized techniques of psychological education" (McClelland, 1975, p. 270).

Training Charisma

All forms of leadership training have two basic functions. First, they provide an individual with an awareness of the nature and dynamics of leadership and with the various behaviors involved in it. Furthermore, through training the individual discovers his or her own standing with respect to these behaviors and thereby his or her potential for developing leadership qualities. This is the information function of training. The second basic function of training is to build the requisite skills for fulfilling leadership roles. In order to achieve this skill-building function, training must provide opportunities to develop new modes of behavior and attitudes and to practice matching them to a predetermined standard.

In the context of charismatic leadership, the information function of training should provide information on the what, how, why, and when of charismatic leadership; an assessment of the trainee's predisposing attributes, such as goal commitment, involvement, power and esteem motive patterns, and so on; and an assessment of the trainee's basic abilities regarding various charisma-related skills or behaviors. With regard to skill building, training should emphasize the development of generalizable cognitive skills in visioning and strategy-making, interpersonal sensitivity and communication skills, and practice in empowering and impression management techniques. Several training devices and testing programs are already available for this purpose. Some of these devices, such as films and case studies, are most suitable for providing information, and others, such as management simulation games and role playing, are more appropriate for skill building. Any training program must incorporate these two functions to be effective.

In Chapter Three, we described the three key stages of the leadership influence process, and within each stage we identified certain behavioral components that distinguished charismatic from noncharismatic leaders. To develop charismatic leadership, training programs should focus on building these behavioral components in a leader. These components can be broken down into five key areas of competency that must be addressed in such a training program. The key skill areas are: (1) critical evaluation (of a context) and problem-finding skills, (2) visioning (goals) and planning (tactics) skills, (3) communication (articulation and interpersonal sensitivity) skills, (4) exemplary personal behavior and impression management skills, and (5) empowering skills. In each area, there is a set of cognitive and behavioral skills that can be developed through training. However, we feel, as House, Woycke, and Fodor suggest in Chapter Four, that certain base line dispositional attributes, such as goal commitment and work involvement, may be necessary for effective training. Diagnostic tools for determining such base line dispositions are available in the literature (see, for example, Kanungo, 1982); these can be used for prognostic assessment of the training programs.

Critical Evaluation and Problem Detection Skills. The literature on charisma suggests that any transition can facilitate the emergence of charisma. In other words, charismatic leaders may either take advantage of an existing situational crisis or, at times of stability, create a crisis or an opportunity to bring about revolutionary changes in a system. This implies that these leaders have a great sensitivity to crisis and serious problem situations. They are also more perceptive than others of deficiencies in the status quo. Very often, they may formulate a crisis by actively searching out potential problems in an existing situation and then use these problems as springboards for advocating their future visions. Therefore, detecting deficiencies and defining problems in an existing situation are necessary skills of a charismatic leader. Thus, training programs must provide opportunities and practice in critical evaluation and problem finding in existing organizational contexts. In addition, such training should instill in trainees a belief that they can always improve things for the organization. Beliefs such as this become the motivational force behind deliberate attempts at problem finding. Problem-finding skills can be developed through the use of such techniques as "synectics" (Gordon, 1961) and "Janusian thinking" (Rothenburg, 1979). These techniques can help develop cognitive skills in reconceptualizing situations and redefining problems.

Visioning Skills. The second trainable component of charisma is visioning for the future and planning realistic but unconventional ways of achieving the vision. An analysis of the visioning component has been presented by Sashkin in Chapter Five. For developing skills in visioning, Sashkin's analyses would suggest training leaders to think clearly into the future (or in long-range planning) in terms of specific goals and paths to those goals. As such, organizations must build in opportunities and rewards for managers to think long term—a perspective that is contrary to the North American business mentality. In addition, managers could be selected on the basis of their cognitive ability to think long term using instruments developed along the lines of Jaques's research (Chapter Five).

Besides visioning, the planning of effective unconventional tactics to achieve a vision is also a trainable skill. Organizations can utilize creativity training programs for developing thinking styles conducive to generating unconventional approaches (novel but appropriate to the context) to solving organizational problems. Developing skills for finding unconventional and creative tactics requires two steps: first, unlearning old habits of following conventional pathways and, second, developing fresh and radically different approaches to problems. This can be accomplished in training by creating a climate for autonomy or self-direction and encouraging motivation for achieving unique solutions. Recent work by Anabile (1983) on creativity may provide practical hints for organizational training programs (see also Kohn, 1987).

In addition, Quick Environment Scanning Technique (QUEST) sessions as described by Bennis and Nanus (1985) may be a particularly effective means to stimulate vision and tactics. In these sessions, company managers are brought together to brainstorm and share their views about future external environmental opportunities and threats—especially those with critical implications for strategic positioning. Using this environmental scanning process, managers then identify and choose among the high-priority strategic options available to them. The brainstorming quality of these sessions fosters a broader and longer-range perspective of an industry than would normally be possible. As well, the process can prod managers into discovering and exploring strategic and tactical options that the conventions of their organization may prevent them from seeing. Since QUEST sessions involve management teams and require a degree of consensus around option choices, this process can build a high degree of trust and commitment to the strategies chosen—in other words, to a shared vision.

Communication Skills. The third element of charismatic leadership training—communication skills—involves a twofold approach. The first focuses on speech and articulation skills and the second on interpersonal sensitivity skills. As we mentioned in Chapter Three, it is through effective articulation of the vision and a sensitivity to followers' needs that the leader's vision is made meaningful and inspiring. In essence, it is not enough to simply have vision. Rather, communicating the vision involves persuading the organization of its importance. As Bennis and Nanus (1985) point out: "A vision cannot be established in an organization by edict or by the exercise of power or coercion. It is more an act of persuasion, of creating an enthusiastic and dedicated commitment to a vision because it is right for the times, right for the organization, and right for the people who are working in it" (p. 107).

Thus, managers must be trained in the skills of artful persuasion and meaning making. While conventional speech courses may be helpful and have the advantage of being widely available, they often lack an emphasis on inspiration-building and meaning-making skills. Yet training in these aspects of speech delivery and content is critical for charismatic leadership. Films of inspirational speakers and training in certain dramatic arts may provide models and experience in delivery. Voice coaching on intonation, pacing, and emotional content also might be helpful.

Speech content skills are also critical. As we noted, the speeches of charismatic leaders are often constructed with scenarios that highlight the shortcomings of the status quo and present, in clear, specific terms, future goals as the most attractive and attainable alternatives. In training, great emphasis then should be placed on meaning making around future goals and simplicity of ideas. Managers must be taught to translate their strategic aims and plans into a perspective and language that are inspiring and meaningful. Pondy (1978) notes: "The real power of Martin Luther King was not only that he had a dream, but that he could describe it, that it became public, and therefore accessible to millions. This dual capacity . . . to make sense of things and to put them into language meaningful to large numbers of people gives the person who has it enormous leverage . . . this capacity to go public with sense making involves putting very profound ideas into very simple language" (p. 95). To some extent, these skills could be developed through an analysis of famous speeches and through training by speech writers. This type of training, however, is contrary to current practice in business organizations in which monotone speakers deliver a litany of statistics.

In order to successfully persuade subordinates to accept a strategic vision and the plans to achieve it, the verbal articulation of the leader must be based on an understanding of subordinates' needs and abilities. Managers in leadership roles should be sensitive to followers' work motivation and to what followers can or cannot do to help achieve the vision. Interpersonal sensitivity can be developed through training programs designed to improve active listening (Rogers and Farson, 1955) and feedback skills (Hanson, 1975; Haney, 1979). These skills are important in building a climate of trust and mutual respect between leader and followers. Active listening skills should also enhance leaders' abilities to scan their environments in a more realistic manner (Bennis and Nanus, 1985), and feedback skills should help in reducing subordinates' resistance to accepting their leaders' vision and plans.

Personal Exemplary Behavior and Impression Management Skills. A leader's charismatic influence is often manifested through the image the leader projects for followers. What the leader exhibits in his or her person is what the followers believe about him or her. Thus, if a leader's charisma represents his or her idealized vision, extraordinary ability to lead, self-confidence, and unswerving commitment and perseverance, then these characteristics must be consistently reflected in the leader's physical appearance and behavior. For this to occur, leaders must develop knowledge and skills in utilizing impression management techniques. In order to present a charismatic image, they should be trained in four major areas: modeling (the use of exemplary behavior), appearance, body language, and verbal skills (with an emphasis on rhetoric [word choice], metaphors, analogies, and paralanguage [word intent]).

In the area of modeling, training should emphasize the use of exemplary behavior involving high personal cost or risk. Kogan and Wallach (1964) proposed that people may differ in their generalized disposition toward personal risk taking or conservatism. Managers can be selected for training programs in charisma based on their risk-taking propensity, particularly in the areas of financial and social risk taking. Charismatic leaders in business often engage in these types of personally risky ventures. In this case, financial risk taking involves the possibility of sacrificing monetary gains and social risk taking involves the possibility of losing esteem in the eyes of others. Diagnostic tools are available to aid the selection process suggested here (Jackson, Hourany, and Widmar, 1972).

After managers are selected for training, educational programs should encourage and reinforce exemplary risky behavior on their part for the sake of realizing their vision. This could be done through simulation games in a format similar to the Looking Glass program developed by the Center for Creative Leadership in Greensboro, North Carolina. Training also should emphasize the management of physical appearance, body language, and verbal skills. These components need to be coordinated with exemplary and personally risky behavior to promote a charismatic image. In order to be effective, each impression management component must consistently express the shared values associated with the vision. The impression management techniques used by Mary Kay Cosmetics are a good example of such coordination and expression of shared values. Mary Kay ventured to promote cosmetics through the use of the color pink (for physical appearance), an emphasis on femininity (for body language), and a glorification of womanhood (in her speeches).

Empowering Skills. A critical trait of charismatic leaders is their ability to empower subordinates to achieve their visions. Empowerment is particularly important because the charismatic's vision is often lofty and difficult to achieve. Stamina and perseverance are required. Only through a belief in their own power and abilities can subordinates hope to achieve the leader's goals. As a result, the leader must be continually reinforcing his or her followers' sense of efficacy. Empowerment implies creating conditions for heightened motivation through the development of a strong sense of personal efficacy.

Leadership practices that have been identified as empowering include: (1) the expression of confidence in subordinates accompanied by high performance expectations (Burke, 1986; Conger, 1986; House, 1977, 1988; Neilsen, 1986); (2) fostering opportunities for subordinates to influence and/or participate in decision making (Block, 1987; Burke, 1986; Conger, 1986; House, 1977, 1988; Kanter, 1979); (3) providing autonomy from bureaucratic constraint (Block, 1987; Kanter, 1979; House, 1988); and (4) setting inspirational and/or meaningful goals (Bennis and Nanus, 1985; Block, 1987; Burke, 1986; McClelland, 1975; Tichy and Devanna, 1986). It has also been suggested by House (1988) that leaders/managers be selected on the basis of their inclination to use power in a positive manner.

Reward systems that emphasize innovative and unusual performance and high incentive values are argued to foster a greater sense of self-efficacy among followers (Kanter, 1979). Jobs that provide task variety, personal relevance, appropriate autonomy and control, low levels of established routines and rules, and high advancement prospects are more likely to empower subordinates (Block, 1987; Kanter, 1979; Oldham, 1976).

Although the preceding discussion emphasizes five key skill areas in which training is needed, the development of skills in each of these areas in isolation will not result in the manifestation of charisma. As indicated in Chapter Four, the various behavioral components must appear in a more integrated constellation to manifest charisma. Thus, training ultimately must emphasize an interweaving of the behavior components in all five areas. Training programs could be designed using a two-step process: In the first step, program members would receive training in each component, and in the second step, a simulated management game would be used to encourage trainees to integrate their training experiences.

Is It Ethical to Train Charismatic Leadership?

Earlier in the chapter, we noted Roberts and Bradley's (Chapter Nine) objections to training charisma on the grounds that it might be used for manipulative and self-seeking purposes. While such a possibility may exist, we feel that the potential benefits to managers of such training far outweigh what we believe would be rare occurrences of misuse of training.

There is a serious shortage of leadership in North American industry today. Our managers have been trained and socialized to be administrators, not leaders. It is imperative that this trend be reversed. Training is one means at our disposal. Charismatic leaders have much to teach about effective leadership skills. If we can distill their more beneficial qualities, we would hope that managers could learn not necessarily to be charismatic leaders themselves but to be more effective managers in their leadership roles.

More important, our concern is that ethical arguments similar to Roberts and Bradley's might be raised against the vast majority of leadership and social influence training programs. Any training that heightens a manager's ability to influence others has the potential of being used in ways that promote either the manager's own ends or the "greater good" (or perhaps both). Such outcomes are dependent largely on the manager's disposition. Some managers are inclined toward personal aggrandizement, and others have more socially constructive intentions. In reality, most managers seek personal reward and achievement within a concern for the overall effectiveness of their work units or organizations. They are motivated by both their personal values and organizational and societal norms. Does one then prohibit training in managerial effectiveness in order to prevent a very small minority of individuals from misusing certain leadership skills? We feel that this is an extreme view. And there are safeguards that can minimize the possibility of managers seeking more self-serving outcomes. First, selection procedures could be used to screen candidates for training programs. For example, individuals could be selected on the basis of the degree of activity inhibition in their expression of power (Chapter Seven). Second, in order to be successful, charismatic leaders must be sensitive to the needs and values of their subordinates. This in itself places, in the majority of cases, a safeguard on a manager's ability to seek purely self-serving ends.

Training programs could emphasize such sensitivity. Third, more senior managers and peers must assume significant responsibility (as they do in reality) for the actions of a manager. In any organization, they are the ultimate safeguards.

Conclusion

Any act of leadership involves risks—for the followers and for the leader. As history has shown, even the greatest of leaders have failed at times, and even they have been driven by their own more personal goals. Allowing anyone to assume a leadership role introduces a risk for those dependent on the outcome. Yet without that leadership it is doubtful that humankind would have advanced as far as it has today. Training managers to be leaders is a risky business—but one without which there would likely be no industrial progress.

References

Anabile, T. M. *The Social Psychology of Creativity.* New York: Springer-Verlag, 1983.

Bennis, W., and Nanus, B. *Leaders: The Strategies for Taking Charge.* New York: Harper & Row, 1985.

Blake, R. R., and Mouton, J. S. *The Managerial Grid.* Houston: Gulf, 1964.

Block, P. *The Empowered Manager: Positive Political Skills at Work.* San Francisco: Jossey-Bass, 1987.

Burke, W. "Leadership as Empowering Others." In S. Srivastva and Associates, *Executive Power: How Executives Influence People and Organizations.* San Francisco: Jossey-Bass, 1986.

Conger, J. "Empowering Leadership." Working paper, McGill University, Faculty of Management, Montreal, 1986.

Gordon, W.J.J. *Synectics: The Development of Creative Capacity.* New York: Collier, 1961.

Haney, W. V. *Communication and Interpersonal Relations.* Homewood, Ill.: Irwin, 1979.

Hanson, P. H. "Giving Feedback: An Interpersonal Skill." In J. E. Jones and J. W. Pfeiffer (eds.), *The 1975 Annual Hand-*

book for Group Facilitators. San Diego, Calif.: University Associates, 1975.

House, R. J. "A 1976 Theory of Charismatic Leadership." In J. G. Hunt and L. L. Larson (eds.), *Leadership: The Cutting Edge.* Carbondale: Southern Illinois University Press, 1977.

House, R. J. "Power and Personality in Complex Organizations." In L. L. Cummings and B. M. Staw (eds.), *Research in Organizational Behavior: An Annual Review of Critical Essays and Reviews.* Vol. 10. Greenwich, Conn.: JAI Press, 1988.

Jackson, D. N., Hourany, L., and Widmar, N. J. "A Four-Dimensional Interpretation of Risk Taking." *Journal of Personality,* 1972, *40,* 483–501.

Kanter, R. M. "Power Failure in Management Circuits." *Harvard Business Review,* 1979, *57,* 65–75.

Kanungo, R. N. *Work Alienation: An Integrative Approach.* New York: Praeger, 1982.

Kogan, N., and Wallach, M. A. *Risk Taking: A Study in Cognition and Personality.* New York: Holt, Rinehart & Winston, 1964.

Kohn, A. "Art for Art's Sake." *Psychology Today,* 1987, *21,* 52–57.

McClelland, D. C. *Power: The Inner Experience.* New York: Irvington, 1975.

Mill, C. R. "The Art of Giving and Receiving Feedback." In L. Porter and C. R. Mill (eds.), *Reading Book for Laboratories in Human Relations Training.* Arlington, Va.: National Training Laboratory Institute, 1976.

Neilsen, E. H. "Empowerment Strategies: Balancing Authority and Responsibility." In S. Srivastva and Associates, *Executive Power: How Executives Influence People and Organizations.* San Francisco: Jossey-Bass, 1986.

Oldham, G. R. "The Motivational Strategies Used by Supervisors: Relationships to Effectiveness Indicators." *Organizational Behavior and Human Performance,* 1976, *15,* 66–86.

Pondy, L. R. "Leadership Is a Language Game." In M. W. McCall and M. M. Lombardo (eds.), *Leadership: Where Else Can We Go?* Durham, N.C.: Duke University Press, 1978.

Rogers, C. R., and Farson, R. E. *Active Listening.* Chicago: Industrial Relations Center, University of Chicago, 1955.

Rothenburg, A. *The Emerging Goddess.* Chicago: University of Chicago Press, 1979.

Tichy, N. M., and Devanna, M. A. *The Transformational Leader.* New York: Wiley, 1986.

Vroom, V. H., and Yetton, P. W. *Leadership and Decision Making.* Pittsburgh, Penn.: University of Pittsburgh Press, 1973.

Conclusion:
Patterns and Trends
in Studying
Charismatic Leadership

Jay A. Conger
Rabindra N. Kanungo

This book signals the beginning of a systematic scientific analysis of charismatic leadership in organizational contexts. As evidenced by the various contributions to this volume, multiple perspectives are offered to help us understand the phenomenon. The complex nature of charisma naturally leads social scientists to view it from different vantage points. As a result, there appears to be no single unified approach at this stage in our understanding. The chapters in the book reflect this reality. Thus, some chapters emphasize the behavioral dispositions and skills of leaders and followers, others emphasize the relational dynamics between leader and followers, and still others deal with contextual and structural aspects of charisma. Some address the delineation of boundaries and limits of charismatic influence, and others highlight the development and training of such leaders. Added to this diversity of emphasis, the various chapters reflect the descriptive and exploratory quality of theory and research at this time.

As is often typical of theories in their early stages of development, it is difficult to draw firm conclusions on the topic.

However, in view of the richness of materials presented in this book, we can draw some general and tentative conclusions concerning points of convergence and divergence among our various contributors. It is our hope that such conclusions might guide future research and management practice.

To provide a framework for our analysis, we view charismatic leadership as an influence process consisting of three structural and three dynamic components, as presented in Figure 1. The three structural components are the leader, the followers, and the environmental context (both inside and outside the organization). The three dynamic components are the relationship between leader and followers, the relationship between the leader and the context, and the relationship between the followers and the context.

The purpose of this concluding chapter is to review the thinking of our contributors with respect to each of these six components. In doing so, we will identify areas in which there is substantial agreement or substantial controversy.

Leader Characteristics

In terms of the distinguishing attributes of charismatic leaders, there appears to be general agreement among the authors of this volume around the following: (1) vision, (2) emotional expressiveness, (3) articulation skills, (4) high activity level, and (5) exemplary behavior. There is more limited agreement around risk taking and unconventional behavior. The principal area of divergence centers on the nature of the visioning process itself. Sashkin argues for a more deliberate, rational process, while Westley and Mintzberg perceive visioning as an emergent process. These differing approaches raise further questions: (1) whether it is possible for both deliberate and emergent visioning processes to occur simultaneously, (2) whether they represent two different but equally effective styles, and (3) whether under certain contextual conditions one process is more appropriate and feasible than another.

Regarding leader predispositions, there appears to be some convergence among the authors on the following qualities:

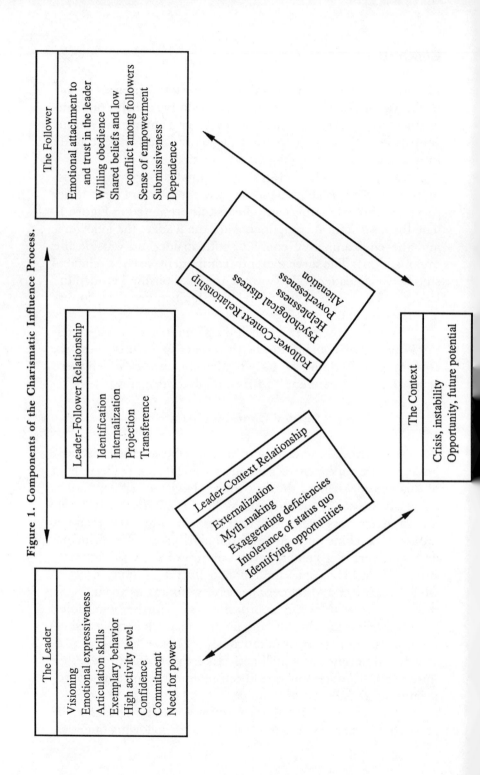

Figure 1. Components of the Charismatic Influence Process.

The Follower

- Emotional attachment to and trust in the leader
- Willing obedience
- Shared beliefs and low conflict among followers
- Sense of empowerment
- Submissiveness
- Dependence

Leader-Follower Relationship

- Identification
- Internalization
- Projection
- Transference

Follower-Context Relationship

- Psychological distress
- Helplessness
- Powerlessness
- Alienation

The Context

- Crisis, instability
- Opportunity, future potential

Leader-Context Relationship

- Externalization
- Myth making
- Exaggerating deficiencies
- Intolerance of status quo
- Identifying opportunities

The Leader

- Visioning
- Emotional expressiveness
- Articulation skills
- Exemplary behavior
- High activity level
- Confidence
- Commitment
- Need for power

(1) high self-confidence and self-determination, (2) a high degree of mental involvement in the mission and the leadership role, and (3) a high need for power. Although there is agreement around a high need for power, there is disagreement around the exact nature of the leader's power orientation. While several authors divide the power orientations of charismatic leaders into two categories depending on their level of activity inhibition (for example, Howell's socialized and personalized categories), we do not feel comfortable with this distinction. For one thing, we feel that such power orientations are not clearly dichotomous in terms of observed behavior and that parallel links to identification and internalization processes (socialized leaders relying on internalization processes with followers and personalized leaders relying on identification) are equally problematic, as we will point out. Secondly, we ourselves distinguish charismatic leaders by their elitist-entrepreneurial qualities—in sharp contrast to the power orientation of the consensus or socialized leader portrayed by Howell. We argue that leaders with a high level of activity inhibition may not be able to develop charismatic appeal. Moreover, we see charismatic leaders as embracing revolutionary rather than evolutionary change (another characteristic of Howell's high activity inhibition and socialized charismatic leader). We question whether an evolutionary leader can be truly transformational or charismatic.

Finally, the notion of a personalized and "pure" charismatic leader versus a transformational charismatic leader is primarily a matter of opinion at this time. Hard empirical evidence is needed before this distinction can be accepted with any degree of confidence. While the dichotomy has a conceptual elegance, it may not withstand rigorous empirical scrutiny. And while we might sort charismatic leaders into "good" and "bad" groupings (which we might then label "transformational" versus "pure" leaders), this distinction is simply a by-product of our own value system. For example, Hitler's actions may have been interpreted by many Germans as "transformational," despite his self-seeking aims. We feel that this conceptualization of charismatic leadership in terms of power orientations requires significant exploration before conclusions can be drawn.

In addition to the issue of power, there is debate among the authors surrounding the charismatic leader's level of internal conflict. Bass describes charismatic leaders as free from internal conflict. This freedom, he argues, allows them to be more confident and directed than other leaders. From a slightly different perspective, Avolio and Gibbons hypothesize that the charismatic (transformational) leader has the capacity to make productive meaning out of all conflict and thereby the ability to resolve it and appear self-confident. For Kets de Vries, the leader's internal conflicts are projected outside of the individual and onto the goals he or she sets. The leader gains a sense of internal psychic freedom through this projection process. We, however, see internal conflict as a universal phenomenon, and we feel that charismatic leaders are no freer from it than anyone else. Further, to distinguish charismatic leaders from others on the basis of internal conflict would require appropriate operationalization of the construct followed by rigorous empirical testing.

Follower Characteristics

Areas of consensus among the authors on the hypothesized effects of charismatic leadership on follower behavior are as follows: (1) high attachment to and trust in the leader, (2) willing obedience to the leader, (3) heightened performance and motivation, (4) greater group cohesion in terms of shared beliefs and low intragroup conflict, and (5) a sense of empowerment. On the empowerment dimension, however, there is disagreement. Some theorists see empowerment as a universal outcome of all forms of charismatic leadership while others (for instance, Howell) tie empowerment outcomes only to one form—the socialized charismatic leader.

There is convergence of opinion regarding the followers' predispositions in a context of charismatic leadership. It is believed that charismatic leaders have followers who tend to be submissive and dependent. Low self-confidence and strong feelings of uncertainty are further thought to characterize such followers; these characteristics foster a receptiveness to the self-confident and directive charismatic leader. However, since crisis is the primary context within which charismatic leaders have been studied, such conclusions may not be entirely correct. For instance, we may find followers in entrepreneurial contexts who are characterized more by predispositions of adventure and confidence than of insecurity and inadequacy. In general, follower predispositions require significant further study.

The Context Characteristic

With respect to the nature of the context in which charismatic leadership manifests, there seems to be a consensus that it often contains crisis situations. Crisis may represent organizational decay, internal dissension and power struggles, or intense and threatening market competition—all of which endanger the survival of the organization. Crisis and its destabilizing effects create the necessary impetus for motivating followers to move toward organizational renewal and change.

Some controversy surrounds the issue of whether charismatic leadership can be manifested in contexts lacking crisis. Bass recognizes the possibility of charismatic leadership without contextual crisis. We concur with Bass in maintaining that unexplored opportunities within the larger context may facilitate the emergence of a charismatic leader. And in his study of charismatic business leaders, Conger (1985) found such leaders in both contexts of crisis and those without crisis. In contexts lacking crisis, the charismatic leaders were associated with high opportunity, entrepreneurial environments. Thus, in our view, both deficiencies and opportunities in the context can account for charismatic leadership phenomena. It remains, however, for future research to determine the extent to which each of these two aspects of context is necessary for the manifestation of charisma.

The Leader-Follower Relationship

Charismatic leadership is characterized by the strong emotional attachment of followers to the leader. There is some consensus among scholars in this regard. The leader-follower relationship is based on an intense emotional bond between the two, often resulting in uncritical acceptance of the leader's influence. The relationship is one of total trust and follower dependence. The dynamics of such a relationship, however, are a subject of controversy. Different explanations have been offered in terms of the followers' identification with the leader (Bass), followers' internalization of the values advocated by the leader (Howell), and more unconscious processes involving projection and transference (Kets de Vries).

Explanations for why and how followers develop and maintain their high emotional involvement with the leader come largely from two sources: social psychological theories of influence processes (French and Raven, 1959; Kelman, 1958) and Freudian theories of ego defense mechanisms (Freud, 1936). We have proposed that the charismatic leader-follower relationship is one of referent power (French and Raven, 1959). Followers accept the leader's influence primarily because they like the leader and identify with him or her. Howell explains the relationship in terms of both identification and internalization using Kelman's (1958) theory of social influence. From the Freudian perspective, a psychological process involving unconscious tendencies has been elaborated by Kets de Vries in terms of projective and transference processes. Followers project their ego ideals onto the leader and, in essence, make the leader their own conscience. These explanations, however, remain at a speculative level and require empirical validation in future research.

One criterion used by Howell to distinguish her two forms of charisma, socialized and personalized, is the nature of the social influence process underlying the leader-follower relationship. According to Howell, followers' identification with the leader defines personalized charisma, whereas their internalization of the leader's values defines socialized charisma. As stated earlier, there is no clear agreement on such a distinction of charisma. Observation of leader-follower relationships might suggest that identification and internalization processes may be operating simultaneously among followers of both socialized and personalized leaders. Although Howell's conceptualization of leader-follower relational dynamics appears intuitively appealing, empirical verification may be necessary to put it on firm footing.

The Leader-Context Relationship

There is overall agreement among the contributors to this volume that charismatic influence stems from a leader's perception of crisis in the environment and from his or her commitment to altering the context in a way that will resolve the crisis. Thus, the leader's relationship with the existing context is one of intolerance and acute dissatisfaction. Little attention, however, has been paid to the dynamics of such a possible relationship.

Kets de Vries has suggested a process of "externalization" to account for the nature of the leader-context relationship. According to Kets de Vries, leaders project their own personal crises and the way in which they wish to resolve them onto the larger context. They then employ historically important and emotionally appealing myths to ground their visions in a way that responds to follower needs.

We have argued that charismatic leaders, because of their intolerance of the existing context or status quo, tend to quickly identify and exaggerate existing deficiencies in the environment and articulate them to subordinates. These leaders are sensitive to shortcomings and are able to discern how environmental constraints frustrate followers' needs. From both psychoanalytical and behavioral perspectives, the identification of crisis is at least partly determined by the way in which charismatic leaders relate to their contexts. In other words, crisis may be, to some degree, the making of the leader's actions and behavior. Such a leader may foster or heighten existing deficiencies and problems to the level of a crisis. Explorations into the dynamics of this leader-context dimension are needed in the future. Both theoretical developments and empirical verification of how and why leaders identify and articulate crises and deficiencies in their environments need to be on the agenda for future research.

Although the authors agree to some degree on crisis-based charismatic influence, there seems to be controversy among them as to whether charismatic influence can come from the leader's perception of unexplored opportunities in the larger environment. On the one hand, Bass, Conger (1985), and ourselves argue for the emergence of charisma based on opportunities. Roberts and Bradley, on the other hand, follow Weber in considering crisis the only necessary contextual condition for the emergence of charisma. For them, the crisis context is a given, and the role of the leader, while relating to the context, is a passive one. We, on the other hand, have argued in favor of a proactive role of the leader in creating and articulating both crises and opportunities in the context.

Perceived crisis and opportunity can be viewed as two complementary aspects of the leader-context relationship. A charismatic leader identifies or articulates crisis in the status quo, but at the same time he or she can identify the potential opportunity within the crisis and articulate an inspiring future vision that plays upon that opportunity. Depending on the emphasis the leader places while relating to the context (either on the status quo or on the vision), he or she could be characterized as a crisis or ideological charismatic. Future attention should be directed toward exploring the extent to which crisis and opportunities in the context are used by leaders to foster their charismatic influence on followers.

The Follower-Context Relationship

The dynamics of the follower-context relationship is perhaps the most underresearched issue of all. Everyone seems to agree that the emergence of charismatic influence is facilitated by contextual cues that cause psychological distress among followers. In other words, when the context evokes feelings of high uncertainty (Conger, 1985), helplessness, powerlessness, and alienation (Kanungo, 1982) among followers, conditions become ripe for charismatic influence within organizations.

Followers become "charisma hungry" when they experience a loss of control over their environment, when their needs and expectations are frustrated because of perceived environmental barriers and threats, when an uncertain future is presented, and when a state of anomie (decline of old values and rituals) arises and results in identity crisis. Iacocca's charismatic influence on Chrysler's employees can be partly explained by the way that Chrysler employees related to their context. They perceived significant future uncertainty (fear of company bankruptcy and the loss of jobs), which caused them to suffer psychological distress and consequently made them more susceptible to Iacocca's influence.

Both Bass and Kets de Vries talk of perceived anomie, upheaval, and crisis in the environment leading to a sense of helplessness and regressive forms of follower behavior, such as unquestioning and blind trust in the leader. However, the psychological processes underlying helplessness (Garber and Seligman, 1980) and alienation (Kanungo, 1982) and the identification of specific organizational conditions (Martinko and Gardner, 1982) that promote such psychological states among followers have received little attention. Future studies should explore this issue in greater depth.

Here we would like to point out that in order for charismatic influence to operate, the context must be viewed differently by leaders and followers. The leader must identify and articulate both crisis in the status quo and opportunities within the larger context to achieve the future vision. The followers, on the other hand, must view the context as representing crisis and/or opportunities that they are unable to achieve by themselves. The experience of crisis or helplessness leads to a state of psychological distress or frustration and consequently to increased follower susceptibility to the leader's influence. Perception by the followers of opportunities that could be achieved on their own would lessen their dependence on the leader, thereby weakening the leader's charismatic hold on them. This mechanism might account for the fading of a leader's charismatic influence with follower empowerment and with the institutionalization of organizational changes. Empowerment reduces the followers' sense of helplessness in relation to their context; institutionalization reduces context instability for followers. Both reduce dependence on the leader.

Some Remaining Issues

While our discussion has covered many of the areas of agreement and debate on the topic of charismatic leadership, several aspects remain to be addressed. The first is the issue of institutionalization or, as Weber describes it, "routinization." This process has been largely overlooked by ourselves and the other contributors to this volume. And with the exception of what we have learned from the Trice and Beyer (1986) study, we know little about the institutionalization of charismatic leadership. There is a significant gap in our knowledge concerning the transition of charisma from leader to institution. Longitudinal studies are needed to chart the processes of routinization as well as the problems that are encountered in institutionalizing charisma.

A second area in need of research attention is the issue of whether charismatic leadership can manifest itself at any organizational level. Bass argues that it is widely distributed at all hierarchical levels. Unfortunately, there is no empirical evidence to support conclusions in either direction. There is also the issue of whether charismatic leadership is a dichotomous phenomenon—either you are a charismatic leader or you are not—or whether it is a matter of degree. Is the phenomenon scalar (Conger, 1985)? We suspect that it is, but the issue needs verification.

The chapters by Roberts and Bradley and Kets de Vries raise important questions surrounding the actual management of charismatic leaders. These leaders appear difficult to control, and their missions may engender tremendous amounts of emotional energy, which only the charismatics may be able to harness effectively. What can senior managers and organizational leaders do to supervise and control these leaders? Such practice implications have been completely overlooked.

Finally, we would like to briefly return to the issue of charismatic versus transformational leadership. This distinction is raised by Avolio and Gibbons, Bass, and Howell. In their conceptualization of the transformational leader, charisma is only one element—albeit the most significant—of the transformational leader's behavior. The other two (considerably less significant) components are intellectual stimulation and individual consideration. The further distinction is made that without these two elements the leader is a pure charismatic driven by personalized or self-seeking aims. In our conceptualization, the qualities of intellectual stimulation and individual consideration are subsumed under charisma itself. In order to become charismatic, we believe that leader must, to a significant degree, be sensitive to follower needs and desires (individual consideration). In addition, he or she must provide a vision and mission that are both mentally and emotionally stimulating (intellectual/ emotional stimulation). A leader who fails to do this will not be perceived as charismatic. In other words, it is not possible for charisma to manifest itself without a degree of individual consideration and intellectual stimulation. These components are interrelated rather than discrete entities, as conceptualized by Bass and others. As such, we feel that the distinction between transformational and pure charismatic leadership may lead to confusion over the concept of charisma itself. It is an issue in need of significant exploration.

Conclusion

It is our hope that this volume will stimulate further thought, debate, and inquiry into what has long been considered an elusive phenomenon. For in our own minds, there is little doubt that charismatic leadership has profound implications— both positive and negative—for organizational effectiveness. We are hopeful that one day much of charisma's mysteriousness will be stripped away and that managers and leaders everywhere will be able to incorporate its more positive qualities into their own skills at building more effective organizations. Our aim has been to initiate that process with this book.

References

Conger, J. A. "Charismatic Leadership in Business: An Exploratory Study." Unpublished doctoral dissertation, School of Business Administration, Harvard University, 1985.

French, J. R., Jr., and Raven, B. H. "The Bases of Social Power." In D. Cartwright (ed.), *Studies in Social Power.* Ann Arbor: University of Michigan Press, 1959.

Freud, A. *The Ego and the Mechanisms of Defense.* (Rev. ed.) New York: International Universities Press, 1936.

Garber, J., and Seligman, M.E.P. (eds). *Human Helplessness: Theory and Applications.* Orlando, Fla.: Academic Press, 1980.

Kanungo, R. N. *Work Alienation: An Integrative Approach.* New York: Praeger, 1982.

Kelman, H. C. "Compliance, Identification, and Internalization: Three Processes of Attitude Change." *Journal of Conflict Resolution,* 1958, *2,* 51–60.

Martinko, M. J., and Gardner, W. L. "Learned Helplessness: An Alternative Explanation for Performance Deficits." *Academy of Management Review,* 1982, *7,* 195–204.

Trice, H. M., and Beyer, J. M. "Charisma and Its Routinization in Two Social Movement Organizations." *Research in Organizational Behavior,* 1986, *8,* 113–164.

Name Index

Subject Index

A

Absenteeism, and organizational culture, 141

Affective Communication Test, 47

Alcoholics Anonymous: charismatic relationships in, 60; routinization in, 59

American Management Association, 153

Analogy, for strategic vision, 191-194

Apple Computer, charismatic leader of, 3

AT&T, Management Potential Study at, 218, 292

Attention, focused by visionary leader, 142

Authority: charismatic, 13-17, 59-60; in existing institutions, 21; and formal versus informal organization, 16-17; ideal types of, 13-14; rank versus personal, 14; rational-legal, 14-17; and rational versus heroic revolution, 14-15; stable versus transitory, 15-16; traditional, 14-17

B

Behavior: of charismatic leaders, 25, 26, 27, 28-29, 104-105; competencies trainable in, 313-319; consequences of, 147; dimensions of, 78-97, 104-105; and effectiveness, 98-121; exemplary, 317-318; formula for, 123; interactions of, 146-147; of leader, 98-121; social learning theory of, 298-299; of socialized and personalized leaders, 222-225; theories of, 25-31; of visionary leader, 142-148, 152-153

Black and Decker, and market competition, 131

C

Cabinet members, study of, as followers, 105-116

California: charisma and credibility study in, 68; Manson followers in, 50

California, Los Angeles, University of, and visionary leader, 145

Canada. *See* Quebec

Center for Creative Leadership, Looking Glass program of, 318

Change: and development, 280; and visionary leaders, 132, 134, 137, 138-139, 141

Charisma: accounting for limits of, 266-270; aftermath of, 58-62; antecedents of, 55-58; as attribution by followers, 79; background on, 237-240; behavioral dimensions of, 80-89; and collective power, 258-259, 261; and communion, 258, 261, 267-268; components of, 43, 90; concepts of, 105, 214-215, 216, 237, 256, 259, 271; conceptual framework for, 7-8; conclusions on, 249-250, 272-273; as constellation of behaviors, 89-92; creation of, 241, 272; and crisis solution, 55-57;

345